The
EARLY CHILDHOOD
Curriculum
A REVIEW OF CURRENT RESEARCH

Carol Seefeldt
Editor

TEACHERS
COLLEGE
PRESS

Teachers College, Columbia University
New York and London

Published by Teachers College Press, 1234 Amsterdam Avenue,
New York, N.Y. 10027

Library of Congress Cataloging-in-Publication Data

The early childhood curriculum.

  (Early childhood education series)
  Bibliography: p.
  Includes index.
  1. Education, Preschool—United States—Curricula.
2. Education, Preschool—United States—Curricula—
Research. I. Seefeldt, Carol. II. Series.
LB1140.4.E27 1987   372.19   86-14510
ISBN 0-8077-2819-5

Manufactured in the United States of America

92 91 90 89 88 87   1 2 3 4 5 6

Contents

Preface

In an effort to learn ever more about children, and how to use this knowledge to foster children's growth and development in an early childhood setting, theoreticians and researchers continue their work. *The Early Childhood Curriculum* is a compilation of the research and theory in the curriculum content areas. It has been designed to give the graduate student in early childhood education an overview of the various theories, research base, and practice of early childhood education in the curriculum areas of content.

Each chapter presents an overview of the theory, research, and implications for practice in a specific curriculum content area. Leslie R. Williams in the first chapter, "Determining the Curriculum," describes how society's attitudes and view of the nature of children has always influenced the curriculum. The social forces that led to varying views of children, and thus curricula, are described. The idea of the curriculum being inseparable from the whole child provides the basis for this chapter.

Teachers' interactions with children—what teachers actually do, how they reach decisions about appropriate educational experiences, and the strategies they use as they interact with children—are potent directors of the curriculum. Margaret Lay-Dopyera and John E. Dopyera present the history, theory, and practice of teaching strategies in the chapter "Strategies for Teaching."

"But all they do is play!" Some believe play is the only mode of learning children have; others disagree and see it as a waste of time. Describing the theories, research, and values of play, in her chapter, "Play," Doris Pronin Fromberg builds a convincing rationale for its importance in the curriculum.

Language, probably the most important vehicle through which children are educated, is a complex and multidimensional activity. Celia Genishi, in "Acquiring Oral Language and Communicative Competence," fosters an understanding of how children acquire language and the role of the teacher in facilitating language growth.

Nita Barbour presents an overview of the theory, research, and practice of how children learn to read and how teachers facilitate their moving into the reading process. The questions of when children should learn to read, and by what methods, are described in "Learning to Read."

The idea of the whole child and an integrated curriculum is found in George Forman's and Melissa Kaden's chapter, "Research on Science Education for Young Children." Science is compared to art as work is compared to play. How children gain an understanding of the scientific attitude, through specific concepts in science, is presented.

"Early Mathematics Education," by Alberta M. Castaneda, builds on the concept that the science of mathematics is an integral part of children's growth, development, and learning. In this chapter the controversy over what mathematics is and how children should be taught basic concepts is discussed.

Art, as well, is an integral part of the curriculum. The theories, values, and importance of art, as well as research and its implications for teaching children art, are presented in "The Visual Arts" by Carol Seefeldt.

Clifford D. Alper discusses the crucial implications of current theories in music education for young children in "Early Childhood Music Education." He reviews the Orff, Kodaly, and Dalcroze methods of teaching music and evaluates critically the contemporary problems with music education research.

The history and current understanding of teaching social studies are described by Blythe Hinitz in "Social Studies in Early Childhood Education." How children develop and are taught concepts from the content areas of geography, history, and economics, as well as the social skills of learning who they are and how to relate with others, are found in this chapter.

Sandra R. Curtis, in "New Views on Movement Development and the Implications for Curriculum in Early Childhood," explores the research and theory of the new techniques for analyzing children's movement development. The shift in focus from the tasks children are performing to a focus on children themselves is described.

A concluding chapter summarizes the knowledge of curriculum we now have and offers suggestions for future research and work. Together, the chapters provide an overview of an integrated approach, each chapter presenting a separate and distinct area of the curriculum and all building a case for an integrated, child-centered curriculum. The vast amount of research and theory in the curriculum content areas presented in this text provides a rich resource for educators to draw on as they determine directions for the curriculum.

CHAPTER 1

Determining the Curriculum

LESLIE R. WILLIAMS
Teachers College, Columbia University

"Curriculum" is a word that evokes many images in the minds of teachers, administrators, and parents. For most early educators, though, "curriculum" has a single powerful association—the image of "the whole child." Consideration of what that phrase means to those who work with young children (children from birth to age eight) and how it came to have so particular a connotation reveals some of the distinctive characteristics of early education, and explains what for other educators may be considered the idiosyncratic nature of the field's curriculum literature. In early childhood education, the curriculum and the whole child tend to be seen as inseparable.

Most early educators understand "the whole child" to mean the child's complete integration of intellectual (cognitive), emotional, social, and physical capabilities. Learning in any one of these domains must necessarily involve all the others. Effective teaching, as a consequence, must draw upon those inner connections, with recognition of the distinctive ways in which young children take in and utilize knowledge of the world around them.

The task of determining the early childhood curriculum, therefore, hinges directly on discovering the nature of children. *What* young children learn is dependent upon *how* they learn. As this concept has evolved, how children learn has also increasingly come to be seen in relation to a *context*, a broad social and cultural base for children's emerging knowledge, skills, feelings, and attitudes. Experience has taught early educators that young children thrive on acknowledgment and use of their unique capacities for learning, and that they show themselves to be capable of strong performance in all areas of accomplishment when taught as unitary, integrated beings.

The idea of educating the whole child reflects a rich tradition of comprehensiveness that has characterized early education from its beginnings. This tradition arose as a response both to social conditions adversely affecting the lives of young children and to the moral, spiritual, pragmatic,

1

and eventually scientific streams flowing through Western society over the past 200 years.

Historian Philippe Ariès (1962) suggests that before the Romantic period, children by the age of five or six were viewed as miniature adults and were expected to learn in the same entirely language-based mode used in adult education. The one classical distinction that was made by both Plato (427–347 B.C.) and Aristotle (384–322 B.C.) was that children required strict training of character as a proper foundation for learning. In a similar vein, preparation of young scholars in medieval Europe was expected to be grounded in spiritual disciplines, so that the training of the mind would reflect the order of the Creation or divine intent. While these provisos implied the integration of the faculties of human learning, translating that assumption into curricula was not seen except in sporadic instances—for example, in the seventeenth century, Luther's incorporation of vocational instruction into courses of study; and Comenius's use of pictures as concrete referents to vocabulary studied (Braun & Edwards, 1972).

A clear demarcation in the image of the child came with the popularization of the work of Jean-Jacques Rousseau (1712–1778). In his educational treatise *Emile* (1762), Rousseau departed from the view of children as being like adults, and presented them as moving through a succession of stages, each of which had its own internal order and coherence (Gutek, 1972). Equally important was Rousseau's insistence that children learned not through the abstractions of the written word, but through direct interaction with the environment. He took the extreme position that only the natural world provided guidance in this interactive process and that society corrupted children, tarnishing their innate nobility of spirit. He recommended that children be raised in situations where contact with nature could be frequent and prolonged, where children could play without social restraint until reaching the age of reason (approximately puberty). At that time formal studies could commence without danger of distortion of the true nature of the child (Rousseau, 1969).

While Rousseau's main interest was in reforming society's total conception of education and did not focus specifically on young children, his work is important to understanding the inner structures of early childhood curricula because he anticipated several of the themes that characterize work in the field to this day. His awareness of the emergence of developmental stages and stage-related learning has already been mentioned. In addition, his presentation of learning as an interactive, sensorially based process, and his recognition of play as a medium for learning, were powerful intimations of the directions to be taken in the future.

Like all issues of import in education, however, conceptions of play and processes in learning, and their relationship to the idea of teaching the whole child, have evolved over time. Ensuing changes have been responsive to broad social patterns, needs, and priorities. In every era, new program designs and curricular formulations have revealed both unique and cumulative perceptions of the role of each of these in suiting instruction to the distinctive characteristics of young children. Tracing the path of that evolution can contribute to our understanding of the fundamental questions behind curriculum research in early childhood education today.

Returning, therefore, to the predecessors of modern practice, we see that from the mid-eighteenth century onward, there was a clear line of development in the image of the whole child. Emphases on interactive processes and play became more and more apparent in the fabric of early childhood education, as each innovator passed insights to a new generation of persons serving, nurturing, and educating the young child.

Rousseau's work deeply influenced the thinking of Johann Pestalozzi (1746–1827), an Italian-Swiss schoolteacher who founded one of the first European schools to acknowledge children's developmental characteristics. Pestalozzi was convinced of the profound effect of social environment on children. When his novel *How Gertrude Teaches Her Children* was first published in 1801, he was promulgating the then revolutionary notion of an intimate teaching connection between parents and their children. He assumed that children were the pliant recipients of parental instruction and were in danger of corruption by society if that teaching were not of the highest moral character.

The curriculum "Papa" Pestalozzi designed for his children equated parental guidance and strong morality with the work ethic. The result was a high-intensity work training program that prepared children to face a rapidly changing economy. Manual dexterity was stressed as a survival skill in the newly emerging industrial revolution (Gutek, 1968).

The structure behind Pestalozzi's program was even more unconventional for its day than was its outward form. Pestalozzi saw the purpose of his work as the development of children's moral, physical, and intellectual powers. While the first two were fostered through the approach described above, intellectual growth was stimulated through *Anschauung*, a perceptual-ideational process through which concepts or clear ideas were formed. *Anschauung* involved three levels of operation. Most immediately, it represented the reception in the mind of direct sensory impressions from interaction with the external environment. One step removed from that was the formation of ideas by combining sense impressions with attention, or mental concentration and arriving at concepts by association. At the third level of operation, mental ideas would appear without a concrete referent. *Anschauung* was developed in children through guided observation and representation of the natural world. Practice in recording the numbers and forms inherent in objects and the language associated with them led to refinement of mental capacity and its application in the physical and moral realms. Thus, the whole person was educated and became a competent and coping human being (Gutek, 1968).

Friedrich Froebel (1782–1852) studied with Pestalozzi; but he, designing a curriculum in 1837, fifty years after Pestalozzi's first work, found his teacher's vision of the child inadequate to capture the spirit of the new age. He molded and changed that vision to encompass "self-actualization" as a legitimate goal of early childhood education. Young children, said Froebel, arrive on this earth with an impressive repertoire of inborn knowledge and skills. The role of the teacher was to bring these capabilities to fruition by making children consciously aware of and able to use all that they know.

Froebel created a curriculum that was fascinating both in its complexity and in its inherent appeal to the children of his day. It consisted of a carefully sequenced set of manipulative materials known as the *Gifts*, complemented by an equally carefully sequenced set of handwork projects which he called the *Occupations*. The Gifts and Occupations together were designed to illustrate fundamental mathematical principles which Froebel believed were part of the creative human spirit and which echoed essential workings of the cosmos, or the mind of God (Froebel, 1887).

Froebel is generally considered the founder of early childhood education not only because he was the first to design a curriculum specifically for young children (Pestalozzi's work encompassed the range from early childhood through adolescence), but because he introduced play as a major medium for instruction. For the first time, children "played" in school, that is, used manipulatives specially designed to teach concepts and skills. Formal games, music, art, and outdoor activities (such as gardening and care of pets) were integrated into the daily program to supplement the use of the Gifts and the Occupations.

Froebel's notion of "play" was substantially different from modern conceptions. He saw play as a teacher-directed process, largely imitative in nature and revolving around predetermined content. But he also understood play to be a form of "creative self-activity," expressing children's emerging capabilities and reflecting their particular way of learning (Froebel, 1887).

Froebel's mystical formulation dominated curriculum design in early childhood education for fifty years. In the 1890s, however, a new generation of persons concerned with the well-being of young children and their families began to challenge the view of the child contained in the Froebelian kindergarten curriculum. While not rejecting the picture of children as innately creative beings, the progressive followers of John Dewey reached backward in time to reclaim some of Pestalozzi's understanding of learning through direct experience with the natural world, and forward into the new century to envision children as builders of a new social order—a democratic society. Progressive educators found the highly defined and teacher-directed Froebelian curriculum to be too removed from the challenges and problems of daily living. Instead, they suggested, a curriculum for young children should be designed to meet the circumstances children faced as members of a group living in a modern world (Dewey, 1966).

Children were thus seen as social beings, and the curriculum became a flexible grouping of activities to promote social problem-solving processes. Examples of such activities were joint efforts in the preparation of food for lunch, or small group work on representation in the classroom of a familiar institution such as the local grocery store. Through such activities, children were expected to develop a sense of mutual responsibility and an understanding of at least some of the workings of the society in which they lived (Dewey, 1902).

New conceptions of play and the use of process in teaching and learning were emerging. The nature of children as learners was being seen in relation to experience (Dewey, 1963). This meant connection with real-life activities that tended to integrate subject areas and require coordination of socioemotional, psychomotor, and cognitive responses from children. Such responses frequently took the form of sociodramatic play, in which the children reenacted what they had observed or directly experienced, often adding new dimensions to the scene in ways that revealed the processes behind their growing understanding.

As the Progressive Movement was gathering momentum in the United States, Maria Montessori in Italy was transforming her observations of the nature of the whole child into another process-oriented curriculum. Like Dewey, Montessori was keenly aware of societal demands on children. Instead of looking at the functioning of children in groups, however, she focused on the promotion of social competence in individuals. She saw children as very sensitive to sensorial stimulation, "capable of sustaining mental concentration when genuinely interested in their work," loving cleanliness and order, "preferring work to play and didactic materials to toys, and having a deep sense of personal dignity" (Standing, 1962, pp. 40–43). Consequently, she designed her curriculum to foster independence in self-care and individual responsibility for one's own learning. Children worked individually or with self-chosen companions, practicing skills on specially made, self-corrective manipulative materials that provided immediate feedback on children's accomplishment.

Montessori had a deep understanding of learning as process. Her curriculum was organized around several "periods" in the child's development, each of which had its particular requirements for interaction with the environment. Assuming a continuum between refinement of the senses and broader intellectual functioning, she devised procedures and didactic materials that were responsive to children's evolving learning characteristics. During the period of the "absorbent mind" (birth to age six), and most especially in the substage of greatest sensitivity and receptivity (three to six years), she engaged the children in exercises of "practical life" and sense training. Practical life work emphasized cleanliness, self-care, and care and maintenance of the learning environment. Work in sense training promoted fine powers of sensory discrimination and developed readiness for the writing, reading, and other academic learnings that followed in the primary grades (Montessori, 1964).

All of the exercises were process-oriented. While the didactic materials were designed to achieve specific outcomes (such as the ability to order cylinders from largest to smallest in height), they were also made to encourage the repetition of tasks, which in young children typically follows mastery. Thus, while specific accomplishment was important, how children achieved mastery was seen to be even more significant to their emerging competence.

Simultaneously with Dewey's and Montessori's separate efforts, the American Child Study Movement, under the leadership of G. Stanley Hall (1844–1924), was starting to influence early childhood practice. Observations of children's behavior in a variety of contexts began yielding powerful data that, in turn, were causing curriculum makers to rethink what were appropriate learning experiences for young children (Kessen, 1965; Weber, 1984). The complexity of "the whole child" was beginning to reveal itself and to require increasingly sensitive applications of integrated approaches to teaching and learning.

As the century advanced, the conception of the child as a social being was expanding to include an accounting of the individual child's physical and psychological growth patterns. From the 1920s through the 1950s, the attention of early educators focused successively on children's social functioning, physical development and maturational milestones, emotional health, and finally on their underlying cognitive skills that signaled stage-appropriate mental functioning. Drawing on the work of Gesell and Ilg, Erikson, and Piaget among others, early childhood educators in the late 1950s generally espoused what came to be known as the "child development" point of view (Braun & Edwards, 1972; Weber, 1984).

Notable during this thirty-year period was the work of such finely tuned educators as Susan Isaacs in Britain and Harriet Johnson, Caroline Pratt, and Lucy Sprague Mitchell in the United States. By mid-century, the names of Lawrence Frank, Daniel Prescott, Arthur Jersild, and James L. Hymes had been added to the list (Weber, 1984). While these early childhood advocates each had a distinct point of view, they did emphasize the centrality of process, and play as an expression of process, in the growth, development, and education of young children.

As understanding of the processes of children's learning became more refined through extended child observation, curriculum content was increasingly linked with the everyday occurrences of children's lives. This was so partly because of the continuing influence of Dewey's thinking on classroom practice, and partly because there was new theoretical support for the power of such content from two giants in the field of child development, Erik Erikson (born 1902) and Jean Piaget (1896–1980). Mentioned above in the context of changing emphases in early childhood education, the work of these two researchers requires particular attention because of the depth and breadth of their influence on curriculum design to the present day.

As a young teacher raised in Europe, Erik Erikson came under the tutelage of Anna Freud. Prepared by her for work in child therapy, he soon became intrigued by the interactions he discerned between the course of psychosexual development in young children as described in classic Freudian literature and the sociocultural milieu in which children were being raised.

Erikson accepted the point of departure of psychoanalytic thought, that the essential nature of human beings is instinctual and manifests itself in the realm of feeling and emotion. Cognition arises from unfullfilled desire, as a secondary characteristic of human nature. He understood socioemotional development as proceeding through the resolution of a series of conflicts, each of which addresses a fundamental issue of the human psyche. Proceeding from trust versus mistrust to autonomy versus shame, to initiative versus guilt and beyond through all eight distinctive "ages of man," children (and adults) strive to achieve integration and maintain balance in the context of the particular demands their society places upon them (Erikson, 1963).

Young children, said Erikson, most commonly work through their current conflicts by reconstructing them in symbolic play. For curriculum developers influenced by Erikson's formulation, play centering on day-to-day events and familiar objects became a critical element in early childhood programs. It provided an arena for children's coming to terms with their existential dilemmas, and encouraged cognition through channeling of childhood fantasy.

Piaget's theory of intellectual development gave a different but equally potent justification for including play in the early childhood curriculum. Piaget concluded that the essential nature of human beings was their power to construct knowledge through adaptation to the environment. From birth, children engage in the reciprocal acts of "assimilation" and "accommodation" in order to form, extend, and expand the structures of their minds. In assimilation, children match information, concepts, and skills arising from interaction with the environment, with previously formed mental structures. Accommodation, on the other hand, requires that these structures be modified in order to make sense of the new information or concepts, or to represent new skills (Piaget & Inhelder, 1969).

These complementary processes are fueled by children's direct activity, said Piaget. Play especially exercises the assimilation process, using action and frequently language as proving grounds for newly acquired ideas. As children proceed through the four periods of intellectual development (sensorimotor, preoperational, concrete operational, and formal operational) described by Piaget, play assumes a variety of forms; and within any one period, it can have multiple functions. Sensorimotor play, for example, generally revolves around practicing physical skills acquired through use of the five senses. However, it can also be used as a medium for establishing social relationships and testing the dimensions of those relationships. During the preoperational period, play might be used symbolically or constructively to solidify physical knowledge of one's surroundings, to practice solving problems in the adult world, to create a microsociety in which to try out new capabilities or to refine social interactions (Piaget, 1962).

Early childhood program designers who accepted Piaget's descriptions of child development found that they could interpret his work according to their own instructional leanings. Piaget himself did not transform his theory into specifications for classroom practice. Curriculum makers, therefore, were free to draw implications leading to a variety of approaches to addressing the cognitive characteristics of young children. The one commonal feature of these approaches was that abundant manipulable materials and ample time for the children to interact directly with them were seen as vital spurs to the children's continued cognitive development.

By the early 1960s, therefore, the concept of teaching the whole child through a process orientation and incorporating play experiences in the curriculum was well established. Many "child development" programs reflected a psychodynamic (Freudian, Eriksonian) or less frequently, a Piagetian point of view that stressed the interconnection of experiences and the roles of emotion, cognition, and maturation in the promotion of learning. Other programs remained more closely aligned to the earlier Deweyan point of view or to the "readiness" rationale stemming from child study. In spite of the variety of theoretical underpinnings, however, classroom practice tended to have common characteristics.

Typically, early childhood classrooms were arranged into "interest centers" such as the block corner, library, art area, family or sociodramatic play corner, and sand/water areas. Daily schedules incorporated both child-initiated and teacher-directed work periods. The areas of the room were stocked with a range of manipulable materials used, according to the orientation of the program, to promote social interaction, skill/concept development or a combination of the two. The curriculum was derived through teachers' observations of the children's interests and developmental needs, through the possibilities presented by the learning materials themselves, and through awareness of the school content that would follow in the first grade.

At this time (approximately 1959–1963), the federal government intervened in early childhood education in ways that altered the course of curriculum development for the next fifteen years. Distressed by descriptions of the depressed physical and intellectual condition of the nation's growing number of poor children, the United States Office of Child Development (now the Administration for Children, Youth and Families) initiated a new federally funded early childhood program—Project Head Start.

Head Start originally espoused the child-development tradition in its early learning centers. The educational program was designed around a flexible schedule of child-initiated play and group-learning experiences, which were generally aimed at connecting the three domains of learning. The purpose of the program was to enable each child to develop as fully as possible all facets of his/her "being," while being prepared for the social, emotional, cognitive, linguistic, and physical demands of the first grade.

The public school expected that children would come to the first grade with a firm command not only of social behavior that would enable them to work effectively in a classroom, but also with premath, prereading, and other "readiness" skills. The very name Head Start implied such a preparation. The public school's conception of curriculum at that time was, generally speaking, not developmental in nature. It was focused instead on the acquisition of specific content (the facts or substance of math, science, language, literature, etc.). If children came to the first grade for some reason not ready to assimilate that content, they were considered to be handicapped.

Head Start's mission was to ensure that children would not fail. Consequently, there were new initiatives among Head Start curriculum makers. Strongly influenced by learning theorists and analysts of school content, some of the curriculum developers in experimental projects turned away from the child development approach to direct instruction in a variety of readiness skills and a high proportion of teacher direction in each day's work. In some of the innovative curriculum models, the interest centers characterizing early childhood classroom disappeared. They were replaced by high-intensity, small-group interactions, by practice with workbook exercises, or by other forms of focus on behavioral sequences geared to the acquisition of skills and attitudes related to upcoming school experiences (Evans, 1975).

In other new curriculum models that made up Head Start's "Planned Variations," the familiar interest centers remained in the classroom, but were used in new ways to promote school-related skills and attitudes. Whatever the case, children who entered the programs were observed or assessed to see what their needs were—that is, where they were lacking skills—and learning experiences were designed to develop those skills in the children. While there were some notable exceptions in program design, many of the recommended learning activities encouraged use of materials commonly found in public school kindergartens and first grades, such as felt circles, squares, and triangles to teach shapes, and monthly calendars to teach passage of time.

Between 1967 and 1973, curriculum research in early childhood education began to take a particular turn. Instead of focusing so heavily on the nature of the child as a learner, psychologists and early childhood educators began to explore which program designs would yield the greatest gains in the children's performance on standardized I.Q. and readiness tests. Some studies indicated that children did equally well in demonstration or experimental programs that were radically different from one another (Weikart, 1969). Other studies indicated that academically based programs that made strong use of direct instruction did result in higher scores on standardized tests (Miller & Dyer, 1975), but that these scores were not generally maintained beyond third grade without follow-up intervention in the public school (Miller & Dyer, 1975; Gray, Ramsey, & Klaus, 1982).

The results of that wave of research raised a number of interesting questions. What were the factors that accounted for some measure of success with some children but not with others in the same classroom? Which programs would be best for children with particular sets of characteristics? (Smith & Bissell, 1970). What were the contextual variables (such as focus on the children's direct experiences and incorporation of culturally derived content into the curriculum) that might account for heightened performance in given situations? (Juárez & Associates, 1982). These and other concerns surfaced through the 1970s, refocusing attention on the complexity of the whole child, and the many dimensions involved in teaching young children.

With the beginning of the 1980s a new curriculum development movement appeared. This initiative arose in response to a growing nation-wide interest in providing all-day kindergartens in public schools. Unlike the Head Start program, full-day kindergartens would address the needs of all children attending public school, regardless of socioeconomic status. While promotion of a longer kindergarten day has been fueled by a variety of political, social, economic, and educational rationales, the net result has been a reassessment of the needs and responses of five-year-olds in such extended programs.

Particularly prominent in this movement has been renewed interest in the use of traditional school subject areas in kindergarten programs. This interest has in fact sparked lively debate between those who feel that formal, academic skills such as reading and computation should be taught in the kindergarten, and those who feel that acquisition of academic skills is not a developmentally appropriate goal for kindergarteners.

The former group believes that school subjects should be presented as soon as possible to young children so that academic achievement can be accelerated. This point of view assumes that young children learn in fundamentally the same ways that older children do, and that the key to their eventual proficiency in the use of basic skills is "time on task."

The latter group, on the other hand, argues that more important than promoting facility with use of symbols is developing young children's underlying thinking processes—the foundations for problem solving that can be applied later to traditional academic learning. The advocates for providing "the foundations" point out that the elements of all the subject areas can be integrated into learning activities designed both to respond to and promote young children's direct engagement with the world around them. Because of children's developmental characteristics, they can best grasp such content when it is highlighted in common events of interest, and when the material is presented in ways that draw upon children's social, emotional, and psychomotor as well as cognitive responses. Incorporation of play into early childhood programs, the developmentalists maintain, should not be abandoned in favor of increased direct instruction, because play serves the function of relating subject matter or content to the children's particular ways of knowing.

Thus, the image of the whole child, and arguments for the roles of process and play in promoting development and learning remain vital to the present day; and the themes that have characterized early childhood program formulations continue to reveal themselves in curriculum research. Opposing ideas introduced in some periods of innovation and exploration have served to sharpen the distinctive viewpoint—that the young child should be approached as an integrated being—permeating the field. The chapters that follow explore that viewpoint both within subject areas and across the themes traced in our brief history. The fundamental curriculum questions and the approaches to their possible resolution provided by each author suggest directions for future early childhood curriculum development.

REFERENCES

Ariès, P. (1962). *Centuries of childhood.* (R. Balkick, Trans.) New York: Knopf.

Braun, S., & Edwards, E. (1972). *History and theory of early childhood education.* Worthington, OH: Charles A. Jones.

Dewey, J. (1902). *The child and the curriculum.* Chicago: University of Chicago Press.

Dewey, J. (1966). *Democracy and education.* New York: Free Press.

Dewey, J. (1963). *Experience and education.* New York: Macmillan.

Erikson, E. (1963). *Childhood and society.* New York: W. W. Norton.

Evans, E. (1975). *Contemporary influences in early childhood education.* New York: Holt, Rinehart and Winston.

Froebel, F. (1887). *The education of man.* (W. Hailman, Trans.) New York: D. Appleton.

Gray, S. W., Ramsey, B. K., & Klaus, R. A. (1982). *From 3 to 20: The early training project.* Baltimore: University Park Press.

Gutek, G. L. (1972). *A history of the western educational experience.* New York: Random House.

Gutek, G. L. (1968). *Pestalozzi and education.* New York: Random House.

Juárez & Associates (1982). *An evaluation of the Head Start bilingual bicultural curriculum development project.* Head Start Bureau, Administration for Children, Youth and Families, Department of Health and Human Services, Contract No. HEW 105-77-1048.

Kessen, W. (1965). *The child.* New York: John Wiley.

Miller, L. B., & Dyer, J. L. (1975). Four preschool programs: Their dimensions and effects. *Monographs of the Society for Research in Child Development. 40. No. 5-6.* Chicago: University of Chicago Press.

Montessori, M. (1964). *The Montessori method.* New York: Schocken Books.

Pestalozzi, J. H. ([1801] 1915). *How Gertrude teaches her children.* (L. E. Holland & F. C. Turner, Trans.) Syracuse, NY: C. W. Bardeen.

Piaget, J. (1962). *Play, dreams and imitation in childhood.* New York: W. W. Norton.

Piaget, J., & Inhelder, B. (1969). *The psychology of the child.* New York: Basic Books.

Rousseau, J.-J. (1969) *Émile or on education.* (A. Bloom, Trans.) New York: Basic Books.

Smith, M. S., & Bissell, J. S. (1970). Report analysis: The impact of Headstart. *Harvard Educational Review 40,* 1 (February).

Standing, E. M. (1962). *Maria Montessori: Her life and work.* New York: Mentor Omega Books.

Weber, E. (1984). *Ideas influencing early childhood education: A theoretical analysis.* New York: Teachers College Press.

Weikart, D. (1969). A comparative study of three preschool curricula. Presented at the biennial meeting of the Society for Research in Child Development, Santa Monica, CA.

Chapter 2

Strategies for Teaching

Margaret Lay-Dopyera
Syracuse University

John E. Dopyera
Cumberland Hill Associates, Inc.

This chapter focuses on the strategies early childhood educators select
and use as they go about their teaching tasks. The term *strategy* as we are
employing it refers to the various approaches teachers use to accomplish
their objectives. There is not, to our knowledge, a previously existing review
of research on teaching strategies that is appropriate for early childhood
educators. The compilations of Joyce and Weil (1980) and Weil and Joyce
(1978a, 1978b, 1978c), which they refer to as "teaching models," are very
valuable but have limited application for teachers of young children. What is
reported and discussed in this chapter has been gleaned from diverse
sources but does not claim full comprehensiveness. We have not, for
example, attempted to review research on alternative strategies for the
arrangement of the environment or the provision of equipment and materials. There are other omissions as well. This issue will be discussed in more
detail at the end of the chapter. The chapter is organized in three sections—
theoretical bases, research bases, and summary and implications.

THEORETICAL BASES

Early childhood educators, like professionals in many fields, have had
little success in articulating what it is that they really do. A case is sometimes
made that it must always be thus, since each teacher and each teaching
situation is different. Some insist that teaching is an art and therefore cannot
be successfully analyzed. The teacher as artist is assumed to create teaching
strategies in response to each new situation. Perhaps such a view would be
more acceptable if there were enough such artists to competently staff our

programs, if there were consensus within the profession as to what excellent teaching is, and if the general public had greater respect for the professional educator. This is not the case. We have very discordant images of teaching even within the education profession. Also, low status and poor salaries suggest that teachers of the young are not perceived as respected professionals. This state of affairs might be remedied were teachers to become more reflective about what they do so that they could better clarify for themselves, and communicate more effectively to others what works, how it works, and with which children.

Donald Schön, a social scientist from the Massachusetts Institute of Technology, in a book entitled *The Reflective Practitioner: How Professionals Think in Action* (1983), provides useful insights for examining the development of professional expertise. In his terms, in teaching as well as in many other occupations, we lack the ability to make sense of what makes practitioners who are artfully competent different from those who are ineffective. He contrasts a professional's "knowing-in-action" expertise with "reflecting-in-action" expertise. Educators, in general, and perhaps early educators in particular, seem to rely on "knowing-in-action." In this mode we use actions that are carried out almost automatically and that we do not think much about before or during their performance. We may be unaware that we ever learned these things. They seem to us to be natural and spontaneous responses to a given set of circumstances. We may once have had an understanding of why a particular action is appropriate in a given set of circumstances, but have long since ceased to think about it. Perhaps we learned through seeing others act in the same ways and never did really come to understand the rationale. In either case, we are unable to effectively describe what it is that we do. Nor can we adequately explain why we do it.

The development of self-confidence and earning respect from others for professional expertise, according to Schön, is more likely to be related to a "reflecting-in-action" mode. This means one notices what one is doing while doing it, and thinks about how it is working, and perhaps changes the way things are being done to determine what these changes bring about. Reflecting-in-action often involves practical theorizing and experimentation—some in advance of action but much of it on the spot. Sometimes a different way of seeing the situation emerges which then suggests a different action. Through these processes, Schön proposes, legitimate professionalism can be developed.

We propose that the consideration of research findings on teaching strategies, some of which may run counter to one's expectations, may be useful in leading toward a reflective stance; in addition, the conscious development of a repertoire of teaching strategies is an essential step toward reflecting in action. By *repertoire*, we refer to the array of alternative actions of which an individual is capable. The systematic planned expansion of repertoire requires a shift away from an assumption of a "best" way and to a gradual adoption of additional strategies. Without a repertoire of alternative strategies for potential teaching situations, the practitioner has little decision-making flexibility.

In early childhood education, practitioners' teaching strategies are sometimes so closely tied to the preferred orientation toward child development (Kohlberg, 1968; Langer, 1969; Lay-Dopyera & Dopyera, 1982), that they may not scrutinize their methods. If the orientation is interactional (cognitive-developmental, constructivist), certain strategies are accepted without question; if the orientation is behaviorist (environmentalist, cultural transmission), another set of strategies are assumed and seldom questioned. The maturationist (romantic) holds to yet another set. Too often, in our opinion, these beliefs become a rigid ideology, seldom questioned and ineffectively articulated. We concur with Schön that the advancement of the profession and the enhancement of the education and development of young children would be furthered by a more active and reflective stance.

Schön also discusses the relationship between research and practice and the need for a partnership between researchers and reflective practitioners. The agenda, he says, will be generated out of dialogue between the groups and from their joint efforts. Much of the research reviewed in this chapter was initiated by researchers on the issues in which they are interested. This may have little relationship to the teaching tasks as they might be viewed by practitioners. Were practitioners to adopt a stance in dialogue with researchers, a different and more extensive set of research findings would be found in such a chapter as this. The following body of research, as viewed from this perspective, must be seen as partial and suggestive.

RESEARCH BASES

The research will be considered under the following subtopics: teacher-child relationships; classroom management strategies; teacher-child dialogue strategies; and lesson presentation strategies.

Teacher-child relationships

Early childhood texts and other professional literature often assert that teachers' relationships with children have a critical influence on children's development and learning. Within this concept, which is often based on something rather close to the Freudian notion of identification, it is said that the ideal relationships are those in which teachers convey warmth, acceptance, and nurturance. Agreement is not universal, however. According to the Montessori tradition, the ideal teacher is friendly but somewhat detached. Montessori children are expected to be motivated by the tasks in which they are involved, not by their relationship with the teacher. Clearly, teachers have alternative possibilities to consider as they decide how they will relate to the children in their classrooms.

And what does the research say about this issue? An early exploration of the benefits of a nurturing supportive relationship with teachers was reported by Thompson (1944), who established and studied two different nursery school curricula for matched groups of children. In one curriculum, the teacher had minimum contact with the children, permitting them to work independently throughout the program day and giving them assistance only when requested. In the other curriculum, the teacher attempted to become a warm friend who actively guided and participated in the children's play experiences in helpful and interested ways. At the end of an eight-month experimental period, the children who experienced the friendly, helpful teacher were found to be more constructive and more ascendant, showed more participation and leadership, and showed less destructive behavior than those in the other group.

A number of similar studies across the decades have used a variety of dependent measures. Comparable findings come from a recent study. In two day care programs housed within the same university, Tzelepis, Giblen, and Agronow (1983) compared one program, with an abundance of adult-initiated contacts of a positive (less restrictive) nature with another program in which there was much less interaction. Observations of children's behavior were made during the first and fourth weeks. Where there was greater adult involvement, there was more interaction with peers, adults, and activities, less time spent in transitions between activities, and longer periods spent in a given activity. Where there were fewer adult-initiated contacts, children's interactions with each other and with activities were dramatically less than in the other group. Differences were also noted in peer affiliation. In the program in which adults initiated more friendly supportive actions, peer interaction was more complex.

Teacher attention and warmth, the above studies suggest, seem to benefit children, at least in the short term. There may be longer-term consequences as well. Shipman (1976), in a longitudinal study of economically disadvantaged children from preschool age through third grade, compared children doing better than expected and those performing more poorly than expected. Those children who did better than expected had teachers during prekindergarten and primary years who were at least moderately warm, enthusiastic, and well prepared. While only suggestive and partial, since other factors may have been as influential, this evidence does support the idea that teacher-child relationships are very important to social and emotional development and that teacher warmth may be critical in those relationships.

Montessori programs which, as previously mentioned, place less emphasis on teacher-child relationships, were compared by Chattin-McNichols (1981) with non-Montessori programs:

> The Montessori program performs equal to or better than other programs in certain areas such as divergent production and school readiness, and is inferior in some respects to specially designed programs, for example, in comparison to Piaget-oriented programs in producing Piagetian conceptual development. Vocabulary recognition, and ratings of verbal-social participation are other areas in which programs other than Montessori produce higher gains. In the development of attentional strategies, general intelligence, achievement in academic areas, . . . the Montessori method performs as well as any other program. (p. 65)

It should be pointed out that there are many additional differences between Montessori and non-Montessori programs besides teacher-child relationships.

There are other ways of describing teacher-child relationships, of course. Within a behaviorist tradition, the ideal teacher-child relationship is often characterized in terms of interchange, such as reinforcements from the teacher, particularly the extent to which those reinforcements relate directly to the appropriateness of children's behavior. Attention, appropriately directed, has been repeatedly found to be effective in changing preschool children's behavior. Warmth, in these situations, may be experienced by children but only when their behavior is in line with the teacher's expectations.

On the other hand, interesting contrasting evidence suggests that adult attention may, in some instances, prevent children from fully exercising their own resources. Garvey (1977) noted, in children as young as age three, how children surrounded by adults seemed to use more restricted language, in contrast to the extensive conversations the same children held by themselves in a playroom. These findings bring to mind earlier evidence (Siegel & Kohn, 1959) that dyads become more aggressive when a friendly interested adult is present but does not interfere with their aggressive actions than when there is no adult present. Pellegrini (1984) similarly has found that adult presence is related to less mature forms of play than when children are alone. It appears than an adult who is passively present, even though friendly in orientation, does not motivate children to rely on their own resources. To build children's repertoire for independent action, however, the active involvement of a warm, friendly, attentive adult may be very important.

It is clear that teachers can bring about diverse effects by the attention strategies they choose. Although the teacher's child development orientation might be expected to accurately predict teacher-child relationships, research suggests that the patterns may not be as clear-cut as one might expect. For example, Miller and Dyer (1975) learned as they compared the program processes and effects of contrasting program models, that the program that most emphasizes teacher-child relationships, the "traditional" nursery school model, had highest ratio of negative-to-positive feedback to children. Soar and Soar (1972) also point out the high rate of negative feedback given to children in the more "open" Follow-Through classrooms in which they observed. Fagot (1973) found a similar result in a preschool study.

Rather than identifying themselves as warm, accepting teachers and simply assuming that this is the case, reflective teachers might do well to observe themselves in action to determine when and under what conditions they are warm and supportive and when they become harsh and rejecting. And the reflective teacher, whether behaviorist or otherwise, might also observe how children's behavior and learning are influenced by their own warmth and attention, contingently or noncontingently given.

Strategies for Classroom Management

Classroom management may be described as teacher behavior aimed at keeping children engaged appropriately and reducing the likelihood of behavior that requires the teacher to give children negative feedback. Much of the research on classroom management has been conducted in elementary schools rather than early childhood settings. It seems likely, however, that there are some important commonalities. On the other hand, it should be noted that in the elementary school studies, effectiveness is equated with pupils' achievement gains. The relevance of these findings for early education and for nonacademic goals has not been determined.

In a number of studies, effective teachers have been found to be those who plan ahead and who develop in advance clear notions of acceptable student behavior. Anderson, Evertson, and Emmer (1979) report that less effective teachers often appear to be unclear in their own thinking about how they want children to behave and wait until problems develop before talking with the children about what they expect. In the third-grade classrooms in which observations were done over the course of a year, the teachers who emerged as more effective could be identified by their pattern of behavior during the first three weeks of school. These teachers were actively involved in communicating with their pupils about behavioral expectations and classroom procedures. Effective teachers began the year by attending to details such as arranging space for personal possessions and routines for toileting, eating, drinking, and so forth. Emmer, Evertson and Anderson (1979) also point out that effective teachers plan ahead for various possibilities such as the need to rearrange space for special events and for the accommodation of classroom visitors.

Similar findings are reported for prekindergarten programs. Tzelepis, Giblin, and Agronow (1983) also found the early weeks of a day care program to be critical, and proposed that since the initial orientation of children entering a new program is toward adults, adults at this stage can take advantage of this opportunity to informally teach children skills necessary to interact with peers, to express wants, to understand possessions and how to share, to verbalize pleasure and anger, and to begin to resolve conflict. Additionally, adults can redirect children's attention to available materials and activities. Then as children engage in parallel play, adults can encourage constructive peer interaction.

Effective teachers have also been reported by Emmer, Evertson, and Anderson (1979) to engage in the following behavior. They use a variety of means of teaching procedures: modeling, rehearsal, and incentives. And they continue to work on necessary procedures until children master them. They give very specific feedback, both positive and negative, about children's performance rather than general praise. For example, instead of saying, "You've been very good at lunch today" they would give more precise praise, such as: "I notice that you remembered what to do with your cup, plate, and napkin when you finished eating." Good and Grouws (1975) studied third- and fourth-grade teachers and found that effective teachers spend less time on transitions. They also wait until all are quiet to give verbal instructions.

One's position in the classroom is important for effective management. Brophy and Evertson (1976) found that effective teachers move around the classroom more often and, when stationary, regularly scan the entire classroom. By knowing what is going on, the teacher is often able to redirect children's behavior in a constructive way or foresee the need for materials or guidance.

Anderson, Evertson, and Emmer (1979) report that effective teachers can predict what children are likely to pay attention to, or to be confused or distracted by. They use variations in voice modulation, pacing, and movement to attract and hold attention. They prevent confusion by carefully pacing directions so that they are not presenting similar activities at the same time. They require the active attention of every group member when important information is to be given. However, it may also be effective to limit the amount of information presented to young children in groups. Stallings (1975) found that when teachers give instructions to first-grade children on a one-to-one basis, the children are more persistent with tasks than when instructions are presented to a group. The younger the child, the less likely that information presented in a group setting will be efficiently received.

The great advantage in systematic structuring for effective classroom management may be reduced stress for the adult. If adult stress is avoided, children benefit, since the psychological state of the teacher is often communicated nonverbally to children, even though verbal expression is suppressed (Yinger, 1975). By building a repertoire for classroom management, teachers can then reflect in action about other aspects of their teaching responsibilities.

Teacher-Child Dialogue Strategies

Dialogue is essential in teaching young children for a number of reasons. First, children prior to age six or seven are believed to take in information more accurately when that information is directed to them as individuals. Perhaps this is a function of teacher positioning or eye contact in the one-to-one encounter. Or perhaps the teacher talks to the child so as to match the child's ability to understand. Or perhaps it is the self-enhancement that comes from receiving personal attention. Whatever the reason, dialogue does seem to be essential (see Stallings, 1975).

Second, in early childhood programs as well as at home, much of children's time is spent in play activities. Many early educators consider play to be the most effective medium for children's learning. While children are playing, however, teachers have the opportunity to engage individuals and small groups in dialogue. Through such interchanges, children can be helped to pursue their own goals and adults have optimal opportunity for informal teaching. As Almy, Monighan, Scales, and Van Hoorn point out in the following excerpt, it is not sufficient for teachers to merely set the stage and let children play:

> Teachers who . . . justify an important place for play in the early childhood curriculum will not lose sight of their responsibilities as instructors. They will take account of the allure of play but will also recognize children's needs to acquire information and skills in a variety of ways. Bearing in mind Piaget's view of play as assimilation, they will not neglect the accommodative aspects of learning. Preschool children, at their own level, need to encounter the physical and the social worlds in ways that help them to clarify and understand. Teachers have

responsibility in these areas as well as for providing the play opportunities in which children can consolidate and make personally meaningful
the experiences they have had. (1984, p. 22)

Dialogue between teachers and children that contributes to children's
learning also occurs in many nonplay settings. Among the ways in which
teachers constructively enter into dialogue with a single individual or with
small groups are the following: providing descriptive feedback; giving suggestions, coaching and prompting; asking questions; modeling. Each of these
will be described in turn.

Giving descriptive feedback.   There have been many useful guides for
teachers about how to teach informally through talking with children.
Memorable examples are "How to Talk with a Scribbler" (Sparling &
Sparling, 1973) and "Teaching Young Children as They Play" (Anker, Foster,
McLane, Sokel & Weissbourd, 1974). In giving descriptive feedback, teachers observe the child's activity or attention focus and talk to him or her about
it. Since the pace-setting study of Hess and Shipman (1965), which found
that the degree to which parents used abstract and task-specific language was
related to children's success in learning tasks, many other studies have
pursued the same and related issues with similar results. Carew (1980), in a
longitudinal observational study of home-reared and day care children in
their second and third year, found that in day care, as in the home, children's
I.Q. at age three was predicted by the amount of language-focused activity
provided earlier by adults. According to Carew and many other researchers,
appropriate language-focused adult-child interchange appears to be required
to build intelligent behavior.

Reinforcing.   As indicated in the above section on teacher-child
relationships, most early educators recognize the influence of teacher behavior on children's behavior, learning, and development. The most systematic
and comprehensive presentation of research on how reinforcement works
comes, of course, from B. F. Skinner and his associates (e.g., Skinner, 1974;
Bijou & Baer, 1978). Teachers in classrooms reinforce or fail to reinforce
children by the distribution of their own attention and approval. They also
distribute "turns," permissions, and regulate the use of resources. Principles
derived from the research of behaviorists on the management of reinforcers
(positive and negative) versus ignoring and punishment are useful for
teachers to understand, regardless of their own child development orientation. Conversely, teachers are well advised to consider how they themselves
are being influenced by the reinforcement of children's behavior toward
them as well as the other way around. Whether viewed in behaviorist terms

or otherwise, it is obvious that in teacher-child relationships influences go in both directions. Many of the hassles between teachers and children may, however, be more easily understood as reciprocal when viewed according to reinforcement principles. For example, Wittmer (1985b) found teachers of toddlers observed in Title XX Day Care to seemingly be influenced by children's behavior. When children's behavior was positive, teachers behaved toward them in a positive fashion. However, when children's behavior was negative it was predominantly followed by negative teacher behavior. Observers in schools often see this pattern and wonder why it appears to be so persistent. As Wittmer (1985a) comments, "If teachers responded to a higher proportion of child positive behaviors and used more positive techniques in response to child negative behaviors, the outcome could be more emotionally nurturant, intellectually stimulating experiences (p. 3)."

When this situation is examined in practical terms, we note that adults who react to children's negative behavior by scolding, for example, are immediately reinforced by the cessation, however temporary, of the child's misbehavior. This reinforcement leads the teacher to increased use of scolding. And since the scolding is only mildly aversive, it is not an effective punishment. In fact, the teacher's attention may be reinforcing. More negative actions are the result. Children's negative behavior followed by the teacher's negative behavior become cyclical in far too many school settings. As Peters, Neisworth, and Yawkey (1985) point out: "Teachers of young children have hundreds of opportunities daily to reinforce developmentally appropriate behavior; the devilish other side of the coin is that there are also hundreds of opportunities accidentally to reinforce inappropriate and developmentally destructive behavior" (p. 105).

Coaching, prompting, and giving suggestions. While children are engaged in pretending and other active classroom pursuits, teachers can, through judicious observation and interjection, add to children's understanding and extend the children's repertoires for subsequent similar situations. The goal of intervening in children's dramatic play is to develop their abilities to engage in social interactions more adequately and to pretend, both of which are related not only to success in play but also learning and thinking skills.

Much of the research has focused on the consequences of training "disadvantaged" children how to play. Smilansky (1968), Feitelson and Ross (1973), Rosen (1974), Rubin, Maioni, and Hornung (1976) have all reported less frequent involvement and less complex sociodramatic play in children from low socioeconomic backgrounds. Smilansky (1968) reported that training significantly improved the quality of Israeli children's play. A number of other studies of what is sometimes called "play-training" have reported positive effects on verbal I.Q. (Saltz, Dixon, & Johnson, 1977), creative thinking (Feitelson & Ross, 1973), social-role conservation (Fink, 1976), conservation of quantity (Golomb & Cornelius, 1977).

Two types of intervention, inside and outside, as suggested by Smilansky (1968) were emphasized by Christie (1982). In outside intervention, the teacher does not take a role in the play episode but comments to a child about specific play behaviors that might be used. Comments may take the form of questions: "What are you going to cook for dinner?" suggestions: "You might cook spaghetti for dinner," directions: "Put some water in the pan and then put it on the stove," or coaching: "Tell the doctor what is wrong with the baby." In inside intervention, the teacher takes a role and actually joins in the children's play and shows the children how to play roles, to use one object to represent another, to pretend particular actions, and to communicate about particular actions and roles to others involved in playing.

Rosen's study (1974) demonstrated that when teachers become actively involved with individual children during free play in modeling role playing, in asking leading questions and offering suggestions, and in greater role playing, the results are gains in group productivity and problem solving. In the Rosen intervention, teachers often directed their attention within the group to those weakest in skills. To the group they introduced new problems, ideas, themes, or incidents. For example, in house play they interjected the illness of a family member; in a mountain-climbing episode, they suggested that a member of the group had fallen over a ledge, leaving the rest of the group to consider how to help.

Coaching, prompting, and giving suggestions are viable teaching strategies in many other situations as well. The teacher's ability to enter skillfully into children's involvement with materials such as puzzles, table toys, paints, and so forth, is also significant. Interrupting a child's activity for dialogue is worthwhile if teachers can use their comments and children's responses as a basis for mutual learning. The teacher can learn about how children are thinking and children can be helped to extend their concepts and language. Guidelines provided by Marian Blank (1969, 1973) are particularly useful in building these skills.

Asking questions. Questions were used extensively by Piaget and were considered by him to "constitute the fundamental factor in cognitive development" (1977, p. 17). Questions, within the comprehension realm of the child, that create discrepancies, pose contradictions, and require a shifting of perspective would be expected to have maximal impact on children's thinking and learning. Kamii and DeVries (1978) suggest four types of questions that encourage children to think about relationships between objects and events: for example, asking the child to make predictions ("What do you think will happen if you —— ?"), asking the child about creating desired effects ("Can you do —— ?"), asking about how actions are connected with events ("How did you do ——?"), asking about causes ("Why does —— happen?").

Questions that focus children's attention on transformations are also recommended by Foreman and Kuschner (1977). They further propose emphasis on questions that encourage the child to think about the opposite of what he or she is talking about. The child says, "I want to play with the ball outside." The teacher might say in response, "Does that mean that you don't want to play with the bike outside?" or "Does that mean that you don't want to play with the ball inside?" Perhaps such teacher intervention, when used judiciously, challenges the child toward greater metalinguistic and conceptual awareness.

Siegel and Saunders (1979), in a comprehensive summary of questioning as an informal instructional model, point out that asking questions directly confronts the child's current point of view, thus leading the child to restructure his or her thoughts. They further point out the importance of waiting long enough between question and answer, accepting answers without posing alternatives, and showing approval of thoughtful answers even though they may be wrong. They advise pursuing the thinking behind incorrect answers, since both the teacher and child benefit. The teacher learns more about the child's view and the child examines his/her own beliefs more fully. Responses to questions a child asks can also be important if the teacher takes advantage of the opportunity to get the child to consider past experiences, find appropriate information, or figure out answers independently. Children's questions can lead to genuine dialogue. Siegel and Saunders (1979) note the positive results of programs that emphasize question asking.

Modeling.   Modeling, as used in this context, refers to adults' conscious enactment, for children's observation, of desirable behavior. If the person doing the modeling is admired, and/or if rewards are observed to follow the behavior, imitation of the modeled behavior can be anticipated. The efficacy of modeling has been fully documented by Bandura and Walters (1963; also Bandura, 1969, 1973). Teachers are potent influences for children, often without realizing it. The extent to which nonrelevant as well as relevant behavior is picked up and faithfully imitated is testimony to the efficacy of modeling. The teacher who sniffs and rubs her eyes because of allergy problems while showing children how to do something sometimes finds sniffing and eye rubbing incorporated by the children as part of what they have learned. The teacher's behavior and especially the behavior of admired peers or older children are potent influences for good or for ill.

Teachers will generally benefit from greater awareness of how to use modeling. For example, according to Zimmerman and Rosenthal (1974), simple modeling, involving only observations of a model, as contrasted with guided practice, is more effective for helping young children learn new procedures. Zimmerman and Rosenthal (1974) also report that four-year-olds, unlike seven-year-olds, are helped in learning from a model by being led to verbalize what is being demonstrated. Much has been written (e.g., Ross, 1981) about the effects of models, the characteristics of a good model, and ways to facilitate modeling effects that teachers may find useful.

Strategies for Group Lessons

When, for one reason or another, it is desirable to have a group of children together in an activity that a teacher intends to actively lead, various strategies may be used. These include direct instruction, deductive lessons with advance organizers, inductive lessons, modeling lessons, and open-ended group discussion. Each of these will be discussed below.

Direct instruction. Direct instruction undoubtedly has many variations but has been characterized generically by Jacobs and Welsh (1984) as using attention signals, instances and noninstances, response signals, feedback, reinforcers, pacing, pauses, rhythm, response rates, volume, body language, enthusiasm, stimulus change, surprises, intentional mistakes, and mastery. The efficacy of direct instruction with low socioeconomic students for accomplishing specific academic and other similar objectives has been well documented (Bereiter & Engelmann, 1977; Becker & Gersten, 1982; Rosenshine, 1979).

In the direct instruction approach, initially proposed by Bereiter and Engelmann (1966) and commercially packaged under the DISTAR label, the teacher's behavior is predetermined via a prepared script provided with the teaching materials. Very specific steps leading to final objectives are specified. The basic techniques, however, may also be employed by teachers for lessons they design with very specific objectives. The direct instruction lesson often starts off with contrasts—children are verbally presented with discriminations or labels along with examples of where these can be applied, as well as instances in which they cannot be applied. The presentations begin with extreme contrasts and go toward finer and finer gradations. For example, children may be asked initially to discriminate between ice-cream cones and the letter *m*, but eventually, between the letters *m* and *n*. The students' role is to learn the right response and the teachers' role is to tell the pupils whether they are right or wrong and to carefully arrange the presentation so that they will be right most of the time. Lively, rhythmic interchanges and enthusiastic reinforcement are essential to the success of this strategy.

Deductive lessons with advance organizers. For Ausubel (1963; 1966), the most efficient approach for instruction is to begin a lesson with general ideas under which more differentiated ideas can be developed. Children are first given a comprehensive general presentation before seeing how exemplars fit into an overall scheme. This is said to be particularly important for young children since they tend to jump quickly to erroneous conclusions, to generalize from limited experience, and to consider only one aspect of a problem or situation at a time. In this approach children's discovery of knowledge is deemphasized and the meaningful presentation by the teacher of external subject matter is considered essential if misconceptions are to be avoided.

A series of studies conducted by Lawton and associates of Wisconsin Research and Development Center for Cognitive Learning support this approach to the teaching of logical operations and social studies concepts (Lawton, 1977), hierarchical classification (Swadener & Lawton, 1978), and concepts of conservation as identified by Piaget (Lawton & Reddy, 1983). Advance organizer lessons have also been applied to instruction in music, math, science, language, prereading, and social problem solving (Schwadener & Lawton, 1978).

In an advance organizer lesson on classification described by Schwadener and Lawton (1978), the teacher pointed out objects in the room and identified them as to their various properties: differing heights, weights, colors, etc. Children were then given objects to examine, manipulate, and classify according to similar properties. Throughout, there were attempts to relate new concepts or examples to the more general concepts the children gave evidence of understanding.

The preplanning of this approach appears to be most concerned with hierarchical sequencing of presentation. Once the format from general to specific is set, the teacher looks for appealing materials, concrete props, and a variety of related materials. While teaching, the teacher must be very alert to the children's existing understandings so that these may be used as the basis for new learning.

Inductive lessons for concept attainment. As in the concept attainment tasks used by Bruner (1956) to study children's thinking strategies, the concept attainment lesson begins with an assortment of exemplars or non-exemplars. The term *exemplar* refers to particular actions, situations, objects, or pictures selected to represent a given concept. *Non-exemplars* refer to actions, situations, objects, or pictures selected because they do *not* represent the concept. There are two approaches. In the first, the concepts to be "discovered" are predetermined by the teacher. Exemplars representing contrasts are either already grouped and displayed at the point of initial presentation or they are presented one at a time and gradually sorted by the teacher according to some preset criterion, for example, zoo animals versus farm animals, circles versus squares. The criterion for inclusion or exclusion in a particular group of objects is not told to the children. They try to figure out the underlying concept that makes one item identified as A and the next as not A.

In this type of concept attainment lesson, the teacher uses familiar materials, identifies both examples and nonexamples of the target concepts, gives students many examples, provides materials for children to test out their own ideas, and encourages children to discuss each others' ideas. The advantage of the concept attainment lesson is believed to be the development of thinking skills. The mental processes used in this lesson are seen as comparable to those used to discover or invent concepts in everyday learning.

In the second approach, the children are shown a mixed array of pictures or objects selected to represent several possible conceptual dimensions (for example, clothing that might be classified according to gender, season, appropriateness for indoor or outdoor wear). Students sort according to a category they invent and explain their classification rationale to other children in the group. There are, in this approach, no "right" ways to categorize.

Modeling lessons.   There are situations in which a teacher may want to teach a particular skill or procedure to a group of children quite systematically. The modeling procedure cited by Charles (1981, p. 156) provides a pragmatic approach for classroom use. The steps recommended are:

1. Choose a good model (a person who incorporates traits seen as desirable by the children, such as a popular peer leader, a somewhat older child, a favorite adult).
2. Train model in precise behavior to be enacted and have model demonstrate the "target" behavior to the group.
3. Call for verbal group enactment in unison of what was modeled. Ask leading questions regarding critical points, having the model reenact as necessary. Repeat verbal group enactment two or three times making sure all participate.
4. Ask for volunteers (two) to reenact event individually.

5. Draft two nonvolunteers.
6. Have learners immediately apply the skill or behavior to a meaningful situation.

Group discussion lessons. In a group discussion lesson, a social
problem is typically used as a focus. The problem may be a simulated one
requiring description and/or role playing or it may be an actual problem of
concern to the group members. The goal is not necessarily finding the
"right" or "best" answer but to build awareness of the need for solutions and
to develop a repertoire of viable possibilities in problem situations.

Group discussion lessons are part of the training provided by the
Spivack and Shure Interpersonal Problem-Solving Curriculum for four-year-
olds and five-year-olds (Spivack & Shure, 1974; Spivack, Platt, & Shure,
1976; Shure, 1980). The curriculum is effective for increasing children's
awareness of alternatives and consequences. Children become more adept
at generating various strategies that have potential for solving interpersonal
problems. They also learn to evaluate various alternatives in terms of their
prospective consequences. Teachers' ratings indicate that after the training,
children's social competence increases.

The Spivack and Shure lesson scripts include the initial development
of essential vocabulary and concepts for considering and discussing alternatives. Once this has been done, the teacher poses a problem for consideration. One lesson, for example, begins by establishing that it is fair for
children who have been playing with toys to help put them away. The
children are then told about a situation in which one of two children will not
help in putting the toys away. The question that is posed is, "What can
———— do so ———— will help him put the toys away?" Responses are
acknowledged and listed on a chalkboard. After each answer, the teacher
repeats it and all other previous suggestions and asks, "Who's got a different
idea?" (Spivack & Shure, 1974, p. 176). Although the Spivack and Shure
materials consist of a set of detailed scripts, the lesson strategies can be
adapted for use for any problem-focused group discussion.

SUMMARY AND IMPLICATIONS

Howsam, Corrigan, Denemark, and Nash (1976) characterize teaching
as a semiprofession. They point out that teaching, in contrast to occupations
that can be considered true professions, is held in low esteem, has a low
occupational status, a shorter training period, a less specialized and less
highly developed body of knowledge and skills, and less emphasis on
theoretical and conceptual basis of practice. As Spodek (1982) points out,
teachers of early childhood education enjoy even less esteem than those at

other levels. In the introductory section of this chapter, we cited Schön's perspective that greater articulation and examination of work processes are necessary to develop professional expertise. The romantic view of teacher as artist is inadequate to foster either individual professional growth or to enhance teaching as a profession.

As a remedy to this situation, we urge teachers to consciously develop a repertoire for various teaching situations and undertake reflection-in-action. It also seems important that professional groups help to articulate what these alternatives might be, developing vocabulary and concepts to match what has remained a largely intuitive set of practices. From such a thrust we predict benefits for individual teachers, the teaching profession, and children enrolled in early childhood education programs.

The strategies discussed in this chapter should help individual teachers in assessing repertoire areas in need of development. They may also indicate the need for better articulation of what it is we really do in teaching young children. In this chapter we have considered teaching alternatives under strategies for teacher-child relationships, teacher-child dialogue, and group lessons. Teachers may choose whether to establish warm, supportive relationships with children or remain more distant, hoping not to interfere with children's autonomy and integrity; whether to provide attention freely or contingently; and what degree of structuring to provide. The classroom management section delineated areas in which teachers' choices and actions may be critical to children's involvement and learning. For example, how may the first days and weeks of school be used to orient children to procedures and expectations? What advance anticipation and preparation is helpful for effective management? Possible alternatives for teacher-child dialogue were proposed: giving descriptive feedback, coaching, prompting and giving suggestions, asking questions, and modeling. For group lessons we discussed strategies of direct instruction, deductive lessons with advance organizers, inductive lessons for concept attainment, modeling lessons, and group discussion lessons. Of course, this represents a very meager set of strategies; others are referred to in textbooks and articles, but have not yet been researched. There are also, we expect, strategies used by highly competent teachers that are not well recognized and hence little, if anything, has been written about them.

Despite its meager nature, we expect that this collection of teaching strategies may go well beyond the alternatives now available to many individual early education teachers. It is fascinating to consider what else there is. We wish to challenge ourselves and our fellow professionals to engage more often in reflection-in-action so that we may, as a profession, act more intelligently and develop a body of knowledge that helps us become adequate to our tasks of guiding the learning and development of young children.

REFERENCES

Almy, M., Monighan, P., Scales, B., & Van Hoorn, J. (1984). Recent research play: The teacher's perspective. In L. G. Katz (Ed.), *Current topics in early childhood education*. Vol. 5, pp. 1–25. Norwood, NJ: Ablex.

Anderson, L., Evertson, C., & Emmer, E. (1979). *Dimensions in classroom management derived from recent research*. Austin: Texas University Research and Development Center for Teacher Education. ERIC Document Reproduction Service No. ED 175 860.

Anker, D., Foster, J., McLane, J., Sobel, J., & Weissbound, B. (1974). Teaching children as they play. *Young Children, 29*, 203–13.

Ausubel, D. P. (1968). *Educational psychology: A cognitive view*. New York: Holt, Rinehart and Winston.

Ausubel, D. P. (1963). *The psychology of meaningful verbal learning*. New York: Grune and Stratton.

Bandura, A. (1973). *Aggression: A social learning analysis*. Englewood Cliffs, NJ: Prentice-Hall.

Bandura, A. (1969). Social learning theory of identification processes. In D. A. Goslin (Ed.), *Handbook of socialization theory and research*. Chicago: Rand McNally.

Bandura, A., & Walters, R. H. (1963). *Social learning and personality development*. New York: Holt, Rinehart and Winston.

Becker, W. C., & Engelmann, S. (1977). *The Oregon Direct Instruction Model: Comparative results in Project Follow Through: A summary of nine years of work*. Eugene: University of Oregon Follow Through Project.

Becker, W. C., & Gersten, R. (1982). A follow-up of Follow Through: The later effects of the Direct Instruction Model on children in fifth and sixth grades. *American Educational Research Journal, 19*, 75–92.

Bereiter, C., and Engelmann, S. (1966). *Teaching disadvantaged children in the preschool*. Englewood Cliffs, NJ: Prentice-Hall.

Bijou, S. W., & Baer, D. M. (1978). *Behavior analysis of child development*. Englewood Cliffs, NJ: Prentice-Hall.

Blank, M. (1973). *Teaching learning in the preschool: A dialogue approach*. Columbus, OH: Charles E. Merrill.

Blank, M., & Solomon, F. (1969). How shall the disadvantaged child be taught? *Child Development, 40*, 47–61.

Brophy, J. E., & Evertson, C. M. (1976) *Learning from teaching: A developmental perspective*. Boston: Allyn and Bacon.

Bruner, J. S., Goodnow, J. J., & Austin, G. A. (1956). *A study in thinking*. New York: John Wiley.

Carew, J. V. (1980). Experience and the development of intelligence in young children at home and in day care. *Monographs of the Society for Research in Child Development, 45*, no. 187.

Charles, C. M. (1981). *Building classroom discipline: From model to practice*. New York: Longman.

Chatlin-McNichols, J. P. (1981). The effects of Montessori school experiences. *Young Children, 36,* 49–66.

Christie, J. F. (1982). Sociodramatic play training. *Young Children, 37,* 25–32.

Emmer, E., Evertson, E., & Anderson, L. (1979). *The first weeks of class . . . and the rest of the year.* Austin: Texas University Research and Development Center for Teacher Education. ERIC Document Reproduction Service No. ED 175 861.

Endsley, R. C., & Clarey, S. (1975). Answering young children's questions as a determinant of their subsequent question-asking behavior. *Developmental Psychology, 11,* 863.

Fagot, B. I. (1973). Influence of teacher behavior in the preschool. *Developmental Psychology, 9,* 198–206.

Feitelson, D., & Ross, G. S. (1973). The neglected factor—play. *Human Development, 16,* 202–24.

Fink, R. S. (1974). *The role of imaginative play in cognitive development: An experimental study.* Ph.D. diss., State University of New York, Buffalo.

Forman, G. E., & Kuschner, D. S. (1977). *The child's construction of knowledge.* Monterey, CA: Brooks-Cole.

Garvey, C. (1977). *Play.* Cambridge, MA: Harvard University Press.

Golomb, C., & Cornelius, C. B. (1977). Symbolic play and its cognitive significance. *Developmental Psychology, 13,* 246–52.

Hess, R. O., & Shipman, V. C. (1965). Early experience and the socialization of cognitive modes in children. *Child Development, 36,* 868–86.

Houston-Stein, A., Freiderich, L., & Susman, E. J. (1977). The relation of classroom structure to social behavior, imaginative play, and self-regulation of economically disadvantaged children. *Child Development, 48,* 908–16.

Howsan, R. B., Corrigan, D. C., Denemark, G. W., & Nash, R. J. (1976). *Educating a profession.* Washington, DC: American Association of Colleges for Teacher Education.

Joyce, B. R., & Weil, M. (1980). *Models of teaching.* (2nd ed.) Englewood Cliffs, NJ: Prentice-Hall.

Kamii, C., & DeVries, R. (1978). *Physical knowledge in preschool education: Implications of Piaget's theory.* Englewood Cliffs, NJ: Prentice-Hall.

Kohlberg, L. (1968). Early education: A cognitive-developmental view. *Child Development, 39,* 1013–62.

Langer, J. (1969). *Theories of development.* New York: Holt, Rinehart and Winston.

Lawton, J. T. (1977). The use of advance organizers in the learning and retention of logical operations and social studies concepts. *American Education Research Journal, 14,* 25–43.

Lawton, J. T., & Reddy, P. (1983). *Effects of advance organizer and guided self-discovery instruction on preschool children's understanding of conservation.* Presented at the annual meeting of American Education Research Association, Montreal. ERIC Document Reproduction Service No. ED 230 279.

Lay-Dopyera, M., & Dopyera, J. E. (1981). *Becoming a teacher of young children.* (2nd ed.) Lexington, MA: Heath.

Miller, L. G., & Dyer, J. L. (1975). Four preschool programs: Their dimensions and effects. *Monograph for Society for Research in Child Development, 40,* Serial No. 162.

Peters, D. L., Neisworth, J. T., & Yawhey, T. D. (1985). *Early childhood education: from theory to practice.* Monterey, CA: Brooks-Cole.

Piaget, J. (1977). *The development of thought: Equilibration of cognitive structures.* New York: Viking.

Rosen, C. (1974). The effects of sociodramatic play on problem-solving behavior among culturally disadvantaged preschool children. *Child Development, 45,* 920–27.

Rosenshine, B. V. (1978). Academic engaged time, content covered, and direct instruction. *Journal of Education, 160,* 38–66.

Ross, A. O. (1981). *Child behavior therapy: Principles, procedures, and empirical basis.* New York: Wiley.

Saltz, E., Dixon, D., & Johnson, J. (1977). Training disadvantaged preschoolers on various fantasy activities: Effects on cognitive functioning and impulse control. *Child Development, 48,* 367–80.

Schön, D. A. (1983). *The reflective practitioner: How professionals think in action.* New York: Basic.

Schwadener, E., & Lawton, J. T. (1978). The effects of two types of advance organizer presentations on preschool children's classifications, relations, and transfer task performance. Madison, WI: University of Wisconsin Center on Cognitive Learning. ERIC Document Reproduction Service No. ED 152 413.

Shipman, V. (1976). *Notable early characteristics of high and low achieving black low-SES children.* Progress Report 76-21. Princeton, NJ: Educational Testing Service.

Shure, M. B. (1980). Real-life problem-solving for parents and children: An approach to social competence. In D. P. Rathjen & J. P. Foreyt (Eds.), *Social competence.* Elmsford, NY: Pergamon Press.

Siegel, A. E., & Kohn, L. G. (1959). Permissiveness, permission, and aggression: The effect of adult presence or absence on aggression in children's play. *Child Development, 30,* 131–42.

Siegel, I. E., & Saunders, R. (1979). An inquiry into inquiry: Question asking as an instructional model. In L. G. Katz (Ed.), *Current topics in early childhood education,* vol. 2. Norwood, NJ: Ablex.

Skinner, B. F. (1974). *About behaviorism.* New York: Knopf.

Smilansky, S. (1968). *The effects of sociodramatic play on disadvantaged preschool children.* New York: John Wiley.

Soar, R. S., & Soar, R. U. (1972). An empirical analysis of selected Follow Through programs: An example of a process approach to evaluation in early childhood education. In I. Gordon (Ed.), *71st Yearbook of National Society for the Study of Education: Part II,* pp. 229–59. Chicago: University of Chicago Press.

Sparling, J. J., & Sparling, M. C. (1973). How to talk to a scribbler. *Young Children, 28,* 333–41.

Spivack, G., Platt, J. J., & Shure, M. B. (1976). *The problem-solving approach to adjustment: A guide to research and intervention.* San Francisco: Jossey-Bass.

Spivack, G., & Shure, M. B. (1974). *Social adjustment of young children's cognitive approach to solving real life problems*. San Francisco: Jossey-Bass.

Spodek, B., & Saracho, O. N. (1982). The preparation and certification of early childhood personnel. In B. Spodek (Ed.), *Handbook of research in early childhood education*. New York: Free Press.

Stallings, J. (1975). Implementation and child effects of teaching practices in Follow Through classrooms. *Monograph of the Society for Research in Child Development, 40,* Serial No. 163.

Thompson, G. G. (1944). The social and emotional development of preschool children under two types of educational programs. *Psychological Monographs, 56,* no. 5, Whole No. 258.

Tzelepis, A., Giblin, P. T., & Agronow, S. J. (1983). Effects of adult caregivers' behaviors on the activities, social interactions, and investments of nascent preschool day-care groups. *Journal of Applied Developmental Psychology, 4,* 201–16.

Weil, M., & Joyce, B. (1978a). *Information processing models of teaching: Expanding your teaching repertoire*. Englewood Cliffs, NJ: Prentice-Hall.

Weil, M., & Joyce, B. (1978b). *Personal models of teaching: Expanding your teaching repertoire*. Englewood Cliffs, NJ: Prentice-Hall.

Weil, M., & Joyce, B. (1978c). *Social models of teaching: Expanding your teaching repertoire*. Englewood Cliffs: NJ: Prentice-Hall.

Wittmer, D. S. (1985a). *Looking in the window: An analysis of caregiver interactions with twos and threes in Title XX day care*. Ph.D. diss., Syracuse University.

Wittmer, D. S. (1985b). Summary of findings of "Looking in the window: An analysis of caregiver interactions with twos and threes in Title XX day care." Unpublished. (Donna Wittmer, Ph.D., Clinical Assistant Professor, SUNY Health and Science Center, 750 E. Adams Street, Syracuse, NY 13210.)

Yinger, J. (1975). *Problem-solving with children*. San Francisco: Far West Laboratory for Educational Research and Development.

Zimmerman, B. J., & Rosenthal, T. C. (1974). Observational learning of rule-governing behavior by children. *Psychological Bulletin, 81,* 29–42.

CHAPTER 3

Play

DORIS PRONIN FROMBERG
Hofstra University

Why would we want children to play in early childhood classes? How would we provide worthwhile conditions?

There are a number of reviews dealing with research on the play of young children, which are in their various ways intensive, distinctive, and worthwhile (Pellegrini, 1985; Wortham, 1985; Almy, Monighan, Scales, & Van Hoorn, 1984; Christie & Johnson, 1983; Rubin, Fein, & Vanderberg, 1983; Sponseller, 1982; Fein, 1981; Schwartzman, 1978; Singer, 1973; and Millar, 1971). This chapter builds upon these, and other works printed since they were published, in order to present a mildly idiosyncratic perspective. I also attempt to present a consensual sort of synthesis, the purpose of which is to suggest what research might contribute to teaching practice. In turn, there is a discussion of a definition of play and some theories that contribute to our views. I will provide a look at the varied research that these theories generate. The implications for teaching practice are drawn from this material.

DEFINING PLAY

Play functions both as a verb and a noun. Perhaps this is why many researchers have found a problem in defining it. Rather than a category, property, or stage of behavior, play is a *relative* activity.

Perhaps because play is relative behavior, it has been studied by historians (Huizinga), philosophers (Ellul, Dewey, Langer), linguists (Cazden, Chukovsky, Kirschenblatt-Gimblett, Vygotsky, Weir), anthropologists (Aldis, Bateson, Blurton Jones, Schwartzman, Sutton-Smith, Smith), and psychologists (Almy, Monighan, Scales, & Van Hoorn; Bretherton; Bruner, Jolly & Sylva; Fein, Freud, Lieberman, Peller, Piaget, Pulaski, Singer, Werner), to list only some. From these varied perspectives, scholars and researchers have considered the child as solitary, playing with objects or imagination; as well as a social player with one or more peers, with children of varied ages, with parent figures, and with other adults. They have considered the immediate contexts in which play occurs; the content, the interaction of context and content, and the cultural environment. They have differentiated play from exploration. They have divided social play into structured games-with-rules and sports, as contrasted with the more evolving forms of sociodramatic play. This chapter concentrates on representational and interactive play.

As we watch children play, it seems a matter of common sense to ask what it is that they are doing. Yet there is a tendency to mix what they are doing with how significant play may be for other purposes than the immediate purpose of pretense. Indeed, when researchers come to look at play, they have a way of seeing play from the unique perspectives of their own specialties and values. Therefore, different theories of play have come to be. For our purposes, and within this limited space, the focus will be on those theories that are more current than mainly historical, except where contrast may serve to highlight an issue.

First, I propose a definition of play that might suffice as a foil to parry with the various theoretical perspectives. Then, those perspectives can riposte. Following this discussion, there is a synthetic view of how play functions, what dynamics might be present, and what sequential development may be relevant.

A Definition of Play in Young Children

Young children's play is:

Symbolic, in that it represents reality with "as if" or "what if" attitude;
Meaningful, in that it connects or relates experiences;
Active, in that children are doing things;
Pleasurable, even when children engage seriously in activity;
Voluntary and *intrinsically motivated*, whether the motives are curiosity, mastery, affiliation, or others;
Rule-governed, whether implicitly or explicitly expressed; and
Episodic, characterized by emerging and shifting goals that children develop spontaneously.

The content of play is influenced by children's experiences, and also by the context in which they find themselves. Context may include the physical environment, time, other children or adults, and cultural sanctions and expectations. Since context helps to define play, various theorists, taking different perspectives, tend to see the functions of play somewhat differently.

THEORIZING ABOUT PLAY

Two broad theoretical perspectives on play are discussed below—the more or less psychological and the more or less cultural. These theoretical positions emphasize different ways of looking at the same activity.

With a Psychological Emphasis

Jean Piaget, a psychologist who also brought the perspective of an epistemologist and biologist, offers a powerful definition of play that evolved from the structure of his cognitive theory of child development. He sees children taking an active role in forming their play symbols. Building on the object play of solitary children, he proposes that play can be "pure assimilation," but that it is the "ratio," the "relationship," or "predominance," of assimilation over accommodation that defines an activity as play (1962, pp. 90, 103, 164, 150). In this emphasis on assimilation, he sees play as a state of imbalance. Using similar terms, Dewey (1933, p. 285) suggests that play gives "prominence" or places "emphasis" on activity, "without much reference to its outcomes." However, he cautions that when there is no outcome, play can "degenerate into fooling, and work into drudgery." "To be playful and serious at the same time is possible, and it defines the ideal mental condition" (p. 286). His work suggests the following continuum: fooling ↔ play ↔ work ↔ drudgery. For example, work or drudgery may come to feel like play, under certain circumstances.

Play as present with a past- or future orientation. For Piaget, play can "distort" reality to fit the child's current level of understanding (1962, pp. 104, 164). However, other psychologists (Vygotsky, Bruner, Jolly, & Sylva) and anthropologists (Schwartzman, Sutton-Smith) speak of Piaget's description of play as assimilation that "distorts" reality, as if the word "distorts" had a negative connotation. Schwartzman prefers the term "allusion," suggesting that play is an orientation, a defining context "which produces a text characterized by allusion (not distortion or illusion), [and] transformation (not preservation)" (1978, p. 330).

Bruner, Jolly, and Sylva propose that children use the conventions, rules, and sets (in the sense of readiness to act) of play in a creative, "generative" way (1976, p. 277). Sutton-Smith suggests that children assume a "representative set" or "frame" in their play. He proposes that "it constitutes new thought or new combinations of thought" (1979, p. 315).

By "distorting" reality, Piaget 1962 passim, suggests that children's play focuses on past experience "to transform reality" and to deform and subordinate reality "to the desires of the self" (Piaget, 1966, pp. 111–12). In contrast, Vygotsky suggests that children at play act "against immediate impulse" by subordinating themselves to rules. There is a paradox in this dialectic between pleasure in being "emancipated from situational constraints" while acting spontaneously, and subordinating oneself to the rules of play as the "path to maximal pleasure in play" (1978, p. 99). In this way, children at play exercise their greatest self-control and behave "in advance of development" (p. 129). Vygotsky contends that "play creates a zone of proximal development" (p. 102) which is a condition of instruction (p. 130) that is oriented toward the future development of children. Note that Schwartzman, above, also suggests a future orientation when she speaks of "transformation (not preservation)."

If the major benefit of play for Vygotsky is the creation of an advancement of development, the major benefit of play for Bruner is "the combinatorial benefit it bestows on behavior" (1976, p. 153). For Piaget, it would be the ongoing consolidation by children of their experiences, a process which leads toward construction of internal representations of the world.

Piaget posits play as a transition between egocentric thought and the development of reciprocity. Vygotzky propels play as a bridge ("pivot") that joins objects and actions with their representation in thought. Until children can separate the thought from the object or action, they must have something to act as a "pivot" in the form of a meaningful substitute, for example, a stick denoting a horse" (1976, p. 546).

Making connections and substitutions. It is interesting to consider how this process of making connections and substitutions occurs. Piaget suggests the elegant dynamic of "cognitive conflict" (1962, 1976), similar to the concept of "cognitive dissonance" postulated by Festinger (1957). There is an element of novelty or surprise caused by the discrepancy between the partial resemblance and the partial difference which stimulates fresh perception. The contrast and movement between familiar and strange stimulate perception. Cognitive conflict in this sense, and cognitive dissonance in the sense of the discrepancy between what you expect and what you find, represents one of the powerful conditions for learning that is available to teachers.

Wish fulfillment and mastery. Investigators such as Erikson, Freud,

Peller, Piaget, Sutton-Smith and Kelly-Byrne, and Vygotsky have agreed
that children use play to represent wish fulfillment. Vygotsky suggests that
play reflects "generalized affects" rather than "isolated wishes" and that the
"union of affect and perception" is characteristic of early childhood (1976, pp.
540, 545).

They also concur that play helps children to feel in control and to
experience a sense of mastery. From this perspective, children come to
understand the limits of their own power to control the environment.
"Seeing the consequences of one's actions in a game develops the sense of
predictable and controllable environment" (Coleman, 1976, p. 462). Opie
and Opie suggest that children learn to "reconcile" themselves to varied
levels of success and influence (1976, p. 396). Children also control the
intensity of play activity, as in "play fighting" (Aldis, 1975, p. 180). These
views parallel White's (1959) notion that children have a need to feel
competent and capable of influencing their world.

Intrinsic motivation.   In addition, these researchers overlap in seeing
play as intrinsically motivated. Other psychologists have suggested that play
is "autotelic" (self-motivated) as well (Moore & Anderson, 1968). Whatever
the motives at the outset, it is useful to refer to Allport's (1958) construct of
"functional autonomy" in which he noted that activity, perhaps begun with a
distant goal in mind, may become intrinsically satisfying in itself without
reference to the less playful goal. In this way, work or drudgery may come to
feel playful.

By way of contrast, consider that a "less playful goal" may become
"workful" or exploratory. Ellul (1965) and Caldwell (1985) have suggested
that sports as an economic, sometimes stressful or obsessive occupation,
need to be differentiated from games. Still another way to define play is to
contrast it with exploration.

Distinguishing between exploration and play.   Hutt (1976, p. 211)
captures an essential orientation when she states, "In play the emphasis
changes from the question of "what does this object do?" [which is explora-
tion] to "what can I do with this object?" [which is play]. She bases her ideas
on "arousal" theory, associated with Berlyne's (1960) work, which proposes
that when humans face high arousal or uncertainty, they attempt to reduce it
by exploratory behavior which provides information. Hutt sees the investigation of unknown properties in exploration as a way to get information,
where the stimulus is the referent. Play for her "only occurs in a known
environment" where the response is the referent (p. 211).

Wohlwill (1984), citing a pilot study with twenty-one nursery school
children, concurs, contending that exploratory behavior precedes play,

which occurs when arousal stimulation is more moderate. He cites Gibson's (1979) work on "affordance-directed activity" which suggests that manipulative exploration at the physical, rather than at the cognitive or imaginal level, may be transitional between exploration and play in its transformational possibilities. While Collard agrees with these views, she adds, "The infant learns the perceptual properties of objects primarily through exploration and the action or function properties of objects primarily through play" (1979, p. 52).

Assessing play. Ellis (1979) and Ellis and Scholtz (1978) suggest that social activity provides more complexity than objects. Hutt's finding that language use is more complex with peers than with teachers is relevant in the context of their work. At the same time, Ellis (1984) comments on the relative nature of social competences. Having studied play's physical manifestations in heart rate and biorhythms, Ellis (1979) observed that children deemed hyperactive in a traditional classroom were indistinguishable in play. From another point of view, Opie and Opie reported similar findings, that children were more aggressive in school and school playground settings than "in the street or in the wild places" (1976, p. 399). These findings suggest that we might expect children to behave in *relation* to context and constraints.

With a Cultural Emphasis

The preceding positions have emphasized a psychological perspective while there have been contrasts with more sociocultural or anthropological views. Now, play will be discussed from a cultural viewpoint. This perspective emphasizes the contextual and *relative* aspects of play. Some investigators have contended that play is defined in relation to the historical period and place in which it takes place (Csikszentmihayli, 1976; Glickman, 1984; Kirschenblatt-Gimblett, 1979; Lancy, 1984; Vandenberg, 1985, 1981). What may be play in one time and place may be ritual or religious, frivolous or technical, elsewhere. The cultural context also determines who may, or is likely to, engage in various kinds of play (Morgan, 1982; Geertz, 1976).

Play as a frame. The concept of a play frame, background, or context, has been identified by some commentators. Bateson has said that play "is the name of a frame for action" (1979, p. 139). It was he who also used the term "metacommunication," contending that our culture teaches us what to expect and how to categorize (1971, 1972, 1976). Thus, children come to differentiate between reality and fantasy as they play. In this way, he sees play as progress in the "evolution of communication" (1976, pp. 121, 125).

Play and categorization. Bateson suggests that children demonstrate by their behavior that they can categorize play and not-play as they enter into and step outside of the framework of play situations.

Janiv (1976) reports on a relevant, informal survey of Eastern immigrant families in Israel. She found that the parents taught their preschool children to categorize objects, kinship structures, and myths in unique ways that differed from those of European immigrant families. Smilansky (1968) found parallel differences between the play of children from these populations, which seems to confirm the existence of differences in category systems. To understand a child's category system is to appreciate differences, rather than rank-order them.

As children play, then, they engage in and learn more about the rules of playing. The kind of "metacommunication" that takes place in social play makes it possible for children to pretend together as they accept or reject each other's play premises, plans, and suggestions. This "metacommunication" is not the same as metacognition, Piaget's (1976) notion of mature self-awareness. In contrast to Piaget's (1962) position that play as "pure assimilation" reflects development, there is conjecture that young children acquire knowledge and develop cognitively as they engage in social play (Bretherton, 1985, p. 70).

Still another way to consider the fruitful notion of metacommunication in play is to consider that symbolic representation takes place every time children play with objects as "pivots" that bridge the gap between real and make-believe, or when they collaborate with others to "map" a play territory together. The verbal rituals of play that help to categorize oneself and others in the play frame make it possible to transform relationships within the system (Garvey, 1979, p. 109).

Play as leading development. In this respect, play seems to lead development. This is evident when the surface structures of children's play reveal their deeper propositional structure. Garvey proposes that insight into the child's competence level can become apparent "by listening to him play" (1979, p. 112). Dunn and Dale would concur, as a result of their study of twenty families consisting of a two-year-old and a four- or five-year-old sibling. They found that the two-year-olds appeared to understand, cooperate in, and contribute to joint pretend play earlier, and to engage in play with longer themes with siblings at home (1984, pp. 134, 137). It would make sense for those who subscribe to these views to pursue a line of research that studies the relationship of play, language, cognitive functioning, and social competence.

PLAY DYNAMICS AND DEVELOPMENT

Looking at play with a psychological as well as a cultural emphasis reveals the integration of the personal, symbolic aspects, and the shared symbols of social players, as well as their interaction within cultural constraints. Bateson's emphasis on "politics" (context) and Freud's emphasis on "symbolism" (content) are mixed together in play, according to Sutton-Smith (1984).

Transformational Dynamics

The symbolic nature of social play also has been considered in the "script model" which Kreye has studied. For her, "Young children come to represent recurring experiences through event schemata. . . . Event schemata represent meaning in context" (1984, pp. 301, 302). Bretherton sees event schemata as figurative frameworks and contends that the "links between elements of scripts or event schemata are temporo-causal, in contrast to the links between members of . . . classification hierarchies that are based on similarity" (1984, p. 272).

In a way, script theory posits a kind of syntactic structure for sociodramatic play which contains a finite set of *figurative* structures that can generate an infinite set of combinations, a kind of grammar for play. While children understand the signals of play such as voice change, posture, gestures, or facial expression, they seem to follow certain organizational rules that are developmentally more or less complex. Their implicit understanding of the "script" is explicitly represented in their play.

Fein (1985) speaks of "affective representational templates" that differ from "templates" that are more discursive (1985, p. 26). Even though Fein also has identified a developmental progression from more to less prototypical toy preferences, capacity, and actions in her own research (1975, 1979), in a more recent study (1985) she expresses concern and wonders whether script theory may be too convergent, since children's emotional preoccupations are fluid. She prefers focusing on the "moment-to-moment" relative change, yet agrees with Peller that there are "universal affective themes" (1971, p. 26). However, it is not at all clear that the "figurative" structures of script theory and the opportunities for divergent experience in play need to be mutually exclusive.

Nevertheless, the isomorphic nature of script theory has an intriguing potential for leading in divergent directions, which is worth studying. *Isomorphic structures* have been postulated in a number of fields where transformational knowledge has been explored. Dream symbols in psychology (Jung, 1970), autotelic folk models in game theory (Moore & Anderson, 1968), mythic themes in anthropology (Levi-Strauss, 1969a, 1969b), recursive loops in interdisciplinary theory (Hofstadter, 1980), perceptual models in communications theory (McLuhan, 1963) and curriculum theory (Fromberg, 1977, 1982, 1987), generative structures in linguistics (Chomsky, 1972), and DNA in genetics research (Pfeiffer, 1962), indicate the diverse directions in which such issues have traveled.

Several other positions point to the isomorphic character of play. Bruner and Sherwood see play as an opportunity to practice subroutines of behavior. They talk about the "syntax" of the game, which consists of "patterned variation within a constraining rule set [that] seems crucial to the mastery of competence and generativeness" (1976, p. 283). Koestler talks about thinking as consisting of "a fixed set of rules but capable of varied flexible strategies" (1976, p. 182). Sutton-Smith assumes that play is the "precursor of games" by a progression of "ludic infrastructures that lead to the game elements" (1971, p. 299).

Even Piaget posits that intuitive sensory-motor schemas that are related to individual objects evolve into "Infralogical or spatio-temporal operations [that] relate not the objects themselves, but elements of those objects" (1962, p. 271). However, from a gestalt psychology perspective, Levine (1984) takes issue with what she perceives to be Piaget's too practical cognition. She proposes that the logic of play is the logic of metaphor that proceeds by the juxtaposition and connection of sometimes disparate phenomena through their isomorphic relationships. Similarly, Gilmore criticizes Piaget for subordinating imagination to reason (1971, p. 342). Gilmore sees play as an expressive form that functions uniquely even though it may contribute to cognitive development.

Affective considerations. Schwartzman, an anthropologist, has entitled an entire book about play *Transformations* (1978), a name denoting and documenting the generative character of play. She also highlights in another study the affective element in play, as children learn "that contexts influence the authority structure of a relationship" (1979, p. 252). Issues of "control," "manipulation," and "dominance" surface during these communications. She would support the notion that the psychological as well as the social aspects of play change in relation to the content of communication (text) that takes place in the play context.

From another vantage point, Fein attributes an affective relativity to play. Further, she sees "pretense as an orientation in which the immediate environment is deliberately treated in a divergent manner" (1985, p. 21).

Lieberman (1977) proposes that there is a quality of "playfulness" that contributes to divergent thinking. Csikszentmihayli touches on the idea of playfulness when he talks about a "state of flow" in play. He focuses on the experiential state of the person who is playing within "a setting or frame of action" and who has achieved "a subjectively perceived balance" between "challenge and skill," spontaneity and control (1979, pp. 268, 261). This state-of-flow experience may be compared to Dewey's views on art. Dewey says that the dialectic of "spontaneity and order" is common to play and aesthetic experience. However, he notes that art "as esthetic experience . . . involves a definite reconstruction of objective materials" (1934, p. 279). Huizinga also speaks of play as creating order and having an "aesthetic factor" (1955, p. 10). These views would logically point to the study of play as related to associative fluency and creativity.

Some other views of the dynamics that take place when children play have been discussed as part of theorizing about play. They include processes that are predominantly a blend of cognition and affect, such as cognitive conflict, cognitive dissonance, challenge, pivotal, and transformational—including isomorphic—models. Other processes that are predominantly social involve metacommunication, collaborative rule-building, and scripts that connect neatly with isomorphic models of the play process.

These processes lead to varied developmental outcomes. Depending upon one's theoretical position, one sees play as extending cognitive, linguistic, and social learning, or as reinforcing what children have already learned. Children extend their imagination and improve associative fluency, or lack the capacity for imagining that which is not or has not been present. If one holds that intervention in play can improve children's learning and imagination, then one would create a different environment for children than if one held that learning and imagination are uninfluenced by play.

More on Cognitive Dissonance, Cognitive Conflict

There is the possibility that the learning aspects of play reflect the cognitive conflict–cognitive dissonance dialectic. Bruner proposes the notion of "surprising, yet familiar" as part of our subjective experiencing of a creative product (1976, p. 641). Koestler (1976) sees such surprise as a way in which new connections are made by a process of *intellectual challenge* (1976, p. 188).

Eifermann presents challenge as a central feature of play, the point at which the child is able to control the level of conflict between what is known and has been experienced and what is undetermined (1976, p. 454). These views are similar to a definition of "intellectual challenge" as "a perceived invitation, containing both an element of uncertainty and a perceived chance for success, which produces learner motivation to strive toward the attainment of intellectual expansion" (Fromberg, 1965, p. 12). It may, indeed, be that the underlying motives of play and intellectual challenge share common aspects. Perhaps this is reflected in those studies that find play influencing cognition, problem solving, or associative fluency.

There appears to be an oscillation process in this dialectic between surprise and familiarity, partial resemblance and partial difference, what you expect and what you find, that is not unlike the oscillation that takes place in the negotiations of social play. This oscillation between what you expect in somebody else's behavior and what you find stimulates the decentration that characterizes development in both cognition and play. (Decentration, a concept developed by Piaget, is discussed in greater depth later.)

Children, when playing, are continually perceiving and using *contrasts*, an essential aspect of learning. For Freud, "A joke is judgment which produces a comic contrast," and play precedes jokes (1960, pp. 10, 128). McGhee (1984) proposes that humor is an intellectual subset of play. Playing with ideas and creating incongruities require contrasts. In this sense, there is a cognitive dissonance between the expected outcome and the surprise of the incongruous one. Freud also sees contrasts in the child's clear distinction between play and reality. Were a child (or adult) not able to contrast play and reality, he might be daydreaming (1958, p. 45). Clearly, the readiness to perceive contrasts varies from one individual to another.

Individual Differences

The study of individual differences provides another contribution to the dynamics of play. Shotwell, Dennis, and Gardner (1979) and Gardner (1982) have distinguished between the styles of "patterners" and "dramatists" in symbolic play. Patterners appear to be intrigued by the world of objects and the design and mechanical possibilities of materials. Dramatists prefer the world of people and interpersonal events. These researchers suggest that each style appears to be a valid route toward general symbolic competence. They attribute the roots of these unique styles to underlying "mental structures" (Shotwell, Dennis, & Gardner, 1979, p. 130) and personality. These play patterns were identified after a longitudinal case study, involving weekly visits to nine middle-class children between the ages of one and three years. These styles appear to parallel Adler's (1923) introvert-extrovert categories.

Blurton Jones uses naturalistic observations, as do Shotwell, Dennis, and Gardner. He refers to gender differences in play, and suggests the possible development of "two cultures," the male "doers" and the female "verbalists" (1976, p. 362).

J. L. Singer (1973) reports findings concerning a related difference: individuals who display a profile of high or low fantasy in their play. Related research by Freyberg (1973) and Pulaski (1973) supports and develops Singer's findings. In addition, Feitelson and Ross (1973) find that kindergarten children come to school with varied ability to show initiative in using equipment imaginatively.

Singer observed forty-six two- to five-year-old middle-class nursery school children during free play and structured play, and studied forty primary-age middle-class children by using interviews, a storytelling task, and observation in a waiting situation. He and D. Singer have found that high-imagination children report greater contact with parents who model or provide specific opportunities for fantasy play (1979, p. 198). High-imagination children manifest a capacity to wait quietly for a longer period of time, reporting fantasy play as they do so. They also scored higher in imaginative storytelling, made more analogic kinds of statements (p. 199), and were more persevering than low-fantasy children. Recent studies confirm J. L. Singer's 1973 findings (Connolly & Doyle, 1984; Moran, Sawyers, Fu, & Milgram, 1984).

Fein (1985) identifies and studies "master players," defined as children who engage in extended social pretend play, according to their teachers and trained observers. She identifies components of play that are characterized by fluidity, flexibility, risk-taking, and affective relationships.

More on Metacommunication and Context

Piaget (1965) makes the point that when children build rules together as they play, they become more independent and increase their ability to see points of view other than their own. This is the process of *decentering* from oneself and one's immediate environment. Indeed, the ongoing social feedback is a kind of coaching system that helps to build social and cognitive skills.

A study of the natural play of ten middle-class preschool children documented this sort of coaching. Chafel (1984) found that children ask for feedback from one another by various conventional statements that they add to their play-related comments. Statements such as "OK?" "Right?" "Don't we?" and "See?" seek confirmation, information, argument, compliance, and attention. These statements reflect the children's awareness of each other's influence and something of the conventions that are acceptable within the play setting.

As they played, the children were able to move outside the playframe for brief negotiations about how to keep the play going. Giffin, after observing thirty-eight middle-class three- to five-year-olds in a classroom dress-up area, proposed a theoretical metacommunicative continuum of "within-frame" and "out-of-frame" communication (Giffin, p. 80). That is, children agreed to rules that helped them sustain their transformation of reality. The agreement process occurred outside the play frame and maintenance of the pretense occurred while children were engaged in the play.

Giffin observes that children "negotiate transformations with the least possible acknowledgment of the playframe" (p. 88) because children prefer to act "rather than organize if at all possible" (p. 93). Giffin proposes three "rules" by which children act: an "implicit pretend rule," a "strict adherence rule," whereby play transformations are consistent with the script, and an "incorporation rule," when others adapt to the recommended transformations of reality (pp. 89–91).

Nelson and Seidman confirm Giffin's work. For them, "the shared script . . . contributes a background context within which roles are defined, props are specified, and a sequence of actions is understood" (1984, p. 50). They studied six four-year-olds in sandbox play and twenty young three-year-olds in each of three different play contexts. All children were from lower-class homes. Among the younger children, they found that "play events within the longest segments of continuous discourse [for each dyad] in each context were scripted" (p. 58). They suggest that "children have specific scripts for play in different contexts" (p. 59). Among the older children, they found play events with a greater number of more expansive and extended scripts (pp. 64, 67, 69). The content of children's play showed repeated cycles of event action or discourse (p. 50).

Using categories of play utterances, other investigators have made similar observations. They have found "a developmental trend toward greater conversational continuity and coherence" and "transformations [that] become constructed in an increasingly reciprocal way" (Göncü & Kessel, 1984, pp. 18, 19).

As a contrast to studies of children who know each other, Forys and McCune-Nicolich (1984) studied three dyads of almost three-year-olds who were unacquainted before the laboratory play setting. They found "that pretending facilitated the social interaction of unfamiliar young peers [which] has not been reported previously" (pp. 174–75). They did note that one dyad engaged in mainly nonverbal negotiation (p. 166), and recognized that their sample size was small, warranting replication study with larger samples.

The Development of Social Competence

The relative nature of play and development, both culturally and individually, seems to be established. Therefore, as we look at the sequence of play development, it makes sense to expect trends with variations rather than fixed results across the field.

One team of researchers, who studied the symbolic play of thirty children at twenty and twenty-eight months, contends that it is more important "to discover the range of a child's ability under different contextual conditions than to attempt to establish whether he or she has the ability in an absolute sense" (Bretherton, O'Connell, Shore, & Bates, 1984).

Using a laboratory setting as well as home visits, Bretherton and colleagues found that when adults modeled play behavior, the complexity of children's use of toys was enhanced at three levels of reference—"self-reference," where children pretend to feed themselves; "other-reference," where children pretend that the doll is a real baby; and other, "agent–patient," where children pretend to play both roles of a play interaction with two doll or animal figures. The more advanced language of the twenty-eight-month-olds enhanced the playing of reciprocal relations between the two toys. However, these young children did not prefer a less realistic substitute prop, and some of the more sophisticated players protested its presence. Whether the individual children started out more or less object-dependent, which was not measured, or whether the object substitution was a result of adult intervention, the researchers concluded that play can be enhanced or depressed by contextual variation.

Fenson also studied the post-modeling behavior of seventy-two middle-class children, twenty-four each at twenty, twenty-six, and thirty-one months of age in a laboratory setting. He also used two levels of modeling—"other-reference" and "other agent–patient." He proposed a developmental progression that involves the processes of decentering, decontextualization, and integration (1984, pp. 254–55; 1985, pp. 34–35).

In Fenson's view, social pretend play both reflects and contributes to decentration. Development proceeds from a focus on the self toward active, other-directed acts. The indicators of decontextualization are symbolic transformation, substitutions, and inventive acts, as children become increasingly less dependent upon prototypical representation. Integration is characterized by an increasing ability to combine individual action sequences into multischeme combinations. He found that there was no gender effect on language but that there was an increasing predominance of speech in children's pretend play as they grew older. However, he found that there was more evidence of integrative play among girls.

Interaction with objects.   The use of objects and toys alone and with others has followed parallel developmental paths. Fein (1975) studied, in a laboratory setting, the degree of pretend play transformations of sixty-six children between twenty-two and twenty-seven months of age who came from working-class and lower-middle-class homes. In the completed study, forty-eight children participated while the child's mother was present in a passive role. Fein (1985) reported some related findings stemming from a study of children at twenty-four and thirty months of age. She found that it was more difficult for the younger children to pretend substitutions with less prototypical objects or with more than one symbolic transformation. The play of the older children was more diverse and complex. Fein concludes that transformations "designate the process whereby characteristics of the immediate environment become subordinated to what is essentially a mentally initiated activity" (p. 295).

Confirming Fein's (1975) findings, Copple, Cocking, and Matthews agree that "Only in a later stage could a dissimilarity in both form and function be tolerated simultaneously within a symbolic act" (1984, p. 108). They also note, "Verbalizations focusing on the object's suitability as a substitute were nearly twice as common as behaviors that took note of a shortcoming. . . . Older children showed the tendency to note object similarities more than younger children" (p. 115). The experimenters observed a developmental progression of object choices as follows: "functional assimilation" followed by "literal representation," and then "symbolic representation" (p. 120). Their findings were based on a study of thirty children between the ages of almost four years and five and a half years. They observed children individually in a laboratory setting that involved interaction with a familiar experimenter.

Bretherton, O'Connell, Shore, and Bates (1984) also confirm Fein's observations regarding substitution. They would even concur that a double substitution would depress pretend play even more than a single substitution. However, they suggest that there is probably an upper limit to the effectiveness of modeling rather than seeing the context as less influential than individual development.

Wolf, Rygh, and Altshuler observed nine middle-class children longitudinally at home between one and seven years of age. They noticed that children began to treat and talk differently to toys than to persons at around eighteen months. They identified a first phase, between one and five years of age, when children begin to implicitly understand that they are "independent agents" as others are (1984, pp. 205, 208). A second phase involves recognizing that "beyond performing actions, human actors also undergo internal experiences" (p. 205). These symbolic capacities become explicit through language, gesture, and their expression in play (p. 208).

These researchers found gender differences. Boys tended to use a third-person stance, and girls to speak through a character (p. 211). Boys emphasized object use, and girls emphasized internal experience (p. 214). While they used their social understanding differently, by three years of age, all were able to describe their characters as agents and experiencers (p. 210).

Another study of thirty lower-class black boys and thirty middle-class white boys between two and a half and five years of age took place in a laboratory setting with individual children (McGhee, Etheridge, & Berg, 1984). The experimenters suggest that children may be more receptive to less realistic, unstructured toys if they have begun with symbolic rather than realistic objects, but that the reverse does not occur. That is, once children begin with realistic materials, they are less receptive to symbolic substitutions.

Interaction with others.   In dialogue, the investigators cited in the above section might all agree that there is a significant interaction between the child's developmental capacity and the play context. Garvey made a related observation after studying forty dyads of three-year-olds and forty-eight children between almost three and five and a half years of age in a laboratory setting. She found that the younger children's interactive speech showed a more complex, advanced propositional structure than might be apparent from the surface elements of play (1979, p. 112). She used the term "scaffolding" (p. 114) to denote the switches that children make between acting and directing within the play frame. These findings suggest that metacommunication in the play context advances development.

Pellegrini (1984c) reports similar findings in a study of ten three-year-olds and ten four-year-olds from middle-class homes who were observed in art, blocks, and housekeeping activities. He found that the children engaged in more mature social cognitive play when there were other children than when there was an adult present. He suggests that the presence of other children provided more opportunity for cognitive conflicts, a view in support of Piaget's positions (1965, 1976).

At the same time, others have found otherwise—that an adult presence with lower-class children stimulated more complex play and language (Miller & Garvey, 1984; Smilansky, 1968, p. 330; Sylva, 1984). Pellegrini wonders whether his middle-class children were less likely than the lower-class population to express disagreement with an adult.

Beyond siblings, peers, or adults, Fein reports that in a "strange situation, the range and diversity of play became considerably restricted and the tempo was reduced. Nothing happened to the structural variables" (1985, p. 72). She suggests that an array of toys for interaction rather than only one makes a difference in play (p. 74).

Rubin (1985) observes that popular children are more able to solve social problems and engage in more rule-centered group games than more slowly developing isolates. He and Pellegrini both refer to Parten's (1971) sequence of play beginning with solitary, then parallel play, followed by interactive play.

Other researchers also have reported a progression in children's play from solitary (two-year-olds) and beginning joint play, more relatedness and talk (two-and-a-half-year-olds), and then reciprocal role playing (three-year-olds) (Miller & Garvey, 1984, pp. 107–08). Sutton-Smith (1971) suggests a similar progression as a series of reversals beginning at two years of age with "passive-active," to "subject-object," "object-object," and then "self-other" (p. 301).

These studies have focused mainly on what happens when children play. Researchers have also wondered whether play, or "improved" play, could change the course of development. Therefore, there are bodies of studies that have attempted to find out if modeling, or other means of stimulating children to be more playful, could influence creativity, cognitive development, and language development. The sections that follow discuss these attempts.

STUDYING THE RELATION OF PLAY AND IMAGINATION

Feitelson and Ross (1973) begin with the premise that thematic play influences children's creativity, and that it does not develop automatically but that children must be shown such play through modeling. Therefore, they reason that children's creativity could be increased if they were taught to play thematically. They studied twenty-four lower middle-class kindergarten children individually in a laboratory setting. They found that children increased their combinatorial play on post-tests after receiving tutoring and encouragement in the use of combinatorial play and unstructured props.

While Feitelson and Ross pretested children for their predispositions to imaginative play, Pellegrini did not. However, he intervened by asking children divergent questions in order to facilitate associative fluency. In a study of sixty kindergarten children, he found that questions stimulating "descriptive exploration and difference exploration" were "both effective facilitators of associative fluency" (1984a, p. 249). These results were confirmed, along with the observation that using both kinds of questions together was more successful than either strategy alone (p. 251), when he used the same procedures on a transfer task with fifty kindergarten children. The sequence of questions used were first descriptive; next, similar; and then different (p. 252). It may be that the powerful process of learning through contrasts, discussed above, was a contributing variable.

Another intervention study was done by Freyberg in which she trained eighty lower-class five-year-olds to play more imaginatively. Children in groups of four received training around various themes, using unstructured materials, during eight twenty-minute sessions. She found improvements in verbal communication, sentence length and complexity, sensitivity to others, spontaneity, creative use of play material, inventiveness and originality, labeling, attention span, and positive affect (1973, p. 132). She suggests that "engaging in activities that in themselves involve more organization and longer and more complex schemata would be facilitating to cognitive development" (p. 133).

Other researchers also hypothesize a connection between play and associative fluency. Dansky and Silverman (1976) studied ninety middle-class and upper middle-class nursery school children individually in a laboratory situation. They found that children who played with unstructured materials produced significantly more nonstandard responses in an alternative-uses test than did children in the control group or those who were asked to imitate tasks. Abraham and Lieberman (1985), who compared the baby-doll and Barbie-doll play of nine preschool children, have proposed that the baby-doll play was more structured, whereas the Barbie doll suggested a wider repertoire of play. Therefore, they credited the convergent, narrower range of baby-doll play behavior with stimulating more disruptive behavior. The Barbie-doll content has stimulated a heated correspondence in the journal, *Young Children*.

Pepler and Ross (1981) report similar findings. They studied sixty-four middle-class three-year-olds and seventy-two four-year-olds in a laboratory setting. Those who had engaged in divergent play before testing scored higher on fluency and originality measures. In comparison with children who played with convergent materials which suggested a narrower range of options or observed play with either type of material, the divergent players seemed to be more willing to try alternatives. The convergent materials seemed to constrain the activities of the children. The researchers cautioned that the effects were short-term and that longitudinal study is needed to confirm these findings.

Lieberman (1977) reported that kindergarten children who were assessed to be more playful did better on divergent tasks. She operationally defined playfulness "as physical, social, and cognitive spontaneity, manifest joy, and a sense of humor" (p. 23). The researcher studied ninety-three upper middle-class kindergarten children individually, developed a playfulness rating for each child, and then administered a series of divergent thinking tasks. Similar findings were reported by Hutt and Bhavani (1976) who studied nursery school children and reexamined forty-eight of them when they were between seven and ten years of age.

Pulaski (1973), using procedures similar to those of Singer, above, found that unstructured toys stimulated a greater variety of play themes than more realistic toys. However, high-fantasy children were better able to include more imaginary details in their stories, which were better organized. In comparison with low-fantasy children, they also were able to integrate more than one category of a toy and to become more deeply absorbed in their play, while accepting interruption and change more easily. The data are based upon observations of thirty-six middle-class kindergarten through second-grade children in a laboratory setting.

Thus these studies support the notion that children who are stimulated to play more imaginatively show an improved ability to make new connections.

STUDYING THE RELATION OF PLAY
AND COGNITIVE DEVELOPMENT

Smilansky's position, like that of Feitelson and Ross, leans toward the notion that sociodramatic play depends on cultural and contextual factors, and that children need adult intervention at some point. Smilansky suggests that less advanced sociodramatic play covaries with academic failure and a disadvantaged background. When teachers intervened to stimulate the sociodramatic play of disadvantaged preschool children in their classrooms, they found that children became more flexible planners, used language more elaborately and expansively, sustained play for longer periods, and improved their use of make-believe. Teachers attempted to vary the intervention on the basis of the different skills with which individual children came to school. Smilansky worked through the teachers of 420 preschool and kindergarten children who "taught" sociodramatic play over sixty-seven hours during nine weeks. She attributes the startling results over this brief period to the children's readiness for learning these skills (1968, p. 139). Freyberg agrees with these conclusions (1973, p. 145).

Contrary findings are reported by Eifermann (1971). She used 150 observers of 14,000 elementary school children in informal, unstructured play settings at school and in their neighborhoods. Eifermann found that disadvantaged six- to eight-year-olds in her sample displayed more, not less, social symbolic play than the other children. While Smilansky attributes her findings to the qualitatively different cultural background and socialization process, Eifermann proposes that poor children may develop symbolic play at a later age.

Levenstein, however, hypothesizes that play skills need to be taught, and that mothers of children from lower-class families could learn to assist their toddlers in improving play skills (1976, 1985). She takes the position that children's play is related to problem solving, academic skills, classroom attitudes, and I.Q. Studying fifty-four lower-class children between twenty and forty-three months of age, Levenstein developed a training program for thirty-three mothers and children at home. Toy demonstrators taught the mothers verbal stimulation techniques and how to use materials in various ways with their toddlers. The demonstrators visited each home regularly, showed how to use materials, and left the toys and books. Levenstein found significant increases in the children's I.Q. In addition, she reports four replication studies that support the initial findings.

Schwartzman cautions us to be careful about labeling children as "nonimaginative, noncreative, nonconceptual" (1984, p. 58). She suggests that we look at differences as not necessarily deficient but merely stylistic. However, she agrees with other researchers that play tutoring is useful in some contexts as long as spontaneity and playfulness are maintained (1985, p. 16).

A smaller-scale play intervention with twelve middle-class three-to five-year-olds found that intensive dramatic play, including individual, dyadic, and trio play, for each child resulted in a significant improvement in the number of cognitive constructs elicited from the experimental group on a sorting task (Ghiaci & Richardson, 1980). These findings were sustained in another post-test one month later.

Sylva, Bruner, and Genova studied problem solving with 180 three- to five-year-olds. Treatments involved free play with materials, observing an adult, or no treatment. They found that the children who had prior free-play experience with the materials solved the problem as well as those who had been shown the principle by an adult. While both groups used an orderly approach, observers noted that there were more all-or-nothing strategists among children in the observation group and more systematic progressions from simple to increasingly complex steps among children in the free play group. They concluded that "the effect of prior play seems to be not only in combinatorial practice, but also in shifting emphasis in a task from ends to means, from product to process" (1976, p. 256).

Sociobiologist Wilson (1978) reported that two-year-old chimpanzees who did not have the opportunity to play with sticks similar to those used in the Sylva, Bruner, and Genova study had reduced skills in solving a similar problem (p. 30). The interaction of sequential play and environment which he suggested may be corroborated by a line of research that is developing in children's block play. Reifel (1982, 1983) traced an interesting parallel development between early childhood block play constructions and Piagetian stages of cognitive development.

Believing that opportunities to play could influence development, Golomb (1979), and Golomb, Gowing, and Friedman (1981), developed a strategy to stimulate the conservation of quantity among young children who were pretested and post-tested in a clinical Piagetian manner. (When children learn that a quantity remains the same even though its appearance may change, they are said to be conserving quantity, as for example, when a liquid is poured from a tall, thin container into a short, wide container. Children are able to conserve quantity when they are able to perceive its reversible nature.) The experimenters provided an intervention procedure with nonconserving children, seventy-five three- to five-year-olds and forty-seven four- to five-and-a-half-year-olds. Their use of pretense play with individual children led them to conclude that it facilitated the acquisition of conservation of quantity. They suggested that their subjects used intuitive and unreflective reversibility which they propose are a spontaneous precursor to genuine reversibility of operational thought.

Gender.   The finding of Golomb, Gowing, and Friedman that boys respond best to child-initiated pretense play and girls to adult-initiated pretense play coincides with Serbin's observation that girls tend to follow the teacher. In turn, Serbin observed that teachers reinforce proximity-seeking in girls. When the teacher placed herself in the block corner, usually populated by boys, the block corner after ten minutes was used by both boys and girls. She and her colleagues also observed that "just the presence of a peer, especially an opposite sex peer, is likely to make a child conform to sex-role stereotypes" (1978, p. 90).

Research by Greif (1976) also indicates that, while there were no sex differences in the frequency of imaginative play, the play content of twenty-four middle-class boys and girls differed according to sex by the time they entered preschool. The four-and-a-half-year-old children in this study demonstrated stereotyped role play. Male roles had more status and girls were willing to play them, while boys were less willing to play female roles.

Other investigators have found that boys tend to engage in more active play, rough-and-tumble play, games with rules, and games involving spatial relations (Blurton Jones, 1976; Henniger, 1985; Humphreys & Smith, 1984; Paley, 1984; and Parker, 1984). These observations of sociodramatic play indicate that such play influences cognitive development because the visual-spatial skills that children develop even in block play, a traditional male domain, have been found to be significantly related to mathematical learning (Maccoby and Jacklin, 1974).

Boys' play is dramatically different from the predominantly housekeeping play of girls. Cazden (1971) reports observations of children's language use during play in a classroom housekeeping corner. While the quantity of language was plentiful, the syntax and language content in this environment were repetitious rather than elaborative and expansive. These observations suggest that we ought to look carefully at ways to revise the traditional housekeeping and block corners from a contemporary, sexually egalitarian, and relativist standpoint. The influence of such sociodramatic play upon children's creativity, cognitive development, and language development, deserves study in classrooms.

STUDYING THE RELATION BETWEEN PLAY AND LANGUAGE DEVELOPMENT

If Piaget (1955, 1959) sees language development following the course of cognitive development, McCune-Nicolich (1981) proposes a similar parallel development and structural correspondence between early vocal articulations and gestures, between early language and symbolic play, and between combinatorial language and combinatorial play. She suggested that investigators should study her prediction that the onset of decentered play and differentiated language use would occur about the same time. McCune (1985) reports that in a study of eighteen children, two-thirds of the population confirmed her hypothesis.

In addition to looking at how language and play coincide developmentally, there has been discussion about the significance of children's play with language itself. Researchers have suggested that children enjoy playing with language because it makes them feel in control (Cazden, 1976, p. 605; Chukovsky, 1963; Freud, 1960, 1959; Garvey, 1977, p. 97; Kirschenblatt-Gimblett, 1979, p. 224; Weir, 1976, p. 615). They have observed such play in the form of sounds or words repeated for their own sake as well as in riddles, jokes, and metaphors. Thus, playing with language may have poetic as well as metalinguistic functions.

The metalinguistic aspect of play has been implied in the discussions of metacommunication and children's play frame competencies. Cazden suggests that, compared with adults, children may treat language with more awareness in play and less awareness in ordinary communications. While there are individual differences in metalinguistic awareness, she proposes a sequence of awareness beginning with words, then syllables, followed by sounds, and then rules dealing with structure (1976, p. 604).

Play and story recall. Also, there have been intervention studies concerning how play influences the recall of stories. Pellegrini and Galda found that children's story comprehension improved after training in thematic fantasy play. Adult-led discussion was less effective. They suggested that role playing facilitated the ability to retell stories because it stimulated the verbal skills that children needed for recall (1982, p. 451). They imply that the metacommunication involved in the play frame made it possible for the children to move between their own role and their peers' role interpretations.

Williamson and Silvern (1984) concur with these findings and stress the importance of giving children repeated opportunities to play out stories in small groups. Basing his conclusions on a study of 192 lower-class children, in a later review Pellegrini (1984b) proposes that peer-directed play as well as adult-directed play facilitates story recall. In a more recent review, Pellegrini adds that the most effective play training includes a combination of fantasy, verbalization, and conflict (1985, p. 117).

Marbach and Yawkey (1980) would agree, adding that children show fuller story recall when they engage in imaginative play actions themselves, rather than having puppets act. Their study was done with sixty middle-class five-year-olds. Mann varied the training to improve story recall after forty middle-class preschool children heard a story. After hearing the story, children rehearsed it using both realistic and unrealistic props. The experimenter, while finding a significant correlation between recall—a problem-solving task that required divergent thinking—and realistic props, inferred that when subjects used unrealistic props, they relied upon their "imaging capacities to a greater extent" (1984, p. 373). This study reports no pilot testing or second observer to strengthen the reliability of observations. Whether the sequence of exposure to realistic toys was a significant variable in Mann's study is a question that begs for longitudinal research.

Although McGhee, Etheridge, and Berg (1984) found that unstructured toys elicited more pretend play, children played with them longer only when they were presented before the structured toys. They wondered if a longitudinal study might reveal that children had a longer attention span with unstructured toys after they had had enough time with the structured toys for the novelty to pass.

IMPLICATIONS FOR RESEARCH

Some Limitations

Size of samples.   With few exceptions, most of the studies of play have involved small samples. When you consider that eighty subjects may have been involved in three or four treatments, findings shrink to the twenty subjects who confirmed the investigator's hypotheses.

Context.   Since most of the studies in the literature have been carried out in a laboratory setting, we need to consider whether, for young children in particular, a familiar adult presence would make a difference. Many of the studies of solitary players may need to be replicated in the context of peer group interaction. Inasmuch as play is a relative activity, it would make sense to account for the human as well as the physical context in which studies take place.

Moreover, many of the laboratory studies reflect very brief encounters between experimenter and subjects. Therefore, we need ways to understand what happens to children in alternative contexts over longer periods. There have been increasing calls for observations of children in a variety of their natural habitats (Blurton Jones, 1976; Eifermann, 1976; Schwartzman, 1984; Singer, 1973; Smith & Simon, 1984). Schwartzman (1985) recommends that children need to be familiar with study settings. For investigators, this may mean catching things when they happen rather than trying to induce them to occur in ways that fit into a busy schedule.

In naturalistic observations, the researchers may focus on a particular sort of behavior as it appears. However, they can understand it more fully because of its context in terms of time, sequence of activity, relationships of the protagonists, and how typical it is for that population.

Collaborative Research

Using a collaborative, naturalistic approach, researchers should reassess and reformulate the role of early childhood teachers working with college teachers as coresearchers. To have the most relevant impact on curriculum, researchers should consult teachers to identify those questions that need answering in order to improve the conditions of children and teachers in school. Teachers, with some job redefinition, are in an exceptional position to collaborate in the collection of data.

For an example, Paley, a kindergarten teacher, documented sociodramatic play in her own classroom (1984). It would be illuminating if such a naturalistic observation could take place simultaneously with an outside observer, and if children's impressions could also be studied. There is a precedent for this approach in the triangulation research of Stenhouse (1980), Elliott (1979), and colleagues at the Cambridge Institute of Education.

Another role for teachers, which has been tapped only minimally in the research on play, is to participate in designing and implementing intervention studies. Smilansky reports that teachers played a significant role in her study, albeit after initial resistance to trying things with their school children that they had done more comfortably with their own offspring at home.

If teachers come to play a more significant role in intervention studies, it is likely that the administrators of such studies can undertake a longer-term commitment to longitudinal research and to timely post-tests and pretests in order to find out the extent to which the intervention was stable over time or was transferred to other tasks. Moreover, such participation will make it possible to study many more than the comparatively small numbers of children who have been studied until now.

Studying Play Content and Context

Functional study.   Beyond looking at the frequency of play behavior and correlations between kinds of possible behavior, we would do well to use such opportunities to consider the diversity of play. Beyond seeing that children make symbolic substitutions and transformations, we would do well to distinguish between transformations based on the surface elements of the objects and the functional relations between them.

Integrative study.   Another way to look at research is to look at play as an integrative experience. Studies have tended to look at either the affective, cognitive, social, linguistic, or other specific aspect of play. We need to plan studies that investigate the interaction of affect, cognition, and play; of social, linguistic, cognitive development, and play. An integrative approach can better provide a body of evidence to support a balanced curriculum that refers to real rather than dissected human beings.

McCune-Nicolich and Fenson (1984, pp. 85, 101) suggest studying the developmental trends that occur in individual children over time from several perspectives—decentration, decontextualization, and integration. It is worthwhile to investigate the interrelation of trends, the relative sequence of their appearance, and their relation to other areas, such as language. This kind of approach is useful when we consider the relative nature of play. Moreover, as we try to find out why certain events take place and how children's play develops, we need to consider children's accomplishments relative to the context in which we study them rather than as absolute or fixed phenomena (Bretherton, 1984, p. 294).

The contextual studies concerned with metacommunication and script models begin to deal with more interactive elements than the solitary study of children in laboratory settings. However, as this body of literature evolves, it would be useful to explore alternative intervention treatments in classrooms. The level of prop structures, the identification of concrete activities that generate cognitive conflict during different developmental phases, the identification of isomorphic patterns underlying children's natural play, and the identification of individual variations, are just a few of the directions that can give us the information necessary to make better curriculum decisions.

It is also likely that we need to extend the literature on the relationship of play, associative fluency, and the young child's artistic-poetic development. Singer reminds us that "our conventional methods are biased towards particular aptitudes that are symbolic and concrete" (1973, p. 201). Implications for curriculum are discussed below within the context and limitations of existing research, theoretical formulations, and my own bias.

IMPLICATIONS FOR CURRICULUM DEVELOPMENT

Teacher Attitude Is Playful

The research on play indicates that it is an important part of the lives of young children. Play has lymphatic, in the sense of pervasive and interconnected, implications for their education. While the research on play has not dealt directly with the impact of teacher attitudes toward play, Torrance (1962) reports that teachers perceive creative children as more of a problem than the garden-variety achiever. We expect that the spontaneous nature of play will be a burden to teachers with this attitude. At the same time, recent commentators tell us that there is a "flatness" to schools in general (Goodlad, 1984; Sadker & Sadker, 1984). More teachers need to be joyful and playful as they work with young children, ready to accept the unexpected connection or alternative with good humor and patience.

Teacher Intervention Is Relative

Modeling. Teachers need to model play behavior that stimulates development through challenge. This would mean attracting children to play by providing a variety of options with which they can feel comfortable and in which they perceive a chance for success. The best options are those which children can actively structure and for which there may be more than only one possible outcome. Rather than try to "motivate" the children by gimmicks, let the materials and activities entice the children to be intrinsically motivated.

While children's ability to transform their play from more realistic to less realistic materials has been documented, part of the teacher's task is to vary the level of structure for different children in order to stimulate varied enactments and symbolic progress. Tizard makes the point that teachers need to help children extend rather than merely replay and repeat what they bring to school (1977, pp. 205–06).

Since children come to school with different experiences, providing materials and opportunities will yield different outcomes. It makes sense to observe how children categorize and play out their experiences. Therefore, beyond providing a "stimulating school environment," teachers need to actively bring children into play activities in varied ways, sometimes by taking roles, creating contrasts, or entering a play frame with a suggestion.

Questioning. A teacher can suggest various kinds of play through example. Modeling also takes place when a teacher asks questions that stimulate a variety of possible responses. Therefore, questions that suggest more than a single acceptable response, situations that suggest to children that they can work things out, are likely to encourage an openness to various solutions to problems. If there is only one material or method, children receive the message that independent thinking is unwelcome. When there is an array of possibilities, then their play is stimulated to progress.

Planning. Children need enough time to play out their themes. Therefore, one or more long blocks of time during the school day need to be provided. Paley (1984) found that some of her kindergarten children needed unusual amounts of time to engage in sociodramatic play before they could focus on art work at a table. Other children need some time to be alone in the unique fantasy world we create in classrooms. Therefore, space needs to be organized for privacy as well as for participation with others. Gardner (1982) describes one child who engaged in pretend play throughout his drawing and another child who created dramatic action with words and gestures after a minimal drawing. Thus, while their teacher provided the materials and the opportunity, the children were able to create their own structures and pace.

Teachers create classroom cultures that define and tolerate different levels and types of play. When teachers find children making opportunities to play at unplanned times or in unexpected places, it is likely that children need more time to play or that immediate expectations are daunting to them.

The playfulness of games and sociodramatic play can stimulate children's focused involvement in activities. When effective teachers use such games with young children, they focus in a comfortable way on the game-playing process rather than only on the outcome. Kamii and DeVries (1980) and Kamii and DeClark (1984) offer many useful activities and suggestions to teachers of young children.

Playing with language. In addition to questions, modeling, materials, time, and space, teachers should encourage children to play with words. In the face of community pressures to acquire basic skills, research findings that support a playful attitude with language are important public relations.

Certainly, poets and linguists would recommend encouraging and appreciating the nondiscursive use of language by children.

Teachers of small groups of children can improve story comprehension by playfully questioning and predicting what might happen in stories, telling the stories, and then having the children play roles. Practice improves this process: a teacher who plays a bigger role as an example can later reduce her or his participation. Paley (1984) reports harnessing rough-and-tumble and superhero play with which she felt uncomfortable by asking the children to "save" their ideas. In a group setting, she and the children collaborated in creating language-experience dialogue of their own which they then played out in a more constructive format. While Paley's way is one way, it is of course not the only way.

Teacher Provisions Are Deliberate

Children need the time and opportunity to explore new materials and situations as well as to play. In order to strike a balance, teachers need to infuse novelty, variety, and fresh challenges as required by the varied backgrounds of the children. There is much skill involved in making such opportunities available to children in ways that they can perceive as relevant.

When teachers pace the *contrasts* between the strange and the familiar effectively, children are able to perceive a new figure when it is contrasted clearly against a known background. When children have opportunities to explore together, their joint exploration can lead to the control needed in social play. To the extent that children construct their learning in these self-directed ways, they acquire increasingly realistic expectations about the future and a sense of confidence.

Teachers Provide for Cooperative Play

Peer play and interage play help children to learn "in advance of development" as they see attainable models. In a sense, playmates are natural examples of new figures highlighted against familiar backgrounds. Therefore, teachers try to help children who tend to be isolates to move into parallel and then collaborative play with other children. For isolates as well as other children, playing with children of different ages may assist the development of more complex and extended play forms.

Schwartzman (1985) reminds us that interage play has traditionally been more common than our relatively recent practice of grouping children according to the calendar. Lieberman (1977) has conjectured that group playing with ideas may aid the creative process. "Brainstorming" is one such practice. Certainly, the development of decentration and reciprocal relations depend upon opportunities to experience cognitive conflict in social play situations.

In addition, teachers should consider ways to plan sociodramatic play areas that involve more varied imaginative settings such as a hospital, a restaurant, and a store rather than play areas that encourage only housekeeping. Teachers should plan for girls as well as boys to feel welcome in the block corner by being present and supportive.

Teachers Provide Worthwhile Experiences

This is a time when extreme views are pressing on early childhood education. There is a push in one direction toward limiting the function of public schools to the three R's and stating facts, crisply advanced. There is advocacy from the opposite direction for a folklorist tradition in early childhood education, vaguely propounded.

We need a more valid basis for developing curriculum than decision making that is based upon what children can learn, or what certain factions want them to learn, or what tradition has dictated. We need to consider what is worthwhile for children to learn. This is the deeper moral issue that can guide us to an ethical decision.

There is abundant evidence, accruing meteorically, indicating the power of play as a developmental lymphatic system. In the course of early childhood development, play almost seems to be a cauldron in which, at different times and in different contexts, various proportions of cultural, social, cognitive, linguistic, creative, aesthetic, and emotional ingredients blend.

Providing balanced activities. Perhaps we might playfully entertain the notion that play serves to merge the hypothetical functions of the right and left hemispheres of the brain. In this way, normal children manage to maintain a balance in their experience as human beings.

Taking the brain model a bit further, consider the implications of the current interest in imagery and metacognition as part of the public concern for children to have "thinking skills." *Imagery* is the creative aspect of experience and the capacity of human beings for making connections. For young children, it is an early form of symbolic representation in such activities as sociodramatic play and personal analogy. Analogy is a primary teaching tool to help children extend their imagery (see Gordon, 1961; Gordon & Poze, 1972). There has been conjecture that the right hemisphere of the brain, dealing with metaphoric and aesthetic ways of knowing the world, can be developed and strengthened by imagery. *Metacognition* is the development of self-awareness about one's own thinking. It takes place in a gradual process as we have experiences, get feedback from our environments, and experience cognitive dissonance. Piaget (1976) suggested that children attain this capacity around the ages of eleven and twelve years, but that development is continuous beforehand. There has been conjecture that the left hemisphere of the brain, dealing with logical ways of knowing the world, can be developed and strengthened by improved metacognition. Working jointly, these processes function in the service of problem solving.

However, to attempt to "teach" young children these integrative skills separate from direct, concrete experiences, is akin to trying to learn to ride a bicycle when the only instruction is a stationary exercycle. To use workbooks for these functions that develop naturally with healthy play is to be irrelevant if not downright abusive.

For young children, play in school, like anywhere else, is a way to strengthen worthwhile meaningful learning and cooperation with others rather than merely acquiring facts alone. Play may well be the ultimate relativist integrator of development. As a moral issue, the role of play as a part of early education touches the development of competence, a sense of self-worth and efficacy, creative potential, problem-solving skills, social learning, cognitive learning, linguistic development, and the sheer joy of living fully. The transformational potential of play in itself is a powerful lever for making new connections in a rapidly changing world.

Thus, teachers of young children have an ethical responsibility to create conditions that can help to improve the conditions of learning and life in schools. Therefore, we need to intervene in indirect and playful ways to the extent of our own potential capacities for professionalism and playfulness.

REFERENCES

Abraham, K. G., & Lieberman, E. (1985). "Should Barbie go to preschool?" *Young Children, 40,* 12–14.

Adler, A. (1923). *The practice and theory of individual psychology* (P. Radin, trans.). London: Routledge & Kegan Paul.

Aldis, D. (1975). *Play fighting.* New York: Academic Press.

Allport, G. W. (1958). "The functional autonomy of motives." In C. L. Stacey & M. F. DeMartino (Eds.), *Understanding human motives.* Cleveland: Howard Allen, 68–81.

Almy, M., Monighan, P., Scales, B., & Van Hoorn, J. (1984). "Recent research on play: the teacher's perspective." In L. G. Katz (Ed.), *Current topics in early childhood education,* vol. 5. Norwood, NJ: Ablex, 1–25.

Barnett, L. A. (1984). "Research note: young children's resolution of distress through play." *Child Psychology and Psychiatry, 25,* 477–83.

Barnett, L. A., & Kleiber, D. A. (1984). "Playfulness and the early play environment." *Journal of Genetic Psychology, 144,* 153–64.

Bateson, G. (1971). "The message 'this is play.' " In R. E. Herron & B. Sutton-Smith (Eds.), *Child's play.* New York: Wiley, 261–66.

Bateson, G. (1979). *Mind and nature.* New York: E. P. Dutton.

Bateson, G. (1972). *Steps to an ecology of mind.* New York: Ballantine.

Bateson, G. (1976). "A theory of play and fantasy." In J. S. Bruner, A. Jolly, & K. Sylva (Eds.), *Play—its role in development and evolution.* New York: Basic Books, 39–51.

Beckwith, L. (1985). "Parent-child interaction and social-emotional development." In C. C. Brown & A. W. Gottfried (Eds.), *Play interactions.* Skillman, NJ: Johnson & Johnson, 152–59.

Berlyne, D. E. (1960). *Conflict, arousal, and curiosity.* New York: McGraw-Hill.

Blurton Jones, N. (1976). "Rough-and-tumble play among nursery school children. In J. S. Bruner, A. Jolly, & K. Sylva (Eds.), *Play—its role in development and evolution.* New York: Basic Books, 352–63.

Bretherton, I. (1985). "Pretense: practicing and playing with social understanding." In C. C. Brown & A. W. Gottfried (Eds.), *Play interactions.* Skillman, NJ: Johnson & Johnson, 69–79.

Bretherton, I. (Ed.) (1984). *Symbolic play: the development of social understanding.* New York: Academic Press.

Bretherton, I., O'Connell, B., Shore, C., & Bates, E. (1984). "The effect of contextual variation on symbolic play development from 20 to 28 months." In I. Bretherton (Ed.), *Symbolic play: the development of social understanding.* New York: Academic Press, 271–98.

Bruner, J. S., Jolly, A., & Sylva, K. (1976). *Play—its role in development and evolution.* New York: Basic Books.

Bruner, J. S., & Sherwood, V. (1984). "Peekaboo and the learning of rule structures." In I. Bretherton (Ed.), *Symbolic play: the development of social understanding.* New York: Academic Press, 277–85.

Caldwell, B. M. (1985). "Parent-child play: a playful evaluation." In C. C. Brown & A. W. Gottfried (Eds.), *Play interactions*. Skillman, NJ: Johnson & Johnson, 167–78.

Cazden, C. B. (1971). "Language programs for young children: notes from England and Wales." In C. S. Lavatelli (Ed.), *Language training in early childhood education*. Urbana, IL: ERIC, 119–53.

Cazden, C. B. (1976). "Play with language and meta-linguistic awareness: one dimension of language experience." In J. S. Bruner, A. Jolly, & K. Sylva (Eds.), *Play—its role in development and evolution*. New York: Basic Books, 603–08.

Chafel, J. A. (1984). " 'Call the police, okay?' social comparison by young children during play in preschool." *Early Child Development and Care, 14,* 201–16.

Chomsky, N. (1972). *Language and mind* (enl. ed.). New York: Harcourt, Brace Jovanovich.

Christie, J. F., & Johnson, E. P. (1983). "The role of play in social-intellectual development." *Review of Educational Research, 53,* 93–115.

Chukovsky, K. (1963). *From two to five* (M. Morton, Trans. & Ed.). Berkeley: University of California Press.

Coleman, J. S. (1976). "Learning through games." In J. S. Bruner, A. Jolly, & K. Sylva (Eds.), *Play—its role in development and evolution*. New York: Basic Books, 460–63.

Collard, R. R. (1976). "Exploration and play." In B. Sutton-Smith (Ed.), *Play and learning*. New York: Gardner Press, 45–68.

Connolly, J. A., & Doyle, A. (1984). "Relation of social fantasy play to social competence in preschoolers." *Developmental Psychology, 20,* 797–806.

Copple, C. E., Cocking, R. R., & Matthews, W. S. (1984). "Objects, symbols, and substitutions; the nature of the cognitive activity during symbolic play." In T. D. Yawkey & A. D. Pellegrini (Eds.), *Child's play: developmental and applied*. Hillsdale, NJ: Lawrence Erlbaum, 105–23.

Csikszentmihayli, M. (1976). "The Americanization of rock-climbing." In J. S. Bruner, A. Jolly, & K. Sylva (Eds.), *Play—its role in development and evolution*. New York: Basic Books, 484–88.

Csikszentmihayli, M. (1979). "The concept of flow." In B. Sutton-Smith (Ed.), *Play and learning*. New York: Gardner Press, 257–74.

Curry, N. E., & Arnaud, S. H. (1984). "Play in developmental preschool settings." In T. D. Yawkey & A. D. Pellegrini (Eds.), *Child's play: developmental and applied*. Hillsdale, NJ: Lawrence Erlbaum, 273–90.

Dansky, J. L., & Silverman, I. W. (1976). "Effects of play on associative fluency in pre-school children." In J. S. Bruner, A. Jolly, & K. Sylva (Eds.), *Play—its role in development and evolution*. New York: Basic Books, 650–54.

Dewey, J. (1934). *Art as experience*. New York: Capricorn.

Dewey, J. (1933). *How we think*. Boston: Heath.

Dewey, J. (1930). *Human nature and conduct*. New York: Modern Library.

Dunn, J. & Dale, N. (1984). "I a daddy: 2-year-olds' collaboration in joint pretend with sibling and with mother." In I. Bretherton (Ed.). *Symbolic play: the development of social understanding*. New York: Academic Press, 131–57.

Eifermann, R. K. (1976). "It's child's play." In J. S. Bruner, A. Jolly, & K. Sylva

(Eds.), *Play—its role in development and evolution*. New York: Basic Books, 442–55.

Eifermann, R. K. (1971). "Social play in childhood." In R. E. Herron & B. Sutton-Smith (Eds.), *Child's play*. New York: Wiley, 270–97.

Elliott, J. (1979). "The implications of classroom research for the professional development of teachers." Cambridge Institute of Education. Unpublished.

Ellis, M. J. (1979). "The complexity of objects and peers." In B. Sutton-Smith (Ed.), *Play and learning*. New York: Gardner Press, 157–74.

Ellis, M. J. (1984). "Play, novelty, and stimulus seeking." In T. D. Yawkey & A. D. Pellegrini (Eds.), *Child's play: developmental and applied*. Hillsdale, NJ: Lawrence Erlbaum, 203–18.

Ellis, M. J., & Scholtz, G.J.L. (1978). *Activity and play of children*. Englewood Cliffs, NJ: Prentice-Hall.

Ellul, J. (1965). *The technological society*. (J. Wilkinson, Trans.) New York: Knopf.

Erikson, E. H. (1976). "Play and actuality." In J. S. Bruner, A. Jolly, & K. Sylva (Eds.), *Play—its role in development and evolution*. New York: Basic Books, 688–703.

Fein, G. G. (1985). "The affective psychology of play." In C. C. Brown & A. W. Gottfried (Eds.), *Play interactions*. Skillman, NJ: Johnson & Johnson, 19–28.

Fein, G. G. (1979). "Play with actions and objects." In B. Sutton-Smith (Ed.), *Play and learning*. New York: Gardner Press, 69–82.

Fein, G. G. (1981). "Pretend play in childhood: an integrative review." *Child Development, 52*, 1095–1118.

Fein, G. G. (1984). "The self-building potential of pretend play or 'I got a fish, all by myself.' " In T. D. Yawkey & A. D. Pellegrini (Eds.), *Child's play: developmental and applied*. Hillsdale, NJ: Lawrence Erlbaum, 125–41.

Fein, G. G. (1975). "A transformational analysis of pretending." *Developmental Psychology, 11*, 291–96.

Feitelson, D., & Ross, G. S. (1973). "The neglected factor—play." *Human Development, 16*, 202–23.

Fenson, L. (1985). "The developmental progression of exploration and play." In C. C. Brown & A. W. Gottfried (Eds.), *Play interactions*, Skillman, NJ: Johnson & Johnson.

Fenson, L. (1984). "Developmental trends for action and speech in pretend play." In I. Bretherton (Ed.), *Symbolic play: the development of social understanding*. New York: Academic Press, 249–70.

Festinger, Leon. (1957). *Cognitive dissonance*. New York: Harper & Row.

Forys, S. K., & McCune-Nicolich, L. (1984). "Shared pretend: sociodramatic play at 3 years of age." In I. Bretherton (Ed.), *Symbolic play: the development of social understanding*. New York: Academic Press, 159–91.

Freud, S. (1959 [1928]). *Beyond the pleasure principle*. (J. Strachey, trans.) New York: Bantam.

Freud, S. (1960 [1916]). *Jokes and their relation to the unconscious*. (J. Strachey, trans.) New York: W. W. Norton.

Freud, S. (1958 [1925]). *On creativity and the unconscious*. New York: Harper & Row.

Freyberg, J. T. (1973). "Increasing the imaginative play of urban disadvantaged children through systematic training." In J. L. Singer (Ed.), *The child's world of make-believe: experimental studies of imaginative play*. New York: Academic Press, 129–54.

Fromberg, D. P. (1977). *Early childhood education: a perceptual models curriculum*. New York: Wiley.

Fromberg, D. P. (1987). *The full-day kindergarten*. New York: Teachers College Press.

Fromberg, D. P. (1965). *The reactions of kindergarten children to intellectual challenge*. Ed.D. diss., Teachers College, Columbia University.

Fromberg, D. (1982). "Transformational knowledge: perceptual models as a cooperative content base for the early education of children." In S. Hill & B. J. Barnes (Eds.), *Young children and their families*. Lexington, MA: Lexington Books, 191–206.

Gardner, H. (1982). *Art, mind, and brain: a cognitive approach to creativity*. New York: Basic Books.

Garvey, C. (1979). "Communicational controls in social play." In B. Sutton-Smith (Ed.), *Play and learning*. New York: Gardner Press. 109–25.

Garvey, C. (1977). "Play and learning." In B. Tizard & D. Harvey (Eds.), *The biology of play*. Philadelphia: J. B. Lippincott, 74–99.

Geertz, C. (1976). "Deep play: a description of the Balinese cockfight." In J. S. Bruner, A. Jolly, & K. Sylva (Eds.), *Play—its role in development and evolution*. New York: Basic Books, 656–74.

Ghiaci, G., & Richardson, J.T.E. (1980). "The effects of dramatic play upon cognitive structure and development." *Journal of Genetic Psychology, 136*, 77–83.

Gibson, J. J. (1979). *The ecological approach to visual perception*. Boston: Houghton Mifflin.

Giffin, H. (1984). "The coordination of meaning in the creation of a shared make-believe reality." In I. Bretherton (Ed.), *Symbolic play: the development of social understanding*. New York: Academic Press, 73–100.

Gilmore, J. B. (1971). "Play: a special behavior." In R. E. Herron & B. Sutton-Smith (Eds.), *Child's play*. New York: Wiley, 311–19.

Glickman, C. D. (1984). "Play in public school settings: a philosophical question." In T. D. Yawkey & A. D. Pellegrini (Eds.), *Child's play: developmental and applied*. Hillsdale, NJ: Lawrence Erlbaum, 255–71.

Golomb, C. (1979). "Pretense play: a cognitive perspective." In N. R. Smith & M. B. Franklin (Eds.), *Symbolic functioning in childhood*. Hillsdale, NJ: Lawrence Erlbaum, 101–16.

Golomb, C., Gowing, E.D.G., & Friedman, L. (1982). "Play and cognition: studies of pretense play and conservation of quantity." *Journal of Experimental Child Psychology, 33*, 257–79.

Goodlad, J. I. (1984). *A place called school*. New York: McGraw-Hill.

Göncü, A., & Kessel, F. (1984). "Children's play: a conceptual-functional perspective." In F. Kessel & A. Göncü (Eds.), *Play dialogue: new directions for child development*, No. 25. San Francisco: Jossey-Bass, 5–22.

Gordon, W.J.J. (1961). *Synectics: the development of creative capacity*. New York: Collier.

Gordon, W.J.J., & Poze, T. (1972). *Strange and familiar*. Cambridge, MA: Porpoise Books.

Greif, E. B. (1976). "Sex role playing in pre-school children." In J. S. Bruner, A. Jolly, & K. Sylva (Eds.), *Play—its role in development and evolution*. New York: Basic Books, 385–91.

Hay, D. F., Ross, H. S., & Goldman, B. D. (1979). "Social games in infancy." In B. Sutton-Smith (Ed.), *Play and learning*. New York: Gardner Press, 83–107.

Henderson, B. (1984). "The social context of exploratory play." In T. D. Yawkey & A. D. Pellegrini (Eds.), *Child's play: Developmental and applied*. Hillsdale, NJ: Lawrence Erlbaum, 171–201.

Henniger, M. L. (1985). "Preschool children's play behaviors in an indoor and outdoor environment." In J. L. Frost & S. Sunderlin (Eds.), *When children play*. Wheaton, MD: Association for Childhood Education International.

Hofstadter, D. R. (1980). *Gödel, Escher, Bach: an eternal golden braid*. New York: Vintage.

Huizinga, J. (1955). *Homo ludens: a study of the play elements in culture*. Boston: Beacon.

Humphreys, A. P., & Smith, P. K. (1984). "Rough-and-tumble in preschool and playground." In P. K. Smith (Ed.), *Play in animals and humans*. New York: Basic Blackwell, 241–66.

Hutt, C. (1976). "Exploration and play in children." In J. S. Bruner, A. Jolly, & K. Sylva (Eds.), *Play—its role in development and evolution*. New York: Basic Books, 202–15.

Hutt, C. (1979). "Exploration and play (#2)." In B. Sutton-Smith (Ed.), *Play and learning*. New York: Gardner Press, 175–94.

Hutt, C., & Bhavnani, R. (1976). "Predictions from play." In J. S. Bruner, A. Jolly, & K. Sylva (Eds.), *Play—its role in development and evolution*. New York: Basic Books, 216–19.

Janiv, N. N. (1976). "Kedmah." Presented at the Bicentennial Conference on Early Childhood Education, Coral Gables, FL.

Jung, C. G. (1970). *Analytical psychology*. New York: Kamii, C., & DeClark, G. (1984). *Young children reinvent arithmetic*. New York: Teachers College Press.

Kamii, C. & DeClark, G. (1984). *Young children reinvent arithmetic*. New York: Teachers College Press.

Kamii, C., & DeVries, R. (1980). *Group games in early childhood*. Washington, DC: National Association for the Education of Young Children.

Kirschenblatt-Gimblett, B. (1979). "Speech play and verbal art." In B. Sutton-Smith (Ed.), *Play and learning*. New York: Gardner Press, 219–38.

Koestler, A. (1967). *The ghost in the machine*. New York: Macmillan.

Kreye, M. (1984). "Conceptual organization in the play of preschool children: effects of meaning, context, and mother-child interaction." In I. Bretherton (Ed.), *Symbolic play: the development of social understanding*. New York: Academic Press, 299–336.

Lancy, D. F. (1984). "Play in anthropological perspective." In P. K. Smith (Ed.), *Play in animals and humans*. New York: Basil Blackwell, 293–303.

Langer, S. (1948 [1942]). *Philosophy in a new key*. New York: Mentor.

Levenstein, P. (1976). "Cognitive development through verbalized play: the mother-child home programme." In J. S. Bruner, A. Jolly, & K. Sylva (Eds.), *Play—its role in development and evolution*. New York: Basic Books, 286–97.

Levenstein, P. (1985). Mothers' interactive behavior in play sessions and children's educational achievements. In C. C. Brown & A. W. Gottfried (Eds.), *Play interactions*. Skillman, NJ: Johnson and Johnson, 160–67.

Levine, S. (1984). "A critique of the Piagetian presuppositions of the role of play in human development and a suggested alternative: metaphoric logic which organizes the play experiences is the foundation for rational creativity." *Journal of Creative Behavior, 18,* 90–107.

Levi-Strauss, C. (1969a [1949]). *The elementary structures of kinship* (J. H. Bell, Trans.). Boston: Beacon.

Levi-Strauss, C. (1969b [1964]). *The raw and the cooked* (J. Weightman & D. Weightman, Trans.). New York: Harper Torchbooks.

Lieberman, J. N. (1977). *Playfulness: its relationships to imagination and creativity*. New York: Academic Press.

Maccoby, E. E., & Jacklin, C. N. (1974). *The psychology of sex differences*. Stanford, CA: Stanford University Press.

McCall, R. B. (1979). "Stages in play development between zero and two years of age." In B. Sutton-Smith (Ed.), *Play and learning*. New York: Gardner Press, 35–56.

McCune, L. (1985). "Play-language relationships and symbolic development." In C. C. Brown & A. W. Gottfried (Eds.), *Play interactions*. Skillman, NJ: Johnson & Johnson, 38–45.

McCune-Nicolich, L. (1981). "Toward symbolic functioning: structure of early pretend games and potential parallels with language." *Child Development, 52,* 785–97.

McCune-Nicolich, L., & Fenson, L. (1984). "Methodological issues in studying early pretend play." In T. D. Yawkey & A. D. Pellegrini (Eds.), *Child's play: developmental and applied*. Hillsdale, NJ: Lawrence Erlbaum, 81–104.

McGhee, P. E. (1984). "Play, incongruity, and humor." In T. D. Yawkey & A. D. Pellegrini (Eds.), *Child's play: developmental and applied*. Hillsdale, NJ: Lawrence Erlbaum, 219–36.

McGhee, P. E., Etheridge, L., & Berg, N. A. (1984). "Effect of level of toy structure on preschool children's pretend play." *Journal of Genetic Psychology, 144,* 209–17.

McLuhan, M. (1963). "We need a new picture of knowledge." In A. Frazier (Ed.), *New insights and the curriculum*. Washington, DC: Association for Supervision and Curriculum Development, 57–70.

Mann, B. L. (1984). "Effects of realistic and unrealistic props on symbolic play." In T. D. Yawkey & A. D. Pellegrini (Eds.), *Child's play: developmental and applied*. Hillsdale, NJ: Lawrence Erlbaum, 359–76.

Marbach, E. S., & Yawkey, T. D. (1980). "The effect of imaginative play actions on language development in five-year-old children." *Psychology in the Schools, 17,* 257–63.

Millar, S. (1971). *The psychology of play*. London: Penguin.

Miller, P., & Garvey, C. (1984). "Mother-baby role play: its origins in social support." In I. Bretherton (Ed.), *Symbolic play: the development of social understanding*. New York: Academic Press, 101–31.

Moore, O. K., & Anderson, A. R. (1968). "The responsive environments project." In R. D. Hess & R. M. Bear (Eds.), *Early education*. Chicago: Aldine, 171–89.

Moran, J. D., III, Sawyers, J. K., Fu, V. R., & Milgram, R. M. (1984). "Predicting imaginative play in preschool children." *Gifted Child Quarterly, 28*, 92–94.

Morgan, R. (1982). *The anatomy of freedom: physics and global politics*. Garden City, NY: Anchor.

Nelson, K., & Seidman, S. (1984). "Playing with scripts." In I. Bretherton (Ed.), *Symbolic play: the development of social understanding*. New York: Academic Press, 45–71.

O'Connell, B., & Bretherton, I. (1984). Toddler's play, alone and with mother. In I. Bretherton (Ed.), *Symbolic play: the development of social understanding*. New York: Academic Press, 337–68.

Opie I., & Opie, P. (1976). "Street games: counting-out and chasing." In J. S. Bruner, A. Jolly, & K. Sylva (Eds.), *Play—its role in development and evolution*. New York: Basic Books, 394–412.

Paley, V. G. (1984). *Boys and girls: superheroes in the doll corner*. Chicago: University of Chicago Press.

Parker, S. T. (1984). "Playing for keeps: an evolutionary perspective on human games." In P. K. Smith (Ed.), *Play in animals and humans*. New York: Basil Blackwell, 271–93.

Parten, M. (1971). "Social play among preschool children." In R. E. Herron & B. Sutton-Smith (Eds.), *Child's Play*. New York: Wiley, 83–95.

Pellegrini, A. D. (1984a). "The effects of exploration and play in young children's associative fluency: a review and extension of training studies." In T. D. Yawkey & A. D. Pellegrini (Eds.), *Child's play: developmental and applied*. Hillsdale, NJ: Lawrence Erlbaum, 237–53.

Pellegrini, A. D. (1984b). "Identifying causal elements in the thematic-fantasy play paradigm." *American Educational Research Journal, 21*, 691–701.

Pellegrini, A. D. (1985). "The relations between symbolic play and literate behavior: a review and critique of the empirical literature." *Review of Educational Research, 55*, 107–21.

Pellegrini, A. D. (1984c). "The social cognitive ecology of preschool classrooms: contextual relations revisited." *International Journal of Behavioral Development, 7*, 321–32.

Pellegrini, A. D., & Galda, L. (1982). "The effects of thematic-fantasy play training on the development of children's story comprehension." *American Educational Research Journal, 19*, 443–52.

Peller, L. E. (1971). "Models of children's play." In R. E. Herron & B. Sutton-Smith (Eds.), *Child's Play*. New York: Wiley, 110–25.

Pepler, D. J., & Ross, H. S. (1982). "The effects of play on convergent and divergent problem solving." *Child Development, 52*, 1202–10.

Pfeiffer, J. (1962). *The thinking machine*. Philadelphia: J. B. Lippincott.

Piaget, J. (1976). *The grasp of consciousness*. Cambridge, MA: Harvard University Press.

Piaget, J. (1962). *Play, dreams, and imitation in childhood*. (C. Gattegno, & F. M. Hodgson, trans.) New York: W. W. Norton.

Piaget, J. (1966). "Response to Brian Sutton-Smith." *Psychological Review*, 73, 111–12.

Piaget, J., et al. (1965). *The moral judgment of the child*. (M. Gabain, trans.) New York: Free Press.

Pulaski, M. A. (1973). "Toys and imaginative play." In J. L. Singer (Ed.), *The child's world of make-believe: experimental studies of imaginative play*. New York: Academic Press, 73–103.

Reifel, S. (1983). "Spatial representation in block construction." Presented at the annual meeting of the American Educational Research Association.

Reifel, S. (1982). "The structure and content of early representational play: the case of building blocks." In S. Hill & B. J. Barnes (Eds.), *Young children and their families*. Lexington, MA: Lexington Books, 171–89.

Rubin, K. H. (1985). "Play, peer interaction, and social development." In C. C. Brown & A. W. Gottfried (Eds.), *Play interactions*. Skillman, NJ: Johnson & Johnson, 88–96.

Rubin, K. H., Fein, G. G., & Vanderberg, B. (1983). "Play." In P. H. Mussen & E. M. Hetherington (Eds.), *Handbook of child psychology*, vol. 4. New York: Wiley, 693–774.

Sadker, D., & Sadker, M. (1985). "Is the O.K. classroom O.K.?" *Phi Delta Kappan*, 66, 358–61.

Schwartzman, H. B. (1985). Child-structured play: a cross-cultural perspective. In C. C. Brown & A. W. Gottfried (Eds.), *Play interactions*. Skillman, NJ: Johnson & Johnson, 11–19.

Schwartzman, H. B. (1984). "Imaginative play: deficit or difference?" In T. D. Yawkey & A. D. Pellegrini (Eds.), *Child's play: developmental and applied*. Hillsdale, NJ: Lawrence Erlbaum, 49–62.

Schwartzman, H. B. (1979). "The sociocultural context of play." In B. Sutton-Smith (Ed.), *Play and learning*. New York: Gardner Press, 239–55.

Schwartzman, H. B. (1978). *Transformations: the anthropology of children's play*. New York: Plenum.

Serbin, L. A. (1978). "Teachers, peers, and play preferences: an environmental approach to sex typing in the preschool." In B. Sprung (Ed.), *Perspectives on non-sexist early childhood education*. New York: Teachers College Press.

Shotwell, J. M., Wolf, D., & Gardner, H. (1979). "Exploring symbolization: styles of achievement." In B. Sutton-Smith (Ed.), *Play and learning*. New York: Gardner Press, 127–56.

Singer, J. L. (1973). *The child's world of make-believe: experimental studies of imaginative play*. New York: Academic Press.

Singer, J., & Singer, D. (1979). "The values of imagination." In B. Sutton-Smith (Ed.), *Play and learning*. New York: Gardner Press, 195–218.

Smilansky, S. (1968). *The effects of sociodramatic play on disadvantaged preschool children*. New York: Wiley.

Smith, P. K. (Ed.) (1984). *Play in animals and humans*. New York: Basil Blackwell.

Smith, P. K., & Simon, T. (1984). "Object play, problem-solving and creativity in children." In P. K. Smith (Ed.), *Play in animals and humans*. New York: Basil Blackwell, 199–216.

Sponseller, D. (1982). "Play and early education." In B. Spodek (Ed.), *Handbook of research in early childhood education*. New York: Free Press, 215–41.

Stenhouse, L. (Ed.) (1980). *Curriculum research and development*. London: Heinemann.

Sutton-Smith, B. (1966). "Piaget on play: a critique." *Psychological Review, 73*, 104–10.

Sutton-Smith, B. (1971). "A syntax for play and games." In R. E. Herron & B. Sutton-Smith (Eds.), *Child's Play*. New York: Wiley, 298–307.

Sutton-Smith, B. (1977). "Towards an anthropology of play." In P. Stevens, Jr. (Ed.), *Studies in the anthropology of play: papers in memory of B. Allan Tindall*. Proceedings from the second annual meeting of the Association for the Anthropological Study of Play. West Point, NY: Leisure Press, 222–32.

Sutton-Smith, B. (Ed.) (1979). *Play and learning*. New York: Gardner, 1979.

Sutton-Smith, B. (1984). "Text and context in imaginative play and the social sciences." In F. Kessel & A. Göncü (Eds.), *Play dialogue: new directions for child development*, No. 25. San Francisco: Jossey-Bass, 53–70.

Sutton-Smith, B., & Kelly-Byrne, D. (1984). "The phenomenon of bipolarity in play theories." In T. D. Yawkey & A. D. Pellegrini (Eds.), *Child's play: developmental and applied*. Hillsdale, NJ: Lawrence Erlbaum, 29–47.

Sylva, K. (1984). "A hard-nosed look at the fruits of play." *Early Child Development and Care, 15*, 171–84.

Sylva, K., Bruner, J. S., & Genova, P. (1976). "The role of play in the problem-solving of children 3–5 years old." In J. S. Bruner, A. Jolly, & K. Sylva (Eds.), *Play—its role in development and evolution*. New York: Basic Books, 244–57.

Tizard, B. (1977). "Play: the child's way of learning." In B. Tizard & D. Harvey (Eds.), *The biology of play*. Philadelphia: J. B. Lippincott, 199–208.

Torrance, E. P. (1962). *Guiding creative talent*. Englewood Cliffs, NJ: Prentice-Hall.

Vandenberg, B. (1981). "Play: dormant issues and new perspectives." *Human Development, 24*, 357–65.

Vandenberg, B. (1985). "Beyond the ethology of play." In C. C. Brown & A. W. Gottfried (Eds.), *Play interactions*. Skillman, NJ: Johnson & Johnson, 3–10.

Vygotsky, L. S. (1978). In M. Cole, V. John-Steiner, S. Scribner, & E. Souberman (Eds.), *Mind in society*. Cambridge, MA: Harvard University Press.

Vygotsky, L. S. (1976). "Play and its role in the mental development of the child." In J. S. Bruner, A. Jolly, & K. Sylva (Eds.), *Play—its role in development and evolution*. New York: Basic Books, 537–54.

Weir, R. (1976). "Playing with language." In J. S. Bruner, A. Jolly, & K. Sylva (Eds.), *Play—its role in development and evolution*. New York: Basic Books, 609–18.

Werner, H. (1948). *Comparative psychology of mental development* (rev. ed.). New York: International Universities Press.

White, R. W. (1959). "Motivation reconsidered: the concept of competence." *Psychological Review, 65*, 297–333.

Williamson, P. A. & Silvern, S. B. (1984). "Creative dramatic play and language comprehension." In T. D. Yawkey & A. D. Pellegrini (Eds.), *Child's play: developmental and applied*. Hillsdale, NJ: Lawrence Erlbaum, 347–58.

Wilson, E. O. (1978). *On human nature*. Cambridge, MA: Harvard University Press.

Wohlwill, J. F. (1984). "Relationships between exploration and play." In T. D. Yawkey & A. D. Pellegrini (Eds.), *Child's play: developmental and applied*. Hillsdale, NJ: Lawrence Erlbaum, 143–70.

Wolf, D. P., Rygh, J., & Altshuler, J. (1984). "Agency and experience: actions and states in play narratives." In I. Bretherton (Ed.), *Symbolic play: the development of social understanding*. New York: Academic Press, 195–217.

Wortham, S. C. (1985). "A history of outdoor play 1900–1985: theories of play and play environments." In J. L. Frost & S. Sunderlin (Eds.), *When children play*. Wheaton, Md.: Association for Childhood Education International, 3–7.

CHAPTER 4

Acquiring Oral Language and Communicative Competence

CELIA GENISHI
University of Texas

Like other children of their age, these four- and five-year-olds in nursery school pretend they're doctors and patients:

PATTY: I have to lay on the bed! But that's all right. I'll lay on the floor.

CHRIS: 'Cause we don't have no bed to play with.

MARY: [TO PATTY] Yeah. And I doctored on you.

TINA: I did too. Mary, we have to give her (Patty) something to go to sleep.

MARY: First I give you a shot. First I give you a shot!

TINA: But don't hurt her, OK?

PATTY: Go put a needle in 'cause there's a little hole. Pretend like there's needles over there, OK? Where you want the needles to be, do it.

Second grader Roy sits behind a screen, describing an arrangement of pictures as he and his partner play a communication game. On the other side of the screen, unable to see Roy or his pictures, his partner sees identical pictures; but only Roy's verbal description can help her figure out the correct arrangement. Unlike the preschoolers creating their own world with words, Roy uses language to refer specifically to these drawings:

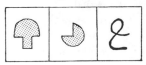

He sometimes uses a geometric term (circle) but often refers to familiar objects (*Pac Man, face, arm, leg*):

> On the top left-hand corner I have something that looks like an arrow, but the part that's supposed to be pointy is a half circle. Next to that in the middle on my left side there's a Pac Man shape that kinda goes up in the air. Next to that on the top row on my right side I have something that looks like a circle on the top and two little—one thing that goes up to the side and one thing to the bottom of the side. One thing that's sitting down without a face and a arm and a leg. (Sykes, 1985, p. 3, based on Glucksberg & Krauss, 1967)

How do children become speakers/learners like Patty, her friends, and Roy? How much language had they learned before they entered the classroom? Should adults expect all children to use language to pretend and describe in the ways that these five have? How large a role has the adult played to encourage talk and interaction? The content of this chapter addresses these questions by focusing on the following topics related to processes of language acquisition: (1) language within the framework of the last twenty years in early childhood education; (2) the nature of language, theories of acquisition, and research on the processes and social contexts of acquisition; (3) the links and gaps between the out-of-school processes of language acquisition and language education; (4) curricula that build on children's oral communication abilities; and (5) conclusions.

INTRODUCTION

In the last twenty years, language has become a special issue in early childhood education in the United States. The social programs and movements of the 1960s and 1970s, including Head Start and the women's movement, affected public expectations for preschool and primary education. People looked to compensatory programs like Head Start as forces for social and economic reform. Social groups outside the mainstream, usually ethnic minorities, participated in changing the structure and look of early education, especially at the preschool level. Parents became an integral part of administrative groups for Head Start and sometimes for day care centers.

Because the dialect or language of minority group children is often different from the English of majority or mainstream children, traditional views of language in schools have been challenged since the 1960s. Twenty or more years ago most people assumed that there was only one kind of English with which teachers needed to be concerned: standard (newscasters' or textbook) English. When educators or researchers wrote about varieties or different dialects of English, they often wrote about them as if dialects were inappropriate and incorrect. For example, in a report of pioneering research about the language of elementary school children, Loban (1963, p. 85) stated in his summary of findings: "For Negro subjects with southern background, using appropriately the verb *to be* proves to be 12 times as troublesome as for northern Caucasian or Negro subjects."

Later, in the 1960s, linguists like Labov (1970) demonstrated that speakers of nonstandard dialects of English, including what many call black English, use forms of the verb *to be* in ways that are consistently different from standard English forms. These different uses are *not* "troublesome" within the black English-speaking community. For instance, leaving out any form of *to be* as in, "Richard sick," conveys the message that Richard is a sickly person, whereas "Richard be sick" suggests that his sickness is temporary; Richard probably is not sickly.

By 1985 a number of books had been written about black English (Brooks, 1985; Burling, 1973; Dillard, 1972; Labov, 1972; Piestrup, 1973). Many authors emphasized the fact that everyone uses a dialect and that the term *dialect* is neutral, not negative. Educators' understanding of variation in language grew, so that they no longer assumed that standard English was the only acceptable dialect for classroom settings. When the federal Bilingual Education Act of 1968 marked the recognition that a growing number of U. S. students spoke a language other than English, the horizons of language education expanded even further. Broadened views of language led educators to reconsider their goals for young children's learning at the same time that parents and practitioners called for "culturally relevant" education. Taking into account the culture and previous experiences of children led to the creation of some innovative programs and curricula, which included the frequent use of languages other than English or the incorporation of black English features into teaching materials (John & Horner, 1971; Simpkins, Simpkins, & Holt, 1977).

By the 1980s, policymakers and the public wondered about the effectiveness of compensatory programs, even though some studies (for example, Schweinhart & Weikart, 1980) showed the long-term benefits of Head Start. As a group, minority children still achieve less well in school than majority or mainstream children. Educators and researchers continue to ask why this happens. They study children's home and school environments as they try to discover what kinds of experiences and curricula might improve learning and teaching for all groups. In recent decades the educator's domain of concern, once limited to the classroom, has clearly expanded. Children's language at home and at school has become part of that domain.

In linguistics and language acquisition research, similar patterns of expansion have developed. Linguists now focus on *functions* of language, along with rules related to its *forms*. Researchers discuss the growth of *communication*, not just language. The processes of acquisition that they study are those of working-class and minority, not just mainstream, children. The findings of researchers whose work is most pertinent to early childhood language education are discussed in the next section.

LANGUAGE AND THE PROCESSES OF ACQUISITION

We take for granted our ability to make language do what we need it to do. In or out of the classroom, language gives our thoughts substance. As we talk to ourselves, language helps us to remember, plan, understand what happens to us, and form our ideas. Language is part of the individual's uniquely human ways of knowing, feeling, being. As we use language with others, it shapes our identities and social lives. The way our own language sounds to listeners leads them to make judgments about where we are from, what our occupation is, how friendly or clever we are.

We easily see what language does, and we can see this without having to describe what it is. Understanding what language is, how it is structured, how it works, is the task of linguists who describe language in terms of components of study. These are summarized below to show just how impressive—for adult and child—the feat of learning a language is.

Each language component is made up of parts and the rules that enable speakers to combine those parts. *Phonology* refers to the sounds of a language. English speakers easily produce the sounds of English and without knowing the word *ruddle* will know that it sounds like a possible English word whereas *fwoodr* does not. English speakers also know the *morphology* of their language, or how words are formed. They know, for example, that to add *-ing* to a certain kind of word means an action is ongoing, as in *looking* or *jumping*. They know that *un-* preceding a word changes its meaning in a specific way, as in *unhappy*. (Words like *happy, look*, or *jump* or parts of words like *-ing* or *un-* are called *morphemes*.) Those who see the morpheme as the main unit of meaning in a language may refer to morphology as the *semantic* or meaning-related component.

The way we combine morphemes in an utterance or sentence is known as *syntax*. We know that in this sentence, "Joan is jumping," the morphemes are arranged in a way that makes sense to English speakers. We say *Joan* before *is* and *is* before *jumping*. We would not ordinarily say "Jumping is Joan" or "Joan jumping is," although we could say "Is Joan jumping?" and change the meaning of the sentence. We are no longer telling; we are asking. Linguists would describe the change from a statement ("Joan is jumping") to a question ("Is Joan jumping?") in terms of the syntactic rules the speaker knows about forming questions. One of these rules for question formation has to do with saying *is* before *Joan*.

Finally, *pragmatics* relates not to combining morphemes within sentences, but combining sentences with other sentences. Here linguists are concerned with rules for carrying on conversations. In other words, the pragmatic component has to do with language as it is used in human interaction. Because rules of usage are different for different groups (e.g., Minnesotans may find appropriate something that Texans think is offensive), pragmatic rules are slippery. They include rules about what kind of answer may follow a question in order to be judged polite or appropriate in a particular situation. For example, saying a simple, "Yes," after someone asks, "Do you know how I can get to Fourteenth Street?" is not appropriate, whereas following the "Yes," with directions to Fourteenth Street is.

We know a great many rules, rules for combining sounds into morphemes, morphemes into words, words into sentences, sentences into conversations. The wonder is that we apply all these rules without being aware of them. We know them in an unconscious way and that knowledge—sometimes called linguistic competence—makes us able to use language as we need to. Most people easily go through life without defining the components of language or reflecting on the marvels of the human mind that enable people to learn and use language. They have no need to study it or understand how an individual learns it. Why should early childhood educators understand what language is and how it comes to be? One reason is that language is a major part of human development. Knowing what the children in their classrooms or centers know and how they have come to know it can aid teachers in planning appropriate activities and teaching strategies. Another reason is that language is at the center of school learning. Every academic area of the curriculum entails language in the learning/teaching process. How do children come to know the language they bring with them to the classroom?

Learning Language Through Interaction

Learning language is enormously complicated. Simple theories of acquisition do not work. For example, according to a strict *innatist* theory, a person's genes are the sole source of language and communicative development; a child born with no physical handicaps would learn language. Unfortunately, researchers know that this is not the case. A child whose physical needs are met but lacks any opportunity for social interaction does not become a communicator (Curtiss, 1977). At the other extreme, a strict *behaviorist* theory bases communicative development on the environment—what is outside the learner. From this point of view, children learn what they hear around them through imitation, repetition, and reinforcement. Children do imitate what they hear, and they learn the language of those around them; but they also say things they have never heard before, such as "goed" or "footses" or "Why you putted it there?" They use these forms even when no one reinforces or encourages them to do so. These forms—what adults would call mistakes—suggest that a full explanation of how children acquire language must include children's ability to think and formulate rules for themselves.

Current theories about language acquisition are neither strictly innatist nor behaviorist. Most child language specialists believe that acquiring language depends on the interaction between nature and nurture, genes and the environment. Human beings are biologically prepared to use language in ways that no other organism is. What is with a person at birth, however, must be cultivated by an environment consisting of other people, objects, and actions, the essentials of interaction and bases of development. The theoretical approach of many researchers of children's communication is, therefore, termed *interactionist* and *constructivist*. The process of acquisition is based on the interaction of inborn abilities to formulate rules, act physically upon the environment, and seek social interaction. The child constructs, through his own activity and thinking, knowledge about how language works.

Early Language or Early Communication?

In the 1960s and early 1970s, child language researchers focused on the development of *language,* primarily the syntactic rules of child speakers. What words did they say first? How did children combine their first two words? Were the combinations similar to adult forms? By the mid-1970s researchers had taken a step back, toward infancy, to investigate the foundations of language. Researchers broadened their focus to study the growth of *communicative competence,* a person's ability to speak and act appropriately in different social situations. This competence depends on many kinds of knowledge: knowledge of linguistic rules (the speaker's linguistic competence), as well as of social rules for appropriate verbal and nonverbal behavior. The complicated rules for communicating develop in a broad range of contexts.

To see how children become communicators, some researchers studied early "conversations" like this one:

MOTHER: Did you ride a horsie yesterday? Horsie yesterday? Did you
see horsies yesterday?

INFANT: Baba daba.

MOTHER: Where was it? It was far away, wasn't it? It wasn't right around here? Noooo.

[Infant babbles]

MOTHER: It wasn't right around here, was it? No.

[Infant babbles]

MOTHER: Yes, you were ridin' an old horsie. Ridin' an old horsie. You saw cows. Did you see co-o-ows? Cows go moooo. Cows go moooo. . . .

The child's construction of communication may be embedded in one-sided conversations like this one between mother and son. With a babbling sound, cry, or vigorous movement of the arms and legs, infants let others know that they have messages to send. To document ways in which communication develops, Stern (1977) watched mothers and children, between birth and age six months, "dance" with each other. From the first weeks of life, each partner accommodated the other; the child's smile was followed by the mother's smile, for example. A gurgle might be a response to mother's question. Taking turns in "conversation" began as mother's behavior alternated with infant's few but powerful behaviors. The child's gaze, for example, was the link to his or her caregiver, who spent about 70 percent of feeding time facing and looking at the child. Facial expressions were another way to communicate. Newborns' muscles conveyed a range of expressions, including anger, sorrow, and joy. These early behaviors are elementary, but researchers believe they are necessary for more complex interaction in the future.

During and after the first six months of life, infants communicate in nonverbal ways. They also vocalize—or coo and babble—using sounds that will eventually be combined into adultlike words. Child language researchers studied this transitional period from prelinguistic to linguistic communication. Bruner, for example, looked carefully at mother-child pairs and concluded that the match between the structure of action and the structure of language—between what is said and what is done—helps the child enter the world of words. Even at two months of age, some infants can follow the adult's gaze, especially if the adult points or talks at the same time (Scaife & Bruner, 1975). In this way caregiver and child share a focus on the same object or event. They both notice who is doing something, what is affected by the action, and when it happens. The adult captures that action-based information through language: utterances contain subjects (doers or agents), verbs (actions), objects (recipients of action), places (locations or locatives). Some time after the first birthday, most children begin to verbalize. They use words like *juice, car,* or *up* to refer to their concrete world. As they become competent communicators, the dance between caregivers and themselves continues as each child expands his or her role in interaction to coordinate words with previously learned nonverbal behaviors and actions.

Nelson (1973) studied early words by documenting the first fifty words of eighteen one- to two-year-olds. She found that most of these words were general nouns like *sock, key,* and *shoe,* which named things that were common in the child's environment, movable and handled by the children themselves. In other words, these objects were the basis for children's actions; first words were grounded in sensory and physical activity. Other researchers (Barrett, 1982; Clark, 1983) proposed alternatives to Nelson's approach. Children may first name common objects in their environment, but to acquire the full meaning of a word, they may need to go through an unconscious analysis of its features. They note features that are functional (how is a shoe used?) and perceptual (what is its shape, size, texture, and so on?). At first, children may refer only to *their* shoes as shoes; then they may focus on noticeable features, for example, the shoe's shape. For a short while they may call both shoes and house slippers "shoes," but over time they are finally able to identify the features that set shoes apart from boots and slippers. At this point, children have acquired the bundle of features and concepts that define the word.

The Development of Syntax

Linguists and psychologists interested in child language in the 1960s focused on rules of syntax, which guide the ways we combine words to form grammatical utterances. Pioneers in this search included Brown and his collaborators (Brown, Cazden & Bellugi, 1969; Ervin & Miller, 1964). These and other psycholinguists recorded and studied thousands of utterances to discover the rules children unconsciously used to combine their first words in conversations. An example is this conversation between Karen, nineteen months old, and her father, who is watching television and attending to his daughter and an adult visitor:

KAREN: Mommy tape. Mommy tape. Mommy tape. Mommy tape. Mommy tape.

FATHER: Invisible mending tape. ["translating" for other adult]

ADULT: Oh!

FATHER: You can have *this* much. [shows with his thumb and index finger how long the piece can be]

KAREN: Daddy knee. . . .   (Genishi & Dyson, 1984, p. 46)

The rules underlying Karen's two-word utterances are part of her early grammar; over a period of years she will construct a number of grammars, not just a single one. Note that by using a simple rule for combining a noun with another noun ("Mommy tape"), Karen has managed to start a conversation about tape. She refers to the mending tape as her mother's; in a few months she may say, "Mommy's tape." In another conversation, she may apply a rule to combine noun and verb, as in "Daddy sleep." Later she might add -ed to all verbs to form a past tense, as in *walked, goed,* or *hided,* probably even to verbs that have irregular past forms (*went, hid*). These children's constructions are especially informative when they occur consistently, since they reveal what the child's own rules are. Well before kindergarten age, then, children's speech reflects their knowledge of basic syntactic rules.

In addition to noting spontaneous child utterances like, "two feets," "Bubba eating," or "Daddy goed," researchers tested children's rules experimentally. Berko (1958) created an ingenious test for tapping children's knowledge of specific rules for combining morphemes, or parts of words, to form other words. Berko used nonsense words, such as *wug, gling,* and *spow,* to see whether children aged four to seven years could look at a picture related to the word and then form an appropriate new word. A child might respond that a picture of more than one *wug* (drawn like a cartoon animal) was a picture of *wugs.* Or the experimenter might show a picture of a man doing something he called *spowing* to see if the child could say that the man *spowed* yesterday. Berko concluded that children who were able to produce such forms as plural, progressive, and past with nonsense words also knew rules for producing these forms with ordinary English words. Along with their spontaneous "mistakes" (*goed, hided*) in conversation, children's responses on the Berko test prove that children learn language by means other than strict imitation of adult forms. Instead they unconsciously construct and apply the rules of their developing grammars.

Researchers in the 1970s shifted their focus from syntax to meaning, or semantics. Their question became: What do children's early word combinations mean? One syntactic structure could have more than one meaning; for example, "Daddy juice" could mean, "Daddy's juice," or "Daddy, give me juice," and so on. Describing "daddy juice" as a noun + noun and "kitty sleep" as a noun + verb combination did not answer questions about the meanings of children's utterances. Brown believed a more satisfactory explanation was based on a "rich interpretation." According to this view, young speakers are able to convey a variety of basic meanings and relationships (Brown, 1973). "Daddy juice" might express the relationship technically called possessor + object possessed, or agent + object. At other times children use language to convey the meaning of nomination (naming things, as in "this doggie") or of nonexistence (remarking on the disappearance of a person or object, as in "allgone car"). Behind the technical terms describing these utterances, Brown believed there was always an active, thinking, meaning-seeking, and meaning-creating child.

Later Syntactic and Semantic Development

Most research on language acquisition has focused on children under five years old, and most recently on children under two years of age. Still there is much "complexification" that develops after the early stages. Somewhere between two and four, for example, children not only use multiword utterances, they also begin to use complex sentences that include more than one idea or proposition. Instead of saying two separate simple sentences, "I see the toy. The toy is new," the child can say, "I see the toy, and the toy is new," or—using more advanced rules for combining ideas in a single sentence—"I see the toy that is new." "I'm going to sleep. Then my mom's going out," later can be stated, "I'm going to sleep before my mom goes out." In order to accomplish these combinations, children master certain rules of syntax that enable them to eliminate some words, add others, and change the word order if necessary. By learning a few rules about incorporating one sentence or idea within another, children can eventually produce countless numbers and varieties of sentences that they could not before.

Children also learn rules for forming other types of sentences. When they can consistently say, "Dan have the book?" instead of, "Dan has the book?" they speak as if they know a basic rule for forming questions. That is, they must use a form of *do* and invert the order of subject and verb ("Does Dan have . . ." instead of "Dan have . . ."). Another form children master is the negative sentence. A six-year-old's utterance, "I don't want to sleep any more," shows mastery of adult rules for negative sentence formation, whereas her earlier, "I not sleep," does not. Researchers have come to realize that such rules may develop over a period of years. In the case of special structures, requiring the use of *ask* and *tell*, for instance, children may not master adult constructions until age nine or ten (C. Chomsky, 1969). In experimental settings, children under nine years may confuse the meanings of *ask* and *tell*, so that they interpret "Ask Joan what her address is," the same way as "Tell Joan what her address is." Part of the dialogue between experimenter and child might sound like this:

ADULT: Ask Joan what her address is.

CHILD: [addressed to Joan] 4 Maple Street.

ADULT: Now tell Joan what her address is.

CHILD: [addressed to Joan] 4 Maple Street.

The child here responds to *ask* as if it means the same as *tell*. Classroom teachers have observed similar confusions, especially when they require children to *ask* questions. Children often *tell* an answer instead. The problem seems to be that the child does not fully understand the meanings of *ask* or *question* in a testlike situation.

Differences in word meaning that seem obvious to adults may be unclear to children, for throughout middle childhood they continue to work out semantic as well as syntactic puzzles. Semantic development in the school years occurs gradually and, like the acquisition of first word meanings, is bound up with the development of concepts. Children learn new vocabulary through instruction and through unplanned exposure in conversation. Few researchers have studied semantic refinements learned by school-aged children. Asch and Nerlove (1960) provided an interesting study of "double function" words, such as *bright, sweet,* and *cold.* By interviewing children between three and twelve years old, they found that the youngest subjects could talk about the physical definition of such words but not the psychological one. Objects could be *bright* or *sweet,* but people could not. Almost all twelve-year-olds, though, understood both meanings. If the definitions of these dual function words develop over a period of years, full understandings of subtler distinctions must also take time. A first grader, for example, might understand that *skinny* and *thin* are similar in meaning, but for a period of time may not understand what makes a skinny person different from a thin one, as an adolescent or an adult may only gradually learn, without instruction, the nuanced distinction between *fashionable* and *trendy.*

Whether we consider syntactic or semantic development, researchers tell us that no development takes place unless children are actively and thoughtfully engaged with the world around them. We have so far focused on the language that is acquired, with little regard for the characteristics of the world outside the child. The next topic is the social context surrounding the child: what activities and human interactions support the development of language and communication?

Contexts for the Development of Communicative Competence

We know that all physically normal children learn to communicate in a first language. We know too that children learning the same language differ a great deal in the rate at which they learn language but follow the same general sequence as they learn linguistic forms. A particular two-year-old may be able to say more than a three-year-old neighbor, but in the course of development, both will utter one word before two, simple sentences before complex sentences. What in the child's environment is absolutely necessary for this ordered learning to take place? Researchers are far from knowing the answer. This section presents examples of interaction in different contexts to illustrate the range of situations that successfully support communicative development.

ADULT: Bo-o-at. Puppy dog. What's a dog say, Robert? What's a dog say, huh?

CHILD: [Babbles]

ADULT: Hey, Chrissy, what's a dog say? What's a dog say? Arf, arf, arf!

CHILD: [Screams happily]

ADULT: No-o-se. No-o-se. Where's Chrissy nose? Um hmmmm. Bird. Bird. Can you flap your wings like a bird? Like this. That's what birds do. They fly. They go wheeee!

CHILD: [Noises]

ADULT: The birds. Whatcha got, Brian? Whatcha got? Uh boo! Uh boo!   (Genishi & Dyson, 1984, p. 65)

This conversation was overheard in the infant room of a day care center, where the caregiver shared a picture book with three children. Her talk has many of the characteristics, which we may find cute or silly, of "baby talk," or adult-talk-to-children (ATC). Researchers have been interested in this way of adjusting one's speech for young children because they suspect that it provides a simplified model for child language learners (Schachter & Strage, 1982). Some of the features of ATC are:

1. Short utterances
2. Lots of repetition
3. Vowel lengthening (as in *no-o-se*)
4. Exaggerated intonation (extreme ups and downs)
5. Lots of questions.

When adults use this style of speaking, they may unconsciously be helping children "crack" the complex code of language. Much of the research that describes ATC has been done with Anglo-American or British mothers and children. Researchers who have studied other cultural groups have found less ATC like that in the example, but they have found no less ability to learn or use language. For example, Heath (1983b) recorded this exchange in a black American mill town. Lem, eighteen months old, sits on the porch, playing with a toy truck while his mother and her neighbor talk about Miss Lula's visit to the doctor:

LILLIE MAE: Miz Lula done went to de doctor.

MATTIE: Her leg botherin' her?

LEM: Went to [rolling his truck and banging it against the board that separates the two halves of the porch] de doctor, doc leg. Miz Lu Lu Lu, rah, rah, rah.

LILLIE MAE: I reckon so, she was complainin' yesterday 'bout her feet so swelled she couldn't get no shoes on. . . .   (Heath, p. 92)

Here Lillie Mae and Mattie focus on each other, not on eighteen-month-old Lem. He seems to pay attention to and pick up bits of the adults' talk so that he can play contentedly with them on his own. By contrast, in the middle-class day care center the infants Chrissy and Brian were the center of attention. The caregiver spoke energetically to *them* even if their contribution to the "conversation" was a squeal or laugh. Lillie Mae and Mattie, who are no less caring than the middle-class adult, and nevertheless different from her in that they use syntactic features that are not found in standard English. We would expect Lem, then, to use black English features as well. These contrasting interactions illustrate that different communities have their own beliefs about how people should interact, how adults should talk to children, and how children should talk. No one set of beliefs is superior to another, and families in every community rear children who learn the complex ways and rules of their community.

In many middle-class families, whatever their ethnicity, children are expected to participate in conversations. They also take part in exchanges like this one:

MOTHER: What's this? [pointing to part of a picture in a book]

KAREN: Turtle!

MOTHER: A turtle. What's this thing?

KAREN: Cow.

MOTHER: And what's this thing? Are you gonna clap when you get it right? And what's this thing?

KAREN: Turtle.

MOTHER: Yeah, that's a turtle too. What's this? . . .

KAREN: Box.

MOTHER: You knew that was a box? [Surprised] How'd you know that was a box? What's this?   (Genishi & Dyson, 1984, p. 46)

This conversation could have taken place between parent and child or teacher and child. It has one striking feature: the adult is asking many questions to which she already knows the answer. After the child responds, the adult encouragingly asks another question. Researchers have called this and other gamelike exchanges a *routine* (Snow, Dubber, & DeBlauw, 1982) and have found that in some homes, the routine changes over time. When the adult and child first establish the routine, the adult is the initiator. In a few weeks or months, adult and child may switch roles, so that the child may initiate and ask, "What's this?" "What's that?" When the routine is book-reading, the child may eventually memorize part of the text and take the adult's place as "reader," well before he or she is a conventional reader.

Routines are to many adults—especially middle-class adults—a staple of adult-child interaction. Heath (1983a) has called the routines in which the child "fills in the blank"—with a detail about a story just read, a color, or a shape—"talk about nothing." She points out that not every child has engaged in this kind of talk and that adults who are not middle-class may judge this talk to be pointless. A grandmother in a working-class black community had this to say about her grandson Teegie's learning and talking:

> He gotta learn to *know* 'bout dis world, can't nobody tell 'im. Now just how crazy is dat? White folks uh hear dey kids say sump'n, dey say it back to 'em, dey aks 'em 'gain and 'gain 'bout things, like they 'posed to be born knowin'. You think I kin tell Teegie all he gotta know to get along? He just gotta be keen, keep his eyes open, don't he be sorry. Gotta watch hisself by watchin' other folks. Ain't no use me tellin' 'im: "Learn dis, learn dat. What's dis? What's dat?" (Heath, 1983b, p. 84)

In these few sentences Teegie's grandmother captures whole systems of contrasting values. Her own emphasizes the child's ability to figure things out on his own, to "keep his eyes open." That of the middle class depends on lesson-like routines in which initiating adults often ask, "What's this? What's that?" The context for learning language and communication is clearly different for Teegie than it is for middle-class Karen. Heath and others (Miller, 1982; Schieffelin, 1979; Tizard & Hughes, 1984) have provided us with vivid documentation of adults and children in working-class and other contexts. Their studies emphatically remind us that all normal children *do* successfully learn their own community's way of communicating.

To summarize briefly the major points of this section:

1, Imitation is not the key to acquiring language. The active, meaning-seeking, and meaning-constructing child thinker, in interaction with people and things, figures out for her- or himself the intricacies of language and communication.

2. All normal children develop communicative competence within their own communities. Different communities' ways of talking and communicating may vary widely, and researchers are just beginning to study these ways in communities that are not white middle-class.

3. Researchers are far from knowing exactly what in the environment is absolutely necessary for children to become communicators. Thus, we cannot make judgments about what social contexts are "better" than others for children's learning to communicate.

The Educator's Choice

Many researchers and educators celebrate the differences among communities and believe that a child's language and culture are to be respected. This respect is central to the ideal of a pluralistic—genuinely multicultural—educational system. How or whether curricula in schools are truly pluralistic depends on each educator's values. These values can be grouped in at least three ways: First, some believe that the best approach is to treat all children in the same ways, using the same programs or curricula for everyone, regardless of cultural or linguistic background. Children who are different—that is, not standard English speakers and not from majority or mainstream homes—learn the ways of the majority culture, these educators hope, as quickly as possible (Bereiter & Engelmann, 1966). Second, others believe that modifications are necessary to ease the different child's entry into majority culture. For speakers of languages other than English, transitional bilingual education programs are an example of this modification. In the early childhood years, the child's home language is used in the classroom, but after that time he or she is expected to learn in English. Educators with a third perspective not only respect cultural differences, but also seek to maintain them. Thus, the children's home language is always the language of instruction, and their own community's ways of behaving and interacting are the ways of the school. Few educators carry out the philosophy of this third group; more fall into the second group, who attempt modifications for minority children; and many are in the first group, who believe that all children should adapt quickly to ongoing programs.

The position taken in this chapter is closest to the second perspective, because of my own values and because of what research suggests. According to that second, moderate perspective, educators should make modifications when needed to ease children's entry into mainstream schools. Further, one of the school's obligations is to offer all children the option to enter the mainstream. In terms of language, the goal is for children to acquire a level of communicative competence that is personally satisfying. For most people in our society, this means being able to use spoken and written language for a variety of purposes. For some—and only some—purposes, standard English is the most appropriate dialect to use.

Research consistently shows that children who reach a satisfying level of communicative competence (and usually perform adequately in school) come from homes where standard English is used and the ways of interacting are similar to those of the school; or they come from homes in which parents or adults share the values and goals of the mainstream (Durkin, 1982; Heath, 1982; Wells, 1981). Put another way, when there is a *mismatch* between family and school expectations, children find school difficult. To create a *match* between family and school is a persistent challenge, especially for educators who want to respect each child's cultural and linguistic background. For teachers to move toward this match, making modifications in curricula designed for middle-class children seems essential.

In no other area of the school curriculum does the child's out-of-school experience, long called the "hidden curriculum," have as strong an effect as in language and the language arts. Durkin (1982) dramatically supports this fact in her study of economically poor, successful black readers (eligible for free school meals *and* reading at or above grade level in the fifth grade). Many in this unusual group of children had this in common: an adult or older sibling at home who took an interest in reading with the child, often in the preschool years. When asked what had helped them become readers, children named this person, rather than a teacher or a school. We can conclude that this attentive individual provided a hidden curriculum, probably filled with the question-answer routines so typical of middle-class family interaction.

During these routines children learn the structure of many classroom lessons. The adult asks a question to which he or she knows the answer, the child responds, the adult may evaluate the response or praise the child and then asks another question. When routines develop so that children become the initiators and contribute more and more to the interaction, they may begin to control the learning process. They begin to see themselves as question answerers and question askers; they begin to take charge of their own learning (Genishi, 1985). This author believes that the process of becoming a learner who can meet the demands of school happens in classrooms as well as in middle-class homes. It happens when teachers make the hidden curriculum visible and open to children from different communities, when teachers and children ask and answer questions together, about people and objects that interest them. Through their varied interactions, they work toward creating a match between the child's ways of communicating and the school's. The next section discusses the kinds of classroom interactions that expand and support children's communicative competence and learning.

LANGUAGE IN THE CLASSROOM

Language in schools is peculiar. In one classroom it's a stepchild, in another it is mother Eve. Oral language plays stepchild when children are quiet, when tasks are done without talking. For example, classroom A contains twenty-five first-grade children sitting at their desks, quietly filling in a ditto sheet intended to reinforce the child's knowledge of sentences that "tell." In order to complete the exercise with understanding, the child needs to know what a sentence is, as well as to recognize the difference between a statement and a question. Oral language becomes Eve when there is talk between teacher and child and between children, when it is at the center of learning.

Classroom B, unlike classroom A, is noisy. Here, kindergarteners are engaged in four or five activities, including art, science, and dramatic play. Many "do" the activity by talking to each other. Their teacher is conversing with children at the art table.

In classroom C, the teacher is working with a group of five preschool children, while the others sit quietly at activity centers. The teacher says, "This is a house," while pointing to a picture of a house. He calls on a child who then says, "This is a house." The teacher asks, "Is this a house?" pointing to another picture. Another child responds, "No, that is not a house." Children are learning the word *house* and using it in complete sentences.

Of course, the classroom of one teacher could be the setting for all three of these scenes, but the language lessons in classrooms A and C are different from the activities in classroom B in two important ways: the degree of *structure* the teacher or the material provides, and the degree of *complexity* offered in the activity. Completing a worksheet and learning the word *house* are highly structured tasks. The teacher or the curriculum writer has carefully planned the task so that children have little planning or structuring to do on their own, and the adult determines which answer is correct. These two tasks are also not complex. The focus of the lessons is narrow, and thus the lessons don't—and aren't meant to—resemble "real-life" situations. The children's and teacher's activity and talk in classroom B, on the other hand, are not separated from the general flow of interactions in the classroom. Much of the talk could occur outside the classroom. The materials, for example, dress-up clothes or shells in the science center, suggest a structure for activity; but there is no carefully planned script for teacher and child to follow.

Each teacher decides what the balance will be between structure and unplanned activity, complexity and simplicity in the classroom. (For further discussion of structure, complexity, and other aspects of early childhood curricula, see Almy, 1975.) Which classroom, A, B, or C, is most like situations in which children became communicators outside of school? Research shows that children learn to communicate through interaction. When adult and child engage in game-like routines, interactions can be structured and simplified. But if we could document all interactions between adults and children, most of them would be unstructured and complex. Interactions would resemble conversations more often than they would lessons. For both child and adult are too sensible or too busy to spend much time in structured, soon predictable, interactions.

Early childhood teachers, looking to create a match between home and school, also sense that highly structured, pre-scripted activities are only part of a strong language curriculum. They know that structure has some advantages: while participating in highly structured lessons, each child receives the same instruction, which makes teaching evenhanded and evaluation of learning easier. The question-answer sequences give children, particularly those who have not experienced the hidden curriculum, prac- tice in the way many lessons work. In addition, the teacher is provided with a script; she or he need not prepare these lessons. Teachers know too the disadvantages: such a program allows for no modifications for individual children. The child who has not experienced the "talk about nothing" of the hidden curriculum may respond negatively to the rigid and alien question- answer sequences. The child who has experienced this kind of talk may find the sequences dull. All children, regardless of background, need opportuni- ties to structure their own activities/talk if they are to expand their communi- cative competence. Finally, and worst, highly structured lessons leave no room for teachers' creativity and responsiveness to individual children, both so essential for creating a match between home and school. (For an analysis and evaluation of types of preschool language programs, see Cazden, 1971.)

How often do we see classrooms like A, B, and C? Textbook adoption patterns and classroom observations suggest that there are many more situations like A and C than like B. Many oral language programs or textbooks identify skills that children should acquire at a certain grade level. For example, first-grade textbooks include the skills of recognizing letters and shapes, writing sentences, making statements into questions, and learning about subject-verb agreement. Many of these tasks involve talking *about* language. In fact, when the words *grammar* and *language education* are used by some, they are synonyms for ways of talking about language, or using *metalanguage*. This language-about-language is often the content of worksheets and sounds little like real-life conversations in which children are *using language*.

The focus on metalanguage in popular curricula is probably not a result of teacher preference. It grows out of one of the realities of schooling in this country: standardized tests often guide curriculum, that is, teachers feel pressured to "teach to the test." Because metalanguage, including terms like *statement* and *question*, are testable in a written form, textbooks offer ways of teaching the terms. In turn, test makers include such items on tests. The point emphasized here is that despite the strong influence of testing on language curricula, *no one has proven the long-term benefits of teaching children to talk about language forms and learn grammatical terms—that is, to use metalanguage—or to use specific language forms*. Attempts to teach standard English forms in highly structured ways, for example, have not succeeded, whereas teachers' acceptance and encouragement of children's own language forms have led to greater learning (Cullinan, Jaggar, & Strickland, 1974; Piestrup, 1973; Rentel & Kennedy, 1972).

Because there are no widely used group tests of oral language, it is often neglected in schools where oral language is a stepchild. Yet for young children who are just becoming readers and writers, oral language is their best means for demonstrating what they know or don't know. For teachers it is an accessible tool to discover what children know or don't know. Thus, despite the influence of written tests on curricula, *children are likely to learn when teachers provide activities that encourage the use of language— not metalanguage—for different purposes*. Teachers who wish or are required to teach metalanguage have many published programs available to guide them. These programs help them meet prescribed lesson purposes— such as recognizing the difference between statements and questions on worksheets—and testing purposes.

The remainder of this chapter focuses on language-using purposes that are not prescribed by publishers or required by schoolwide testing programs. It focuses on teachers who treat oral language as mother Eve, who provide a language "bath" for children (Lindfors, 1980), to such an extent that their language curriculum becomes hard to distinguish—it becomes seamless. Real-life and lesson language blend with music, science, math, art, play, and so on, and are truly at the center of classroom life.

Language as the Center of the Curriculum

To meet the goal of promoting children's communicative competence, to enable them to use oral and written language for various purposes, a variety of activities in the classroom is essential. The following examples illustrate the possibilities that exist. These interactions occurred in different settings, from day care to primary-grade classrooms, among both minority and mainstream children. What they and their teachers do with and through language should help construct a link between home and school when the two settings differ, and maintain a link when they are similar.

Playing Roles

"In play a child behaves beyond his average age, above his daily behavior; in play it is as though he were a head taller than himself." (Vygotsky, 1978, p. 102). When children engage in pretend or dramatic play, they take on characteristics of people who behave and speak differently from themselves. They may imitate their parents, doctors, or speakers of other languages:

MARI: Hablamos en inglés. Hablamos en inglés. (Let's speak in English. Let's speak in English.)

DIANA: [A little later] I'm gonna call you—I'm gonna friends is you—[talking to toy telephone].

ADELITA: I'm friends.

DIANA: I already told you. I'm gonna call you at H.E.B. [a super-market]. One, two, eight, nine [dialing the toy telephone].

ADELITA: I'm gonna sit me down, OK?

DIANA: OK. Don't cry. You promise to me.

DIANA: [later to Adelita] Ouch, ouch, ouch, ouch. Ouch. Dije que te salieras, Adelita. ¿Sabes qué quiere decir *ouch*? Que te salgas. (Ouch. . . . I told you to get out, Adelita. Do you know what *ouch* means? To get out.)

(Genishi & Dyson, 1984, p. 122)

In this exchange, Spanish speaker Mari gets the others to speak English, though she herself speaks none. Her classmates at a Head Start center in Texas follow her cue and stretch their language so that part of their play becomes a short practice session in English, which is becoming their second language. At first, most teachers and children at the center spoke Spanish, but toward the end of the year, teachers occasionally encouraged children to practice English to "get ready for kindergarten." This was one of the few examples of English use that the author heard in a two-month period. Diana's and Adelita's English was elementary but understandable—regardless of Diana's unique translation of "ouch."

The dramatic play setting, enjoyable and usually free from adult intervention, truly encourages talk that is "a head taller" than the ordinary. It can also push children to take others' points of view, as they create scripts for their characters (Nelson & Gruendel, 1979). Representing through play talk the way others think or present themselves can enrich the child linguistically and cognitively. Thus, opportunities for dramatic play, so often limited to preschools and kindergartens, would also benefit children in the primary grades.

Ms. Raney, eight-year-old Alex's teacher, has her children act out different roles as they read the play, "The Bremen Town Musicians" together:

DOG: Good morning.

[ALEX]
DONKEY: Good morning. Where is your—where's your Mastah?

DOG: I'm running away from her.

DONKEY: That's funnah. I'm runnin' away from mine. For many years it's been nothing but work, work, work. Now that I'm old and tired, he wants to get rid of me. . . . Where are you going?   (Genishi & Dyson, 1984, p. 201)

To teach children about their own language, Ms. Raney audiotapes her children in different speaking situations, so that in some they sound casual and in others they sound more formal, more "how they talk on TV." Alex, as donkey, talks in TV talk, though at another time he described a picture in this way: "Dat cah right dere goin' ta hit da cub [curb] 'n dat cah right dere goin' ta hit da ho'se 'n dat cah right dere goin' to hit da do-ug [dog]" (Genishi & Dyson, 1984, p. 201). As the donkey, Alex uses some features of the sound system of standard English, pronouncing crisply and carefully (*going*, instead of *goin'*), whereas in the second example, he uses many features of his own community's dialect, black English. Ms. Raney believes in the importance of dramatizing plays in standard English and also of accepting the children's own dialect in less formal situations. Without the use of repetitious language drills, she acts upon a belief that children should grow in their communicative competence, as they become readers, writers, and speakers of different dialects.

Telling Stories

Storytelling, the sharing of experiences either real or imagined, is an activity common to everyone. What we may not realize is that the way people tell stories can vary from one group to another. Most middle-class speakers are used to a rather direct style. What happened first is usually told first, so that in a complete and clearly structured story we recognize the beginning, middle, and end. In a kindergarten classroom where the teacher reads the children many stories, she invites children to tell, and later act out, their own. Here is one of Wally's stories:

> Once there was a boy hunter. His little sister didn't like him so he ran away. So he found a baby girl lion. Then he found a girl. "You can both be my sisters," he said. Then they met a good fairy and she turned the girl lion into a girl person so he had two real sisters. They lived happily ever after. (Paley, 1981, p. 29)

We can follow the linear development in this story about family members and fairies: the boy hunter runs away, then other things happen to him, and finally, in the style of many a fairy tale, there is a happy ending.

Other children may tell entertaining stories in quite a different way. Health (1983b), for example, recorded stories like Nellie's, in which the structure is less conventional:

> Once upon a time, uh-er-ah, I uh, saw a monster
> 'n my mamma said
> 'n my mamma said
> 'n my, my mamma had a cockroach in her bed
> 'n she kicked 'im outta de bed
> 'n then it was a big giant mice in my mamma's room
> 'n then I hadda kill 'im
> I got a big giant mice and then I kilt 'im
> We chop 'im 'til he was bleedin'   (Heath, 1983b, p. 299)

The story of first grader Nellie, from a black working-class community, is unlike the stories of trade books or basal readers. If it were, we might expect it to be about the monster Nellie mentioned at the beginning, but it is also about her mamma, a cockroach, and an unlucky mouse. (Note that Wally's more conventional story centered around a single topic, the boy hunter.) Heath and a number of classroom teachers had children like Nellie, along with their mainstream classmates, audiotape their stories. The children then listened to them, compared and discussed them, and modified them if they wished to. Over time, stories that were less conventional became more so. The teachers' curriculum, based on the language of their children, acted as a bridge between out-of-school styles and school style.

Storytelling is often but not always an activity that showcases a single storyteller. Group performance in sharing experiences is characteristic of Hawaiian children, who invite others to construct stories with them. This cooperative style is called *talk story* and has been incorporated into young children's reading lessons at the Kamehameha Early Education Program in Honolulu (Au & Kawakami, 1985). Instead of expecting a response from just one child, teachers accept near-simultaneous responses from several children. In other words, they encourage "calling out." This is another way of bridging an out-of-school style of talking and interacting with the style of most schools. The result in this case has been improved reading abilities.

Children can also tell each other stories, when adults set up book corners and let children take charge of the activity. Mexican-American kindergarteners Erica and Oscar, not yet readers, use puppets to act out the tale of *The Three Little Pigs:*

ERICA: *The Three Little Pigs.* The mother said, " 'Bye, my little pigs got to go." The first little pig met a little man with a bundle of straw. "Please, please leave me have those straw. I can build a house. . . ."

OSCAR: Se lo comió. (He ate him.)

ERICA: "And I'll huff and huff, and I'll blow your house in. . . ." "Little pig, little pig, let me in." "Not by the hair of my chinny, chinny, chin." "Then I'll puff—" [Erica carries on with the story, as Oscar reminds her twice:]

OSCAR: ¡Se lo comio-o-o-ó! Erica, Erica, se lo comió. El, el marranito. (He ate him! Erica, Erica, he ate him. The, the little pig.) [By now Oscar is exasperated with Erica for not noticing the picture that he pointed out, showing the pig's fate.]   (Adapted from Seawell, 1985, pp. 84–85)

Spanish speaker Oscar understands what is happening in this English story, as he and Erica, an English learner, maintain a truly bilingual dialogue.

These examples of storytelling from children of different backgrounds contrast with each other, though their teachers share this belief: children share experiences successfully and tell stories better when they are encouraged to talk in comfortable ways, in the way of their own communities. Teachers may not be familiar with the way of everyone in their classrooms; children may belong to three or four ethnic groups. But the teacher's first step is to provide an opportunity, to let the children talk. Then the stories tell themselves.

Talking About Something

Heath (1983a) calls talk about stories and the cognitive code of colors, shapes, and numbers "talk about nothing." Much school talk is indeed about nothing, but much of it can be about "something," things that children can see and touch or have experienced themselves. The activities of the traditional nursery school or kindergarten—art, math, science, social studies—all provide subjects for shared experiences. A child's drawing easily leads to a description of its content or a conversation about the child's name, which she has written or asked the teacher to write. Or the art table can be the setting for talk about the tooth fairy, a topic of real concern:

SARAH: They're smiling about my loose tooth. You'd better stop smiling about my loose tooth.

[TEACHER]
Ms. COFFEE: They're probably thinking about all of the money you're going to get when you get it from the tooth fairy. Does the tooth fairy come to your house?

[Several children answer.]

CHILDREN: Yeah.

Ms. COFFEE: How much money do you usually get, or have you ever lost a tooth?

SARAH: [Her answer must be negative.]

Ms. COFFEE: Then you don't know how much money you get, do you?

SARAH: I know, but one time I had money, um, when I had my wart fell off . . . when I gave them the wart and then they had to take the wart away, and then they gave me some money.

(Archer, Coffee, & Genishi, 1985, p. 272)

The teacher (Ms. Coffee) attends to Sarah's hurt feelings at the beginning of the conversation, then leads the children to have a talk about money, which was the subject of a recent class unit.

Science for young children is often embedded in nonscience experiences, which lead to discussions about scientific principles. For example, after hearing Marcia Brown's *Stone Soup*, Paley's kindergarteners discuss whether stones do melt when they're cooked. To find out, the class boils three stones for an hour and makes these comments:

ELLEN: They're much smaller.

FRED: Much, much. Almost melted.

ROSE: I can't eat melted stones.

TEACHER: Don't worry, Rose. You won't. But I'm not convinced they've melted. Can we prove it?

MICKEY: Draw a picture of them.

TEACHER: And cook them again? All right. (Mickey and Earl trace the stones on a piece of paper, and I put them back in the water to cook some more. Thirty minutes later the stones *do* look smaller.)   (Paley, 1981, p. 17)

The children persist in their thinking that the stones do change after cooking, although they do not. Through talk, Paley has gotten glimpses of the children's own notions of "science." She is patient, for she knows that telling children the facts of science does not necessarily lead to genuine understanding of concepts. In conversations later in the year, talk will show her whether the children's thinking has changed.

Almost every object or activity presents an opportunity for talk when teachers allow it to. The computer, the object of scrutiny and controversy in some early childhood programs, is a machine that could be socially isolating and impersonal. But like many other things, it can prompt talk. In the following example, first graders are using a computer program to create designs on their screens:

FLORA: Help him. He doesn't know how to do it.

MARGARET: [to Juan] Want me to help you?

JUAN: Yeah.

MARGARET: OK. First, press that one down [demonstrates]. [Juan presses the key while Margaret presses another.] There.

JUAN: I can do it.

MARGARET: OK, and you keep pushing that one [goes back to own computer, but quickly checks Juan's again]. Now you need to make your plus [a cross-like shape], so you go up here and you do that, and go here, like that [she touches the screen as she traces a cross]. If you need help, just ask me, OK?

Computer activity among first graders and younger children can be talk-generating and cooperative (Genishi, McCollum, & Strand, 1985; Strand & Gilstad, 1985) The easily viewed computer screen can lead to children's helping and learning from each other.

CONCLUSIONS

Everything in this chapter is in praise of children's enormous accomplishments as communicators at home and school. Researchers still do not know how children manage to become communicators so quickly or what exactly is needed for language to develop, for it develops in so many differing contexts. Returning to our questions about Patty's and Roy's talk at the beginning of the chapter, we do know that like all children, they have become speakers and learners through a complex process. In interaction with people and objects, they have figured out large numbers of rules, related to the phonology, syntax, semantics, and pragmatics of their own dialect. *As active, thinking children, they have been at the core of the learning process.* The examples given throughout the chapter demonstrate that children become communicators in a remarkably short time. By the time they enter nursery school, they are able to carry on conversations, and such conversations are elaborate and quite adultlike by the time they reach the second grade.

We know too that Patty's and Roy's talk demonstrates tiny bits of their communicative competence and that their ways of communicating, ordinary though they sound, are not the ways of every child. Researchers have shown that (1) children's ways of talking and communicating grow out of a long history of interactions within the home and community, and (2) as a result of this history, successful students are usually made, not born. If a person's communicative development could be viewed like a kaleidoscope that is constantly moving, individual teachers would see only a few of the intricate patterns that make up the whole of a child's communicative history. The classroom or center is only one setting in which that history evolves. So much more of it has been embedded in children's own communities where the events and conversations of everyday life have a seamless look and feel. There are few mismatches or gaps from one situation to the next when people share communicative rules and social values. For some children, the seamlessness of the years at home ends abruptly when they enter a center or school where adults talk and behave differently from their parents or friends. Unless there are opportunities to learn "school talk," a center or school may become an uncomfortable and difficult place for the child.

Teachers ease the mismatch when they encourage role playing, story-telling, talk about "nothing" (the cognitive code, stories) and "something" (science, computer use, the tooth fairy). The talk highlighted in this chapter had these characteristics:

1. Talk between adults and children, and between children serves a *variety* of purposes or functions. That is, language is used to inform, tell stories, pretend, have fun, argue, plan, and so on.
2. Since talk flows when people have something to talk about or tell each other, teachers provide for and engage the children in *activities* that are the focus of talk.
3. Conversations are comfortable for both child and teacher. Talk is

fluent because the communicators are absorbed in getting their messages across, and their conversations are *meaning-oriented*, not form-oriented.

Though the language forms that a child uses may not always match those of the teacher, their communicative purposes can match. In this sense, teacher-child interactions resemble those of parent and child, when the child knows little adult grammar.

Parents focus most on the child's meaning; whether or not a specific form (for example, *hided*) is correct is not important. Unlike parents of young children, many language and language arts curricula do focus on correctness of form and the ability to talk or write about forms (the use of *metalanguage*). But research suggests that a focus on language forms is not productive either for early language acquisition in the home or for expanding language at center or school. Instead, a focus on varied activities leads to the use of language for varied purposes, and this variety—not a published language curriculum—leads to greater communicative competence. Educators choose how much variety they can include in classrooms, depending on their own values and views of language.

The teacher plays a critical role in deciding whether oral language is a stepchild or mother Eve in the classroom. The primary goal of the teacher is, after all, to help children learn. Before children read and write with ease, talk is the adult's ready tool for finding out what the child knows and what she or he needs to know. Paley (1981) calls her book, which is full of stories and conversations with kindergarteners, a book about thinking. Her children's thoughts were made concrete by their words, by lots of talk. Paley often attempted to take the point of view of six-year-olds to see what they saw, to try to understand their experiences and the sometimes elusive meanings that talk held for them. These are three tasks for early childhood teachers: to provide activities that nourish talk; to draw on their own knowledge of language and development to communicate clearly with children; and finally, to see what children see, with the goal of helping them see and know more.

GLOSSARY

Bilingual able to understand and speak two languages with ease. In reality, many bilingual persons are fluent in one language and have varying degrees of fluency in the other.

Communication the act of sending and receiving meaning in a given context, through verbal and/or nonverbal means.

Communicative competence unconscious knowledge of both linguistic and social rules that enable one to use language appropriately in different social contexts. In this chapter it refers to both oral and written communication.

Comprehension understanding; the receptive aspect of language.

Curriculum used generally to refer to published programs for any subject matter, including language; teacher-created programs; or to what actually gets taught in the classroom.

Dialect a variant of a language. A single language is spoken in different ways in different geographic regions and social groups (community, social class, or ethnic group). Language specialists say that a dialect contains systematic deviations from the standard form of the language, in phonology, semantics, syntax, and pragmatics.

Form an element of language often named in grammatical terms, such as verb, noun, adjective. Sometimes form is a synonym for structure: a focus on language form refers to a concern with correct (standard) structure, for example, using a singular verb with a singular noun.

Function a purpose for which speakers use language, for example, to make requests, to give information, to tell stories, to ask questions.

Grammar a description of language structure, of the parts or elements of the language (sounds, words), and how those elements are combined to form spoken utterances.

Grammatical rules rules that enable speakers to combine the sounds and words of their language to convey meaning. Linguists traditionally refer to three aspects or levels of these rules: phonological, semantic, and syntactic. They are learned by all speakers of a first (native) language without formal instruction.

Language for purposes of this chapter, a system for human communication that relates sounds to meanings.

Language arts the study and practice of producing and receiving of both oral and written language, generally referred to as speaking, listening, reading, and writing.

Linguistics the study of the structure or grammar of language.

Mainstream of the majority culture in the United States; often called white or Anglo middle-class. It is used descriptively, not positively or negatively, in this chapter.

Minority of social or ethnic groups, generally considered to differ from the majority culture of the United States. Examples are Asian-American, black or Afro-American, Hispanic- or Mexican-American, etc. The term is used descriptively, not positively or negatively, in this chapter.

Morpheme the smallest unit of meaning in the syntax of a language. It may be a word or a part of a word, for example *story* is one morpheme, but *bluebirds* is made up of three: *blue, bird,* and *-s*.

Nonstandard in reference to languages, a dialect that is different from the one found in textbooks or generally used by educated speakers. In English, a well-known nonstandard dialect is black English, used by some black and non-black speakers.

Phonology the aspect of grammar that has to do with speech sounds and the ways they can be combined and spoken in a given language.

Pragmatics sometimes referred to as the fourth aspect or level of grammar, it has to do with rules of language usage, or how language is used in different social contexts.

Psycholinguistics the study of the cognitive or mental processes involved in learning and using a language; a marriage of psychology and linguistics.

Semantics that aspect of grammar that has to do with the meanings of words and sentences.

Social context the situation in which communication occurs. It consists of various factors: number of participants, their relative social status or rank, degree of familiarity with each other, topic, nature of the physical setting, the communicative purpose, and so on.

Sociolinguistics the study of how language is used in particular social contexts, or of how social structure is related to linguistic structure: sometimes used as a synonym for pragmatics.

Standard in reference to language, the speech and writing patterns that are generally used and considered the "correct" form of a language by most speakers. The rules of standard English, for example, are found in dictionaries and school textbooks.

Syntax the aspect of grammar that has to do with the systematic arrangement of elements of language (words and morphemes) to form utterances or sentences that are meaningful to native speakers.

REFERENCES

Almy, M. (1975). *The early childhood educator at work.* New York: McGraw-Hill.
Asch, S. E. & Nerlove, H. (1960). The development of double function terms in children: an exploratory investigation. In B. Kaplan & S. Wapner (Eds.), *Perspectives in psychological theory: Essays in honor of Heinz Werner,* pp. 47–60. New York: International Universities Press.
Archer, C., Coffee, M., & Genishi, C. (1985). Research currents: responding to children. *Language Arts, 62,* 270–76.
Au, K. H. & Kawakami, Alice J. (1985). Research currents: Talk story and learning to read. *Language Arts, 62,* 406–11.
Barrett, M. D. (1982). Distinguishing between prototypes: The early acquisition of the meaning of object names. In S. Kuczaj II (Ed.), *Language development,* Vol. 1: *Syntax and semantics,* pp. 313–34. Hillsdale, NJ: Erlbaum.
Bereiter, C., & Engelmann, S. (1966). *Teaching disadvantaged children in the preschool.* Englewood Cliffs, NJ: Prentice-Hall.
Berko, J. (1958). The child's learning of English morphology. *Word, 14,* 150–77.
Brooks, Charlotte K. (Ed.) (1985). *Tapping potential: English and language arts for the black learner.* Urbana, IL: National Council of Teachers of English.
Brown, R. (1973). *A first language: The early stages.* Cambridge, MA: Harvard University Press.
Brown, R., Cazden, C., & Bellugi, U. (1969). The child's grammar from I to III. In J. P. Hill (Ed.), *Minnesota symposium on child psychology,* vol. 2, pp. 28–73. Minneapolis: University of Minnesota Press.
Burling, Robbins (1973). *English in black and white.* New York: Holt, Rinehart and Winston.
Cazden, C. B. (1971). Evaluation of learning in preschool education: Early language development. In B. S. Bloom, J. T. Hastings, G. F. Madaus (Eds.), *Handbook on formative and summative evaluation of student learning,* pp. 345–398. New York: McGraw-Hill.
Chomsky, C. (1969). *The acquisition of syntax in children from 5–10.* Cambridge, MA: MIT Press.
Clark, E. V. (1983). Meanings and concepts. In P. H. Mussen (Ed.), *Handbook of child psychology* (4th ed.), vol. 3, pp. 787–840. New York: Wiley.
Cullinan, B. E., Jaggar, A. M., & Strickland, D. (1974). Language expansion for black children in the primary grades: A research report. *Young Children, 29*(1), 98–112.
Curtiss, S. (1977). *Genie: A psycholinguistic study of a modern-day "wild-child."* New York: Academic Press.
Dillard, J. L. (1972). *Black English: its history and usage.* New York: Vintage.
Durkin, D. (1966). *Children who read early: two longitudinal studies.* New York: Teachers College Press.
Durkin, D. (1982). A study of poor black children who are successful readers. Reading Education Report No. 33. Urbana, IL: Center for the Study of Reading. ED 216 334.
Ervin, S. M., & Miller, W. (1964). The development of grammar in child language.

In U. Bellugi & R. Brown (Eds.), The acquisition of language. *Monographs of the Society for Research in Child Development, 29* (1, serial no. 92).

Genishi, C. (1985). Talking to learn: the child takes charge of literacy. *Dimensions,* 13(3), 9–11.

Genishi, C., & Dyson, A. Haas (1984). *Language assessment in the early years.* Norwood, NJ: Ablex.

Genishi, C., McCollum, P., & Strand, E. (1985). Research currents: the interactional richness of children's computer use. *Language Arts, 62,* 526–32.

Glucksberg, S., & Krauss, R. M. (1967). What do people say after they have learned how to talk? Studies of the development of referential communication. *Merrill-Palmer Quarterly, 13,* 309–16.

Heath, S. B. (1982). Questioning at home and at school: a comparative study. In G. Spindler (Ed.), *Doing the ethnography of schooling: educational anthropology in action,* pp. 102–31. New York: Holt, Rinehart and Winston.

Heath, S. B. (1983a). Research currents: a lot of talk about nothing. *Language Arts, 60,* 999–1007.

Heath, S. B. (1983b). *Ways with words: language, life, and work in communities and classrooms.* New York: Cambridge University Press.

John, V., & Horner, V. (1971). *Early childhood bilingual education.* New York: Modern Language Association.

Labov, W. (1972). *Language in the inner city: studies in the black English vernacular.* Philadelphia: University of Pennsylvania.

Labov, W. (1970). The logic of nonstandard English. In F. Williams (Ed.), *Language and poverty,* pp. 153–89. Chicago: Markham.

Lindfors, J. W. (1980). *Children's language and learning.* Englewood Cliffs, NJ: Prentice-Hall.

Loban, Walter D. (1963). *The language of elementary school children.* Urbana, IL: National Council of Teachers of English.

Miller, P. (1982). *Amy, Wendy, and Beth.* Austin: University of Texas Press.

Nelson, K. (1973). Structure and strategy in learning to talk. *Monographs of the Society for Research in Child Development, 38* (1–2, serial no. 149).

Nelson, K., & Gruendel, J. M. (1979). At morning it's lunchtime: A scriptal view of children's dialogues. *Discourse Processes, 2,* 73–94.

Paley, V. (1981). *Wally's stories.* Cambridge, MA: Harvard University Press.

Piestrup, A. (1973). *Black dialect interference and accommodation of reading instruction in first grade.* Berkeley: University of California, Language-Behavior Research Laboratory.

Rentel, V., & Kennedy, J. (1972). Effects of pattern drill on the phonology, syntax, and reading achievement of rural Appalachian children. *American Educational Research Journal, 9,* 87–100.

Scaife, M., & Bruner, J. S. (1975). The capacity for joint visual attention in the infant. *Nature, 253,* 265–66.

Schachter, F. F., & Strage, A. A. (1982). Adult's talk and children's language development. In S. G. Moore & C. R. Cooper (Eds.), *The young child: review of research.* Vol. 3, pp. 79–96. Washington, DC: National Association for the Education of Young Children.

Schieffelin, B. B. (1979). Getting it together: An ethnographic approach to the study of the development of communicative competence. In E. Ochs & B. B. Schieffelin (Eds.), *Developmental pragmatics,* pp. 73–108. New York: Academic Press.

Schweinhart, L. J., & Weikart, D. P. (1980). Young children grow up: effects of the Perry Preschool Program on youths through age 15. *Monographs of the High Scope Educational Research Foundation,* no. 7. Ypsilanti, MI: High Scope.

Seawell, R.P.M. (1985). *A micro-ethnographic study of a Spanish/English bilingual kindergarten in which literature and puppet play were used as a method of enhancing language growth.* Ph.D. diss., University of Texas, Austin.

Simpkins, G., Simpkins, C., & Holt, G. (1977). *Bridge: a cross-culture reading program.* Boston: Houghton Mifflin.

Snow, C. E., Dubber, C., & De Blauw, A. (1982). Routines in mother-child interaction. In L. Feagans & D. C. Farran (Eds.), *The language of children reared in poverty: implications for evaluation and intervention,* pp. 53–72. New York: Academic Press.

Stern, D. (1977). *The first relationship: infant and mother.* Cambridge, MA: Harvard University Press.

Strand, E., & Gilstad, B. (1985). Young children's interactions as they used LOGO. Presented at the annual study conference of the Association for Childhood Education International, San Antonio, TX.

Sykes, M. (1985). Referential communication in elementary school children. Unpublished, University of Texas, Department of Curriculum and Instruction, Austin.

Tizard, B., & Hughes, M. (1984). *Young children learning.* Cambridge, MA: Harvard University Press.

Vygotsky, L. S. (1978). *Mind in society.* Cambridge, MA: Harvard University Press.

Wells, G. (1981). *Learning through interaction: the study of language development.* New York: Cambridge University Press.

CHAPTER 5

Learning to Read

NITA BARBOUR
University of Maryland

In 1967 Jeanne Chall published a book entitled *Learning to Read, the Great Debate*. The purpose of the book was to settle the debate then in progress on which was the best method of teaching reading. Chall reviewed the reading research from 1912 to 1965. Though she concluded that phonics methods resulted in children having higher reading achievement, the results were not overwhelming.

Since then, an enormous amount of reading research has been conducted. This vast body of research has been produced in a wide range of disciplines: education, linguistics, sociology, psychology, philosophy, anthropology, and others. However, because this research has been multidisciplinary rather than interdisciplinary, it has not produced an integrated approach to the teaching of reading (Goodman, 1984, pp. 79–80). Thus, the question of which approach is best remains today.

When children should begin reading instruction, and what form this instruction should take, has not been resolved. Fueled by the back-to-basics movement, as well as political, social, and economic forces, a renewed interest in how children learn to read and how they should be taught reading is occurring. Reports have summarized the research, and recommendations for the teaching of reading were made in the 1985 Commission on Reading report. Beginning teacher evaluation studies have prescribed a classroom climate that is conducive to reading achievement. Research on different methods helps the classroom teacher discover activities that are practical for classroom use. Teachers who make constructive use of research are able to interpret how the suggested strategies and techniques help individual children in their classrooms.

The purpose of this chapter is to present a general overview of the research in reading. It is impossible, however, to do a complete review, as reading is one of the most highly researched areas in education. This chapter is limited in its review to examples of (1) various views of reading, (2) theoretical research models developed for understanding the reading process, (3) research on when to begin reading instruction, and (4) research on methods or strategies designed to enhance reading instruction. As teachers reflect on these four areas, they may be able to redefine their own thinking or find support for the methods and strategies they already use to teach reading.

DEFINITIONS OF READING

Reading is defined in different ways; however, nearly all definitions have the common elements of print, language, and comprehension. Authorities also view reading as an activity that involves a combination of certain motor, perceptual, and linguistic functions. For example, Dechant's synthesis is: "Reading is a two-fold process. It is a complex language system; it is a complex cognitive skill aimed at obtaining information. The reader is constantly processing information" (1982, p. 13).

Another important aspect of the reading process is the role played by the reader in the reading process, but theorists often differ as to what that role is. Finn (1985) points out that definitions often fall into three broad categories: empiricist, rationalist, and interactivist. Empiricists concentrate on the relationship of print to language as the important focus in reading. They view the beginning reader as progressing from learning the various parts of words to understanding the whole passage, maintaining that reading is first translating graphic symbols into the corresponding speech sounds. The empiricists believe that only after this task has been accomplished can the learner attach meaning to the symbols (Reed, 1965; Gagne, 1970; Bateman, 1983). These theorists have been strong advocates of the phonics emphasis in teaching beginning reading, and in the current literature are often described as advocating a "bottom-up" approach to reading.

The rationalists focus on the relationship between language and meaning. They see the reader as interpreting and building meaning in context before analyzing the subparts of the graphic form. Smith, representing the rationalist theory, maintains that the act of reading depends upon the context in which the reading takes place. He notes that the reader seeks information and tests out hypotheses in order to answer questions regarding the text. The process of obtaining that information will vary according to the setting—reflecting, in part, the child's previous world knowledge and understanding of the text topic and, in part, the child's knowledge and understanding of the text structure (1978, pp. 176–77). These theorists advocate the "meaning" or holistic approach to beginning reading and in the present literature on reading are often described as advocating a "top-down" approach.

Interactivists have a balanced perspective, maintaining that reading is a transactional process (Goodman, 1984). They believe that a reader must simultaneously extract information about print *as well as* make hypotheses regarding the meaning of the text. Information from both sources interacts until finally the meaning of the text is clear (Rumelhart, 1977).

In summarizing this position, Anderson and colleagues (1985) point out that research indicates that reading requires children to learn letter patterns and the sounds associated with them, to learn to identify words rapidly, and to learn to use their own word knowledge, plus their knowledge of the text structure.

Whatever viewpoint is followed, it is clear that reading is a complex process. It is not a simple linear pursuit proceeding from one subskill to the next until the act of reading is accomplished. It is the accumulation of a wide range of skills that require practice if children are to become active readers who seek information and enjoyment from the printed page.

THEORETICAL RESEARCH MODELS

Since the 1960s, theoretical research models have been developed through which various facets of the reading process may be examined. Research, as well as classroom practice, have been influenced by various positions based on these theories or models. As just described, these positions are the subskill orientation, currently referred to as bottom-up theory, and the meaning orientation or top-down theory.

Singer and Ruddell (1976) and Kamil, Langer and Shanahan (1984) provide detailed descriptions of a number of these theories and models. Four theoretical models are described below as examples of either the subskills theory orientation or the meaning theory orientation.

Subskills Theory Orientation

A comprehensive model described by Holmes in his Substrata Factor Theory of Reading provides a structure of interrelated working systems that shows a hierarchy of major skills and subskills. Holmes indicates that a working system is a dynamic set of subskills set in motion for the purpose of solving a particular problem. The substrata factors are neurological subsystems of brain cell assemblies containing various kinds of information, such as memory for shapes, sounds, and meaning of words and word parts, as well as memory for vicarious and experiential materials, concepts and meaningful relationships stored as substantive verbal units in phrases, idioms, sentences, and so forth (Holmes, 1970, p. 188).

Though Holmes and Singer (1964) noted a common set of subskills in reading, they believed that their own research using the Substrata Factor Model supported the notion that different individuals may use different sets of subskills with equal success in performing the same reading task. In another research study using this same model, Singer determined that a sequential development of the substrata factors did accompany improvement in speed and power in reading (1983, p. 17).

LaBerge and Samuels (1974) developed a partial reading model called Theory of Automaticity in Reading. This model has four elements: raw material of reading, processes for translating the information (visual memory, phonological memory, episodic memory, and semantic memory), ability to store the information, and mental energy for attention to the task. The theory is based on the concept that reading is a complex activity and the unskilled reader does not have enough attention energy simultaneously to decode, extract meaning from the words, and see the words in relationship to the sentence and then to the text as a whole. Therefore the unskilled reader must divide the task into subunits of decoding and comprehension. He/she may even need to divide the decoding into smaller and smaller units. As the reader practices and gains skills in decoding, the demands for this process decrease and the reader is able to attend to larger units until the process of decoding becomes automatic. At this point decoding takes such little energy or attention that the reader can decode and comprehend at the same time (Samuels & LaBerge, 1983, pp. 41–51).

Meaning Theory Orientation

Hansen and Lovitt (1977) suggest an alternate methodology for research in reading: the Applied Behavior Analysis model. This method, concerned with how children learn to read, has four ingredients: direct measurement, daily measurement, individual analysis, and experimental control. The model requires that behavior in reading be measured directly on a daily basis rather than by pre/post-achievement tests. Each student's performance is analyzed and graphically recorded separately so that all of the idiosyncratic behavior patterns are observed. Finally, experimental construct is established by obtaining data several days before intervention is scheduled and then data are collected over several days of intervention (pp. 162–64).

Hansen and Lovitt conducted studies on comprehension using this model and have documented the improvement of the subjects' comprehension skills. Though there are limitations to this type of research design, the authors note that it allows researchers and teachers to investigate current problems in classrooms where reading ordinarily occurs. Teachers and researchers thus have a common language and are able to establish similar patterns for research design and teaching methods.

Conducting research in the classroom is supported by Goodman and Goodman (1979), Carey (1980), and Kantor, Kirby, and Goetz (1981), who agree that research must be relevant to classroom teachers in order to bring improvement. Naturalistic inquiry takes place in a classroom and is more readily interpretable by teachers. Researcher and teacher are often partners in the search for knowledge with "child as informant."

Harste, Woodward, and Burke (1984) present a model for a naturalistic approach to research in language arts learning. This research model has four key theoretical areas upon which curriculum is built: (1) language, (2) language learning, (3) successful language users, and (4) the evaluation of literacy. Assessment entails observation and collecting data about the child's performance in the natural setting. The question asked using this research model is, "In light of what is known about language and language learning, how are language users performing in ——— ?" The curricular support for both study and teaching has offered two forms, "the strategy instruction and the creation of a low-risk classroom aura" (pp. 225–27).

WHEN SHOULD CHILDREN BE TAUGHT TO READ?

Since reading is a complex process, the answer to the question, "When should children be taught to read?" is not simple or straightforward.

Some researchers have examined specific factors to determine if there are relationships between reading achievement and intelligence, gender, visual skills, auditory skills, letter knowledge, word consciousness, cognitive ability, metalinguistic ability or environmental factors. Though establishing a strong correlational link between any of these factors and reading achievement does not mean these factors are prerequisites for reading, research findings help teachers identify which children may need assistance either before specific formal instruction begins or as reading instruction is taking place.

Age

Chronological age seems to have little relationship to when a child is capable of learning to read. Coltheart (1979) reports that the ages at which children are formally taught to read varies from country to country: for example, it is five years in Israel, Great Britain, and Hong Kong; six in France, the United States, and Japan; and seven in Denmark, Sweden, and Ecuador. If there were an optimal age, then the programs in some of these countries would be more successful with beginning readers; no such evidence exists (Coltheart, 1979, pp. 4–5).

In the United States, instruction has tended to begin by age six, since events in the 1930s (for example, major reading studies, the developmental theorists' influence, and the testing movement) led people to believe that a mental age of 6.5 was necessary for reasonable growth in reading. The Morphett and Washburne, and Dolch and Bloomster studies greatly influenced the notion that there was a mental age that children should reach before reading instruction should start. After finding that children with mental ages of 6.5 made better reading progress than did those with less maturity, Morphett and Washburne concluded that if reading instruction were postponed until children reached 6.5 years, this would reduce their chances of failure (1983, p. 169). Dolch and Bloomster found a high correlation between phonic ability and mental age, and concluded that a child could not be expected to use phonics much before the age of seven (1937, pp. 204–05).

Gates (1937) examined different methods of teaching reading and found that if teachers recognized individual differences and adjusted to them, low achievers could successfully learn to read. He concluded that whether the child could learn to read at a particular time depended more on the type of instruction than on a particular mental age.

In spite of this contrast between the Gates study and other studies, the concept of a specific mental age for readiness gained much more prominence in this country than did the concept of adjusting instruction to the child's need. In reviews of "mental" age concept research, Gentile (1983) and Durkin (1983) suggest that the climate of the times allowed the mental age view to be much more widely accepted. The influence of psychologists such as Gesell, Piaget, and Erikson led people to believe that these stages could be pinpointed to specific ages. Second, other studies revealed data that large numbers of children were failing to read at the end of the first grade. It was believed, therefore, that allowing children more time for maturing would reduce the failure rate.

A third factor influencing the identificaton of mental age as a factor in beginning reading was the testing movement, with Binet as its leader. Instruments for determining the child's mental age were developed. The readiness test was to provide teachers and administrators with objective information about when to begin reading instruction for different groups of children. Designed with subskills scores, these tests were supposed to identify specific skills in which children showed strengths or weaknesses.

Since then, the validity of this testing practice has been challenged. Research from the 1940s suggests that, at least for some children, the tests do not predict future reading achievement very well. Teachers' predictions are as good as, if not superior to, readiness test results (Kottmeyer, 1947; Barrett, 1965; Satz & Fletcher, 1979). However, the practice of beginning reading instruction and using tests to predict readiness has persisted in many of America's schools.

In the 1960s there were challenges to the notion that reading instruction should not commence until a child had reached the mental age of 6.5 for fear that these children would have problems once they began to receive school instruction. Research on the early reader was one such challenge.

Dolores Durkin carried out three longitudinal studies of early readers. In the first study, Durkin tested 5,103 children entering first grade to determine if any of them could already read without having had any formal instruction. Forty-nine, or about 1 percent, met the criterion. The backgrounds of these children were investigated to determine if there were any indications as to how and why they could read. The children were also followed through sixth grade to determine if they maintained their advantage as proficient readers. Durkin (1966) reported that the early readers maintained higher reading scores throughout their six years in elementary school. In a second study done in New York, Durkin identified 156 early readers, nearly 3.5 percent of the total population tested. These children also maintained an advantage over other children as they progressed through the grades. In her third study (1977), Durkin examined early readers who had been taught to read in a two-year language arts program before entering first grade. During the first two years of schooling, these children scored significantly higher on reading tests than did their classmates, but by the end of third and fourth grades the two groups did not score significantly differently.

Other studies have been designed to teach reading to younger children. McKee, Brezeniski, and Harrison (1966) reported on a Denver study in which kindergartners were taught to read using some phonic training and letter recognition techniques, but mainly stressing use of context to discover the meaning of unknown words. In first grade, half of the sample was placed in a classroom where the teacher adjusted her instruction to capitalize on the early instruction. The other group had regular first-grade instruction. The children whose instruction was coordinated with their earlier program maintained their progress, while the others did not. Sutton (1969) reported a study that had young children learn to read by providing lots of pre-primers, opportunities for children to share their skills and knowledge with each other, a teacher available to answer questions, and the reward of taking home books they learned to read to share with their families. Sutton found those children who did learn to read continued to show more progress through third grade than did their classmates who started to read in grade one.

The research on early readers makes it apparent that some children do learn to read early and that the mental age of 6.5 is not necessary for all children. The research also indicates that, in most cases, early readers sustain their advantage and learning to read early does not have deleterious effects. However, the research does not support the idea that all preschoolers should be taught to read.

Intelligence

Intelligence is another factor to be considered. On the average, early readers have higher intelligence scores than their peers. High intelligence seems to help, but it is neither a prerequisite nor a guarantee that very young children will profit from beginning reading instruction (Torrey, 1979; Sampson & Briggs, 1981; Durkin, 1977).

Intelligence for *all* readers seems to have some effect on reading. Early studies reported a correlation between intelligence scores and first-grade reading scores that ranged between .45 and .56, with a median of .50 (Gray, 1960; Bond & Dykstra, 1967). Lohnes and Gray (1972) and Tremans-Ziremba et al. (1980) verified these earlier correlations between reading scores and intelligence scores. Ekwall and Shanker (1983) noted that there were higher correlations between reading scores and I.Q.s for students with either very high or very low I.Q.s, but for the vast majority of students the I.Q. score was not a significant predictor of reading achievement. Reading specialists such as Harris and Sipay (1979) point out that some very bright children can have problems that affect their learning to read. Moreover, slow learners are often able to learn to read when instruction is adapted to their learning capacities, a point that William Gray made in the 1930s but that was largely ignored.

Gender

Gender differences in reading achievement tend to be explained by cultural expectations. Girls in the early years of reading instruction tend to achieve higher scores than boys (Gates, 1961; Johnson, 1973–74). One hypothesis offered is that in American culture reading is a sedentary activity and girls are socialized to be more passive than boys. Thus, girls are rewarded for quiet reading behavior.

A second theory is that reading materials are more interesting for girls. Finally, the major role models that children have for reading are their female kindergarten and primary school teachers. From the research there is no clear evidence that boys should begin reading instruction any later than girls (Dwyer, 1973).

Visual Skills

Vision plays an important role in learning to read, but it is difficult to discern to what extent vision is related to reading failures. One important visual factor is visual discrimination. Since visual discrimination is believed to be related to reading achievement, there are many prereading activities in schools designed to improve this. Children perform many activities requiring them to note likeness and difference in objects and pictures, and to relate much of this to size, color, and shape.

Children who are weak in the ability to seek likeness and difference in shapes, patterns, and forms have difficulty in recognizing words and letters (Spache, 1976). Spache argues that there is a developmental pattern of visual discrimination, that is, children progress from discrimination of three-dimensional materials, then to two-dimensional materials, and finally to reproducing and matching two-dimensional forms.

Other researchers have also been attempting to determine if perceptual training could enhance a child's readiness for reading. Barrett (1965) concluded that discrimination of letters and words was a better predictor of reading than discrimination of shapes and forms. A 1978 research review by Weaver and Shonkoff concluded that perceptual training to help children "discriminate, recognize and produce letters of the alphabet" was more helpful than perceptual training to help children discriminate geometric shapes and pictures (p. 40).

Children may need some experience in discriminating similarities and differences in shapes and patterns. However, it appears that these experiences will not necessarily enhance children's readiness for reading. Children need direct experience with discrimination of letters and words as a part of their reading instruction if they are to learn to read.

Auditory Skills

Auditory skills, like visual skills, encompass a number of component parts: auditory acuity, discrimination, blending, comprehension, and memory. Children who have difficulties in one or more of these areas may have some difficulties in learning to read. Research has attempted to determine if auditory discrimination or the ability to hear likeness and difference between the smallest unit of sound (phonemes) is a predictor of reading achievement.

Smith (1978) notes that children do not need skill in auditory perception in order to read. There may be, however, some types of reading instruction that might require the child to have certain auditory skills in order to achieve. The relationship between auditory discrimination—or ability to segment the phonemes into component parts—and reading ability has been studied by Bond and Dykstra (1967), Liberman et al. (1974), and Fox and Routh (1976). They found positive correlations between ability to discriminate phonemes and readiness to read. Paradis and Peterson (1975) and Rozin, Bressman, and Taft (1974) noted that children from lower-income backgrounds and inner-city children had greater difficulty in discriminating between sounds.

Though there is correlational evidence of the relationship between distinguishing sounds and reading, there is no clear indication that a cause-and-effect relationship exists. Phonemic analysis may be greatly improved as one learns to read. Goldstein (1976) determined that phonemic analysis was *both* a predictor *and* a consequence. Children who were sensitive to the differences in sounds were able to read with greater ease, but learning to read also helped improve the ability to discriminate sounds for all the children in the study.

From several reviews of this topic (Groff, 1975; Lyon, 1977; and Ehri, 1979), one can conclude that though auditory discrimination skills seem to be related to learning to read, developing these skills in nonreaders will not assure that they will learn to read. In the studies there were good readers who had poor auditory skills and poor readers who were able to discriminate sounds adequately (Lyon, 1977, p. 570).

Letter Knowledge

Knowledge of letters has been viewed as an important factor in beginning reading and numerous studies have indicated that letter naming and letter recognition are the best predictors of reading success, especially in the primary grades (Barrett, 1965; Richek, 1977–78; Muehl & DiNello, 1976; Nurss, 1979). Studies indicate that early readers have a knowledge of letter names (Torrey, 1979; Bissex, 1980; Lass, 1982; Mason, 1980).

Although there is evidence that letter knowledge is an important factor in reading, teaching of letter names to children does not necessarily result in their successfully learning to read (Speer & Lamb, 1976; Muehl & Kremenack, 1966). Some theorists suggest that letter knowledge is a result of a child's interest in books and his or her intrinsic language competence (Gibson & Levin, 1975).

Most children are surrounded by a great deal of print in their environment, but there is disagreement among authorities as to whether children learn to abstract the necessary graphic clues for reading from this environment in the same natural way that they learn oral language, or whether children need such prerequisite skills as letter recognition or phoneme segmentation before they can read the print.

Goodman and Goodman (1979) and Harste, Woodward and Burke (1984) maintain that children are learning to read in the preschool years as they begin to identify symbols from their environment. For example, they can read things such as the labels on food packages, the Gulf or Exxon signs on gas stations, or the McDonald's sign on the fast-food restaurant. At first children recognize these signs because of the context in which they are found. Gradually, after many experiences, the print itself becomes familiar and the words can be recognized when seen in a new context, and finally individual letters can be segmented out and recognized.

Mason (1980), in a longitudinal study of preschoolers, identified three distinct stages of reading acquisition: (1) dependence upon the context to be able to identify the word, (2) the ability to recognize words found out of context and to recognize and name the letters that match the sounds found in the words, and (3) the ability to read multisyllabic words and to decode printed words.

In a critique of the letter-name knowledge research, Ehri (1983) points out that in the last ten years research on letter-name knowledge has focused on the child's developing awareness of the letter-sound mapping system. English orthography is alphabetic and the sounds of many letters closely resemble the letter names.

That children demonstrate this awareness is clear from the research relating to children's early writings (Harste, Burke, & Woodward, 1982; Chomsky, 1977; Paul, 1976; Vukelich & Golden, 1984). Children who are encouraged to write and to use their spelling will use the letter names they hear in the words in their writings. Thus they might write PPL for people, or KOT for coat, DRD for dirty. Paul (1976) has even suggested that there is a progression in this skill. That is, children seem to note first the initial consonant or long vowel (letter name) sounds, progress to final phoneme or syllable, and then finally begin to separate out short vowel sounds. Thus, a child might progress in recognizing and writing the letters in the word *come* by first writing *k* (representing the initial sound of the word). Then he would begin to write *km*, representing the initial and final letter sounds, and then finally write *kum*, indicating an awareness of the separation of sounds within a word. It would be only after much experience with the word that the child would finally write the correct orthography, *come*. At that stage the child would have learned the word and no longer be writing the word as letter and sound segments. The "invented spelling" seems to be a means for mapping the sound system rather than a means for identifying words.

The question as to whether children need to know the letter name in order to read or whether they can figure out the process by lots of experience with the print environment is not totally clear. Masonheimer, Drum, and Ehri (1984) found that children could be classified into two groups depending on mastery of the alphabet: (1) contextual dependent children had not mastered the alphabet and were unable to read words in isolation, (2) contextual independent children had mastered the alphabet and were able to read words in isolation. It seems that children need to know letter names in order to be able to read words out of context. Nevertheless, it is still not clear whether direct teaching of the letter names helps the children move from contextual dependency to contextual independence, or whether children need to figure out the letter names because of interest and curiosity.

The research does suggest that teachers provide a classroom environment where letter name and recognition are a part of the program and where children have an opportunity to ask questions and receive answers regarding the letters they see in books or printed on various signs and charts in the classroom. Alphabet songs and games also provide children the opportunity for acquiring letter knowledge. Mastering knowledge of the alphabet does not, however, guarantee reading success. Learning letters should be a part of the total reading process, not just a prerequisite to reading instruction.

Word Knowledge

Children entering school have wide variations in their vocabulary development, and certainly language facility plays an important role in later reading success. The extent of a child's vocabulary has been a predictor of future reading success (Artley, 1948; Robinson, 1963). Children who did well earlier on different vocabulary tasks had higher scores later in reading achievement.

Meaningful words are easier to learn to read. Thus, the words selected for sight recognition may affect children's reading achievement. De Hirsch, Jansky, and Langford (1966), Biemiller (1977–78) and Lesgold and Resnick (1982) found a high correlation between first grade reading achievement and children's ability to recognize words they had been taught that had special meaning for them, such as their name, important dates, or words like *monster, candy*.

While vocabulary is important for a child's reading achievement, it is not clear that attempting to teach children an extensive sight vocabulary improves their reading ability. Jackson and Biemiller (1985) concluded from their study comparing the time it took precocious readers and average readers to read letters in isolation, words in isolation, and connected text, that rapid *word* identification facilitated rapid reading and comprehension of text, but was not a prerequisite for it.

Extensive studies are being conducted on word consciousness and how that relates to reading. Many children, when they enter school, are not aware of the subunits of language, that is, that sentences can be divided into words and words into letters and sounds. In addition, children also may have difficulty in interpreting the terminology for teaching reading, such as letter, word, sound, beginning and ending.

Karpova (in Slobin, 1966) identified different stages of word consciousness for children ages three-and-a-half and seven. Younger children regarded the sentence as a total unit and separated ideas by meaning units. During the second stage, they can distinguish subject and predicate. The oldest children divided sentences into words but often left out prepositions and conjunctions, and even sometimes divided words into syllables. Holden and McGintie (1972) and Huttenlocker (1964) concurred with Karpova's results.

Ehri (1979) examined the relationship between word consciousness and ability to read. From several correlational studies, she found that beginning readers did much better on word analysis tasks than did nonreaders. She suggests that there is perhaps an interactive process taking place where learning to read helps the child understand function of words better, and thus adjust to print. At the same time, the child's knowledge and understanding of the spoken word helps with reading the printed language (p. 84).

Cognitive Ability

A relationship between cognitive development and reading ability has been suggested (Dimitrovsky & Almy, 1975; Briggs & Elkind, 1973; Polk & Goldstein, 1980). Children who are able to do Piagetian tasks of conservation achieve better on reading tasks. Since the studies are correlational, there is no strong evidence that conservation is a prerequisite for beginning reading instruction. It may be that as children learn to read they are also developing greater ability in conservation.

Gough, Juel, and Roper/Schneider (1983) suggest that one type of instructional approach may be more appropriate for children who have achieved conservation and another type more appropriate for children who have not. For example, the phonics approach may be more suitable for the child who is better able to conserve, since the approach demands that a child be able to decenter and realize that letters belong to more than one category at the same time.

Children who have difficulty decentering may have greater success learning to read when taught by the meaning approach. These children may need more experience with understanding that print gives meaning and may gradually begin to discern that not only does "McDonald's" mean a place to get hamburgers, but also that it is a word and it has subunits of letters and sounds.

Metalinguistic Ability

The relationship between the child's metalinguistic ability—being able to separate language from its meaning and to analyze and reflect upon the form of language—and reading achievement has recently been explored. According to Flavell, metalinguistics includes the monitoring of the language processes and the selection and regulation of these processes in order to achieve some objective or goal (1976, p. 232).

For example, a child would know that *man* is not only someone like Daddy or Uncle Joe, but also that it is a word and can be separated into both letter and sound parts *(m-a-n)*. Further, he or she would know strategies for segmenting the word. The ability to develop these strategies for this segmentation requires the child to decenter, and recognize that things (ideas, objects) can have more than one characteristic. *Man* can have a "meaning quality," but *man* can also have "linguistic qualities," such as sounds and letters that are arranged in a certain order and that relate to one another (Templeton, 1980).

Ryan, McNamara, and Kenny (1977), Ehri (1979), and Allan (1982) examined the relationship between children's awareness of lexical tasks and their reading achievement. Ryan et al. tested differences between better and poorer readers in awareness of sounds as words and as nonwords. Ehri examined the word consciousness of beginning readers compared to that of prereaders. Though there were some differences, both researchers found high correlations between children's lexical awareness and reading achievement. There seems to be some evidence that children who have not achieved metalinguistic awareness are less able readers. However, as Ehri points out, it is not clear whether teaching children word analytical skills will improve their reading skill. Ehri suggests that it is possible that the child who has acquired some basics in reading has also acquired some word consciousness and succeeds better on word analysis tasks (1979, p. 81).

Fox and Routh (1976), Mattingly (1972), and Helfgott (1976) examined the importance of metalinguistic awareness as it relates to phoneme segmentation for reading achievement. In these studies, children were given tasks to determine whether they were aware of the separate sounds in the word and could tap out the number of different sounds or match these sounds to corresponding printed letters. High correlation between phonic segmentation abilities and reading ability was reported. These segmentation abilities appear to be developmental (Liberman et al., 1974). Liberman (1973) maintains that reading acquisition depends on the child's developing awareness of phonemic segmentation. As in other correlation studies, it is not clear whether phoneme segmentation is a prerequisite for beginning reading instruction or whether a child beginning to read is then able to do better on phoneme analysis tasks.

Some researchers have attempted to determine if reading instruction develops metalinguistic awareness. Alegria, Pignot, and Morais (1982) and Perfetti and Beck (1982) conducted studies in which they compared children's ability in phoneme segmentation and instructional method of reading. From the evidence of their studies, both concluded that phonemic awareness is necessary for reading and reading is important for developing phonemic awareness.

Yopp and Singer (1984) reported quite different conclusions after attempting to determine if children with no linguistic ability can still learn to read. Kindergarten children who had no ability to segment utterances into phonemes were given instruction via a "phonics" or a "whole word" approach, but a post-test found no correlation between linguistic awareness (in this case, the ability to segment utterances into phonemes) and initial reading performance. Yopp and Singer speculate that the stimuli presented in these studies did not require metalinguistic processes and that these particular processes are not needed under certain instructional conditions (1984, p. 155).

Metalinguistic knowledge, as it relates to the discourse level of a whole passage, has also been examined to determine how the discourse affects children's reading comprehension ability. The processes involved in story comprehension and different story grammars, how stories are constructed, have been examined by Rumelhart (1978), Stein and Glenn (1982), Mandler and Johnson (1977), and Thorndyke (1977). A common grammar, for example, is a story set in time and place (which may be indefinite) in which characters are introduced so that a problem is set up, the hero or heroine departs to solve the problem, and through a series of events the problem is resolved. The hero or heroine returns, often wiser for the experience. Children appear to remember better stories that conform to the better-known story formats.

However, metalinguistic knowledge—in this case the ability to construct a story—seems to be developmental. When Applebee (1978) and Nurss, Hough, and Goodson (1981) asked four-year-olds to create their own stories, these stories contained various events but few other narrative conventions. Stein and Glenn (1984) found, however, that the older the children, the more stories they could construct and these stories were more complete.

In an extensive study of reading as a complex system of skills, Forrest-Pressley and Waller (1984) found that performance on reading skills and on the ability to verbalize or strategize increased with grade and reading ability. The ability to *use* the skills tended to be a better predictor of reading ability than did the ability to *verbalize about language* (a metalinguistic function). High performance without high verbalization and vice versa was rarely found. The study did not shed light on whether it is productive to instruct students in metacognitive skills with the intent of improving reading ability. However, since the verbalization measures did help to explain the students' level of reading, the researchers concluded, "The implication of this observation put simply is that teachers, perhaps, should talk to students about how and what they know and why they do things the way they do" (p. 123).

Environmental Factors

The effects of home environment on children's reading achievement have been studied by several researchers. When early researchers examined the relationship between socioeconomic status and reading achievement, high correlations were found (Justman, 1965; St. John, 1970; Chomsky, 1972). Later research studies, however, have examined other factors in home and school, in addition to socioeconomic status, that could account for differences.

Walberg and Tsai (1985) examined nine-year-olds in an attempt to determine some of the factors that affect reading. Socioeconomic status and ethnicity were not highly correlated to reading achievement, but stimulus materials for reading in the home were. Walker and Kuerbitz (1979) noted that children who had been reading at home achieved higher reading scores at the end of the first grade than did their counterparts.

Thus, it has been concluded that socioeconomic background may have some influence, but it is only a minor factor. It is the family background that plays the important role in terms of reading (Teale, 1978; Torrey, 1979; and Tremans-Ziremba, 1980). These studies confirm conclusions from Durkin's study of early readers (1966). Children with higher reading achievement and early readers come from homes where parents read a great deal themselves, read a great deal to their children, and provide a rich print environment. Other important factors are: availability of writing materials, the encouragement to write, responsive parents or siblings when children ask for help in spelling, and educational TV programs that focus on reading. In all the studies there are strong suggestions that the initiative for reading activities comes from the children. They want to be read to and often ask for the same book over and over. They request the information they need in performing both reading and writing tasks.

In summary, the research supports the idea that reading is an accumulation of many skills, that these skills are acquired in an interactive way and that each child's process of learning is unique. There are few, if any, prerequisites for learning to read and no precise time when reading instruction should begin. Reading is an ongoing process, beginning at home as parents respond to the child's interest in books and print, progressing during the school years as teachers facilitate comprehension and interest through helping the child to perfect the subskills of reading, and continuing into adulthood as one practices and refines one's own ability to acquire information and to receive enjoyment from various types of text.

METHODS AND STRATEGIES FOR TEACHING READING

Methods Research

Reading programs in this country have reflected the beliefs of two quite different views of how children learn. One view maintains that the various phonics and decoding models of instruction are the best ways to learn to read. Advocates of this view maintain that children must first learn the subskills or parts of reading before they can progress to gaining meaning from reading.

The meaning approach has been viewed by others as the best way to learn to read. Advocates of this view maintain that children first perceive meaning of print in context and then learn to associate the spoken word to the different parts of that print.

Much of the early method research compared an "innovative" approach (either meaning or phonics) to the current or traditional approach (either meaning or phonics). The results of these studies suggested that the innovative approach produced greater achievement than did the traditional approach (Pflaum, Walberg, Kargianes, & Racher, 1980). Because of inconclusive results of such studies, three major research studies were conducted in the 1960s and 1970s to further assess the best method.

Chall's research (mentioned earlier), while concluding that emphasizing phonics produced better results than emphasizing meaning, noted that the phonics-emphasis approaches were not cure-alls for all reading ills. Many children made excellent progress in the meaning-emphasis approach and many other children failed using a phonics emphasis (1967, p. 307).

During 1964–65, the United States Office of Education conducted a broad-based research project (the Cooperative Reading Research Project).

Five different approaches to reading: Initial Teaching Alphabet, language experience, linguistics, basal plus phonics, and phonics plus linguistics were compared to the traditional basal approach. The results of this study pointed out that teacher effectiveness was an important factor in children's learning to read and that no one approach was best in all situations. Since children learn from a variety of methods and materials, no one approach should be used exclusively (Bond & Dykstra, 1967; Dykstra, 1968).

In the 1970s, the United States Office of Education developed the program, *Follow Through*, because evidence indicated that early gains made by children during the preschool years were not maintained as children progressed through the primary grades. The twenty models varied greatly in their emphasis and goals, but all required development of reading skills as part of their curricula. In contrast to the Cooperative Reading Research project, which specified only the type of reading program to be conducted, the Follow Through project specified the type of classroom environment, materials to be included, role of the teachers, and types of groupings for the students involved. The results of the study were similar to the Cooperative Reading Research results. There were great differences in results of the same model from site to site and each model had sites where reading achievement was high and sites where reading achievement was low. The academically oriented models (when classified together) did tend to have students who scored higher on such subtests as word knowledge, spelling, and language, but no model proved more effective for reading comprehension (Stebbins et al., 1977).

An interesting new study, shared book experience, is an example of a method that combines writing and literature, and one started with kindergarten children. From the earliest experiences in school, children are read to, with the children's favorite stories often reread several times. They are encouraged to "pretend read" familiar books. They play with words and letters in games and songs, and "read" together stories printed in large format. Children are given time to "read" independently and time to create stories and pictures stemming from their experiences with new and old favorite stories (Holdaway, 1979). Holdaway (1982) reports that the experimental study conducted in New Zealand using this method resulted in greater gains for the experimental group in reading achievement on several measures. The greatest significance was the highly positive attitude toward reading of the lower achievers.

From the vast research on what method is best, it has become apparent that no single method or model is superior in developing general reading skills. The fact that, in all the method research studies, there were wide variations among students who were taught by the same approach indicates that many other factors affect reading outcomes.

Observational Research

Observational studies have identified about 350 different variables that affect classroom learning (Dunkin & Biddle, 1974). The variables pertain to such elements as teacher–pupil interaction during instruction, teachers' solutions to problems that arise in the classroom, amount and type of content covered, student's success rate, and general classroom climate (Barr, 1984; Rosenshine & Stevens, 1984). Various other components in addition to classroom environment can affect reading outcome. Samuels (1981) has summarized these as: the human element (teachers, aides, parents, librarians, administrators), materials (textbooks, audiovisual materials, teacher-constructed materials), and procedures (curriculum and evaluation mandates, schedules and routines, school district organization and size).

In the many observational studies, correlations have been noted between many of the different components and reading. Academic learning time (ALT), or the amount of time a child is engaged in an academic task, is one of the components that has been found consistently to correlate with reading achievement or school learning (Carroll, 1963; Wiley, 1976; Fisher et al., 1978). The Beginning Teacher Evaluation Study found that ALT (and thus achievement) was increased when the task the child was to complete was related to a very specific area of learning and was not too difficult for the child. Monitoring of the task by the teacher and giving appropriate feedback also affects the ALT (Fisher et al., 1978). Grouping students for instruction increases the ALT per student and thus reading achievement. In small groups children receive more instruction from the teacher, more praise and more feedback. A combination of these factors is more productive for learning (Stallings & Kaskowitz, 1974; Soars, 1973). Kean et al. found that children in the first through fourth grades had higher achievement if they were in classes that were taught in some combination of small group/large group instruction. These children achieved better reading scores than did their counterparts who were taught in classes where teachers conducted lessons only individually, only in small groups or only in large groups (1979, p. 9).

The amount of materials covered in a program was found to correlate with reading achievement (Anderson, Evertson & Brophy, 1979; Lesgold & Curtis, 1981; Barr & Dreeben, 1983). The pact of the lesson and the fact that children are grouped according to different levels are important considerations of the amount of content covered. It is important, in interpreting the research, that teachers not misinterpret and try to cover content regardless of children's ability level. Brophy and Evertson (1976) and Fisher et al. (1978) found that overall reading achievement was positively correlated with children's success rate. The fewer errors children make in learning tasks, the more time they remain engaged in that task, the more content they are able to cover, and thus the greater their achievement.

Some of the conclusions drawn from the studies point to the fact that successful teachers give more instruction per student, more opportunity for children to practice skills, and more feedback on the correctness of these skills. They also monitor each child's behavior better and keep each child more involved in the reading task (Rosenshine & Stevens, 1984, p. 787).

Strategies Research

No matter what method one uses or what philosophy one espouses, the main purpose of reading is comprehension. However, in order to achieve that comprehension, certain skills must be acquired. Let us consider studies suggesting strategies for developing phonic skills, sight-word identification, comprehension skills, and writing skills which in turn enhance reading.

Phonics. Beginning readers must master rules and generalizations about phonics if the basal reader texts are followed. The utility of phonics generalizations in basal readers has been examined by several researchers. The number of words that have certain letter combinations, and when to apply successfully the rules for those combinations, were noted. For example, Clymer (1963) found that of the forty-five generalizations on words that contain certain letter combinations, only eighteen worked as often as 75 percent of the time. He maintained that many generalizations that are taught are of limited value (p. 258). However, Burmeister (1971) determined that rules which work most often were not always the most useful to teach to elementary children because they may not be reading the words to which these rules apply. She developed a list of different rules that she felt would be most useful to teach (pp. 28–33).

The purpose of phonics is to teach the alphabetic principle, and the rules that children learn should have operational use. From the principles, children should be able to identify known words rapidly and to figure out unfamiliar words. Therefore, only the most important and regular phonic rules should be taught (Anderson et al., 1985). In spite of these studies, basal readers still provide lessons for all forty-five generalizations. Instead of following the dictates of the basals in making decisions about which rules to focus on, teachers need to be aware of the utility of each rule and the likelihood of children finding examples of its application in their reading.

The synthetic approach and the analytic approach are the most common strategies for teaching phonics. In the synthetic approach, sounds in words are identified separately and then blended in order to form words. Children first learn a number of letter sounds from words in their speaking and listening vocabulary, then identify these sounds in isolation. The next step is to separate out the individual sounds from the known words. The final and most important step is blending the sounds together (Englemann & Bruner, 1974).

The analytic approach to phonics instruction never uses the sound in isolation, but teaches the sound as it is heard in a series of words. For example, the letter *b* is the first sound one hears in the words *baby, boy, basket, Billy*. Children are then encouraged to think of other words that they know that begin like *baby, boy,* etc. As they develop skill in thinking of other words, they are encouraged to identify unknown words by their similarity to known words. For example, if children know *cat* and know the sounds of other initial letters, then they should be able to figure out *mat, sat, rat* (Durkin, 1983).

Research as to which method is best is somewhat inconclusive, though Pflaum et al. (1980), Johnson and Baumann (1984), and Williams (1985), in reviewing phonic instruction strategies, concluded that there was increasing evidence that a synthetic approach was more effective in teaching letter sound correspondence and in helping children transfer this skill to unknown words. The most important skill for transferring the phonic analysis skills to new words was the skill of blending isolated letters into recognizable words (Johnson & Baumann, 1984, p. 595). Alternatively, other research has shown that the strategy of substituting letters in known words to figure out unknown words (part of the analytic strategy) is a very effective means of helping children understand how letters combine to make meaningful words (Cunningham, 1977, 1979; Railsback, 1970).

Sight words. Sight words are commonly taught to young children before they begin reading. The rationale for this practice is that children can begin immediately to make meaning from the printed page. Words that children already know can also serve as a starting point for phonics instruction. The research on the most effective way to teach sight words presents conflicting views.

Some advocates of teaching sight words suggest it is better to teach the word in context, using picture clues, oral or written phrases and sentences, so that as children attach meaning to the word they see its communication value and thus remember it longer. This is often viewed as helpful, especially for function words which, in isolation, are difficult to define (Searfoss & Readence, 1985; Ehri, 1978; Goodman, 1967).

Other advocates suggest children learn words best in isolation when their attention is not distracted by other stimuli but is focused on the word so that they note its distinctive features, such as configuration, length of word, and letter placement. These advocates maintain that the child's attention is attracted to the picture or other words in the sentence, when taught in context, and thus the child does not attend to the target word (Samuels, 1967; Singer, Samuels & Spiroff, 1973–74). Rose and Furr (1984) concluded from their study that, especially for the learning-disabled reader, illustrations interfered with their learning isolated words.

Ceprano (1981) reports on a study comparing children's learning of words by the isolation or context method. In assessing the children, she also assessed them on the ability to recognize the words in a sentence and on the ability to recognize words in isolation. She found that children taught by the isolation method did better on the isolation test and children taught by the context method did better on the sentence test. She concluded that learning words in isolation facilitates the child's learning of the graphemes and phonemes, but learning words in context facilitates the child's learning of syntax and meaning (p. 320).

Comprehension. Researchers examining the comprehension process indicate that it is interactive. Various types of knowledge are important to the understanding of a text. The reader interprets the meaning by gathering new information from the text, as well as by using whatever prior knowledge he may have regarding both the content and structure of the text. Text information and the reader's hypotheses are processed at various levels. The text has lexical and syntactic structure and the reader must analyze the structure of the text (Anderson, 1977; Rumelhart, 1977; Bowey, 1984). The reader must be able to process this information at all levels and at all times (Mason, 1984). What the reader knows about text structure and the particular words the writer uses determines, in part, how much the reader will comprehend. The reader brings vast amounts of information about the context of the text to the reading. The reader forms judgments about the meaning from prior knowledge, but as new information is added, the reader adjusts her understanding of the text and also adjusts her own prior knowledge. In addition, a sense of story and a knowledge about different genres facilitates understanding. Thus, comprehension of a text depends as much on a reader's knowledge as it does on the information found in the text (Mason, 1984, pp. 29–31).

In addition to understanding the process of comprehension, teachers need to know how to teach comprehension. Durkin (1978–79), in a survey of fourth-grade classrooms, noted that teachers did much more comprehension testing than teaching. Since most teachers of reading follow the Directed Reading Approach suggested in the manuals (Shannon, 1983; Mason & Osborne, 1982), the following sections review research in specific techniques in keeping with the DRA.

Preparation just prior to reading is usually the first step in the Directed

Reading Approach. Research suggests that an important preparatory step for increasing comprehension is providing prior knowledge or activating the child's existing knowledge. In one study, researchers gave two groups of children different sets of background information about an Indian tribe they were to read about. A third group got information about Spanish people irrelevant to the story. Both groups with Indian information recalled 24 percent more story information than the group with Spanish information. The recall errors of the two groups with Indian information were consistent with their background information. The authors concluded that helping children gain information prior to a story does facilitate understanding and recall of the story, but the information can also color the understanding of the story (Brown et al., 1977, p. 44). Beck, Omanson, and McKeown (1982) had similar findings, but emphasized that information focusing on the central theme of the story was more effective than generalized information.

Prior questioning and establishing comprehension goals before reading the passage are other frequently used preparatory strategies. These questions and goals alert the children to what they should be looking for in the text (Levin & Pressley, 1981). These strategies are especially beneficial if the material to be read is difficult for children to understand (Hartley & Davis, 1976).

A third preparation strategy is clarifying content through pictures that can help "set the stage" for the reading. However, these pictures must be directly related to the text or they may be a hindrance (Rice, Doan, & Brown, 1981). Arnold and Brooks (1976) determined that pictures were more helpful than statements about the reading. Pictures included in the text have also been reported as helping students recall more information about a text (Guttman, Levin, & Pressley, 1977). It seems that pictures are extremely beneficial for slow learners in assisting comprehension (Bender & Levin, 1978).

The second phase in the teaching of reading process is the reading of the text itself. There has been controversy over the form that reading should take. Often the reading is done orally by children, without any prereading, going around the group in what is known as round-robin reading. Some children reading in this fashion stumble over words, read in a jerky manner, and get frequent corrections from classmates or the teacher. Anderson, Mason, and Shirley (1984) suggest that the children who are following along are not paying attention, and thus are not engaged in learning.

During oral reading, teachers are correcting and evaluating children's progress. Correcting errors as children make them has been shown to deter comprehension unless the teacher is careful (Allington, 1984). Anderson et al. (1985) indicate that children show greater gains in reading when corrections are made only for those errors that distort meaning. The child is given time to make the correction, and the teacher provides clues if this is unsuccessful. Finally, it seems important to have the child reread the sentence correctly in order to assure better comprehension (pp. 52–53).

Oral reading can enhance comprehension if children have an opportunity to read the passage silently before reading aloud. Repeated readings have proven beneficial to poor readers, and they have shown marked improvement in their ability to read new selections more accurately and marked improvement in their comprehension skills (Samuels, 1985). Research indicates that the amount of silent or independent reading is related to children's gain in reading (Greany, 1980; Walberg & Tsai, 1984).

Postquestioning and discussion strategies with emphasis on literal, inferential, and critical questions have long been a strategy that teachers have used to assist and/or assess children's understanding of the content of a story. In the Directed Reading Approach, the text manuals give teachers examples of all three types of questions related to the content of the text. Reading experts (Finn, 1985; Lapp & Flood, 1983) recommend that questions be developed that also help children understand the story structure and story grammars.

School-age children and even some preschoolers have a sense of story grammars (Applebee, 1978; Whaley, 1981; Dreher & Singer, 1980). When this knowledge is activated, children are better able to understand and remember details and events from the text (Bower, Black, & Turner, 1979; Rumelhart, 1978; Mandler & Johnson, 1977). These questions and discussions, of either text content or story structure, when they are directed to helping children integrate prior knowledge, have been found to improve reading achievement significantly (Hansen, 1981; Beck, Omanson, & McKeown, 1982). Morrow's (1984) research lends support for providing both types of questions, regarding content and story structure, to aid children's comprehension.

Writing to Read

Writing as a means to assist skill in reading is a technique that is being explored. From the early readers research (cited earlier in this chapter), it was found that early readers were interested in writing and often asked for words to be spelled. As children play with writing, they also are guided into the realization that writing is communication, that to communicate truly certain conventions must be followed if anyone else is to read their writing (Clay, 1977). In writing, children move through stages of "invented spelling" (Chomsky, 1971; Read, 1971). They build to writing words or a series of words representing an idea, first by representing the word or thought unit by the initial letter, next by the first and last letters, then they begin to recognize the medial sounds. Finally, children become more facile at using conventional spelling as they recognize the words they use in writing from their reading and other experiences with print. A sense of letter-sound relationships, alphabetic principle, spacing, synthesizing words and sentences into a story is being developed (Harste, Woodward, & Burke, 1984). Writing thus becomes a complement to reading.

IBM has developed a formal Write-to-Read program for use by kindergarten and first-grade teachers. Children use the computer to write and correct stories even as they are learning to read. ETS has done an extensive study of this program and found that the kindergartners had a significant advantage over the control group in reading. By first grade, both groups of children were doing equally well on standardized tests of reading, but kindergarten and first-grade children in the Write-to-Read programs write creative stories better than children in the regular programs (Murphy & Appel, 1984).

SUMMARY

Reading is a complex process. While research helps identify some of the elements of this process, vast amounts of research have not given definitive answers to such questions as when to begin the teaching of reading, how children learn to read, or what are the best methods for teaching. However, research does offer sound theoretical bases and suggestions, and gives directions that can be helpful to teachers.

While use of the different views of how children learn to read is helpful to teachers, they must still develop skill in observing children, using theoretical concepts as a basis to determine what each child is in fact doing as he or she is acquiring the skill of reading. Age, intelligence, gender, environment, visual and auditory skills, letter and word knowledge, cognitive and metalinguistic abilities are all very important considerations in the reading process. From the research on method and strategy, it appears there is no one method that is better than any other or that will work for all children. However, some ways are illustrated in studies that teachers can use to facilitate more effective learning for children.

REFERENCES

Alegria, J., Pignot, E., and Morais, J. (1982). Phonetic analysis of speech and memory codes in beginning readers. *Memory and Cognition, 10,* 451–56.

Allan, K. K. (1982). The development of young children's metalinguistic understanding of the word. *Journal of Educational Research, 76,* 89–93.

Allington, R. L. (1984). Oral reading. In P. D. Pearson (Ed.), *Handbook of reading research.* New York: Longman.

Anderson, L. M., Evertson, C. M., and Brophy, J. (1979). An experimental study of effective reading in first grade reading groups. *Elementary School Journal, 79,* 193–233.

Anderson, R. C. (1977). The notion of schemata and the educational enterprise. In R. C. Anderson, R. J. Spiro, and W. E. Montague (Eds.), *Schooling and the acquisition of knowledge.* Hillsdale, NJ: Erlbaum.

Anderson, R. C., Hiebert, E. H., Scott, J. A., and Wilkinson, I.A.G. (1985). *Becoming a nation of readers.* The Report of the Commission on Reading. Washington, DC: National Institute of Education.

Anderson, R. C., Mason, J., and Shirley, L. (1984). The reading group: an experimental investigation of a labyrinth. *Reading Research Quarterly, 20,* 6–38.

Applebee, A. (1978). *Child's concept of story: ages 2–17.* Chicago: University of Chicago Press.

Arnold, D. J., and Brooks, D. H. (1976). Influence of contextual organizing material on children's listening comprehension. *Journal of Educational Psychology, 68,* 711–16.

Artley, A. S. (1948). A study of certain factors presumed to be associated with reading and speech difficulties. *Journal of Speech and Hearing Disorders, 13,* 351–60.

Barr, R. (1984). Beginning reading instruction: from debate to reformation. In P. D. Pearson (Ed.), *Handbook of reading research.* New York: Longman.

Barr, R., and Dreeben, R. (1983). *How schools work.* Chicago: University of Chicago Press.

Barrett, T. C. (1965). The relationship between measures of pre-reading visual discrimination and first grade reading achievement. A review of the literature. *Reading Research Quarterly, 1,* 51–76.

Bateman, B. (1983). A commentary on Johns' critique of Gumen and Hughes' study: Measuring the effects of intensive phonics vs. gradual phonics in beginning reading. In L. M. Gentile, M. L. Kamil, and J. S. Blanchard (Eds.), *Reading research revisited.* Columbus, OH: Charles E. Merrill.

Beck, I. L., Omanson, R. C., and McKeown, M. G. (1982). An instructional redesign of reading lessons: effects on comprehension. *Reading Research Quarterly, 17,* 462–81.

Bender, B. G., and Levin, J. R. (1978). Pictures, imagery and retarded children's prose learning. *Journal of Education Psychology, 20,* 583–88.

Biemiller, A. J. (1977–78). Relations between oral reading rates for letters, words and simple text in the development of reading achievement. *Reading Research Quarterly, 13,* 223–53.

Bissex, G. L. (1980). GNYS at WRK: a child learns to write and read. Cambridge, MA: Harvard University Press.

Bond, G. L., and Dykstra, R. (1967). The cooperative research program in first-grade reading instruction. *Reading Research Quarterly, 2*, 5–142.

Bower, G. H., Black, J. B., and Turner, T. J. (1979). Scripts in memory for text. *Cognitive Psychology, 11*, 177–220.

Bowey, J. A. (1984). The interaction strategy and context in children's oral reading performance. *Journal of Psycholinguistic Research, 13*, 99–118.

Briggs, C., and Elkind, D. (1973). Cognitive development in early readers. *Developmental Psychology, 9*, 279–80.

Brophy, J. E., and Evertson, C. M. (1976). *Learning from teaching: a developmental perspective*. Boston: Allyn and Bacon.

Brown, A. L., Smiley, S. S., Day, J. D., and Townsend, M.A.R. (1977). Intrusion of a thematic idea in children's comprehension and retention of stories. *Child Development, 48*, 1454–66.

Burmeister, L. E. (1971). Content of a phonics program based on particularly useful generalizations. In N. B. Smith (Ed.), *Reading methods and teacher improvements*. Newark, DE: International Reading Association.

Carey, R. F. (1980). Empirical vs. naturalistic research? *Reading Research Quarterly, 5*, 412–15.

Carroll, J. B. (1963). A model of school learning. *Teachers College Record, 64*, 723–33.

Ceprano, M. A. (1981). A review of selected research on methods of teaching sight words. *The Reading Teacher, 35*, 314–22.

Chall, J. S. (1967). *Learning to read: the great debate*. New York: McGraw-Hill.

Chomsky, C. (1977). Approaching reading through invented spelling. In L. B. Resnick and P. A. Weaver (Eds.), *Theory and practice of early reading*, Vol. 2. Hillsdale, NJ: Erlbaum.

Chomsky, C. (1971). Invented spelling in the open classroom. *Word, 27*, 499–518.

Chomsky, C. (1972). Stages in language development and reading exposure. *Harvard Educational Review, 42*, 1–33.

Clay, M. M. (1977). *Reading: the patterning of complex behavior*. London: Heinemann.

Clymer, T. (1963). The utility of phonic generalizations in primary grades. *Reading Teacher, 16*, 252–58.

Coltheart, M. (1979). When can children learn to read—and when should they be taught? In G. T. Waller and G. E. MacKinnon (Eds.), *Reading research: advances in theory and practice*, Vol. 1. New York: Academic Press.

Cunningham, P. M. (1979). A compare/contrast theory of mediated word identification. *Reading Teacher, 32*, 774–78.

Cunningham, P. M. (1977). Supplying the missing links from consonant substitution to "real reading." *Reading Horizons, 17*, 279–82.

De Hirsch, K., Jansky, J. J., and Langford, W. S. (1966). *Predicting reading failure*. New York: Harper and Row.

Dechant, E. Z. (1982). *Improving the teaching of reading*. Englewood Cliffs, NJ: Prentice-Hall.

Dimitrovsky, L., and Almy, M. (1975). Early conservation as a predictor of later reading. *Journal of Psychology, 90,* 11–18.

Dolch, E. W., and Bloomster, M. (1937). Phonic readiness. *Elementary School Journal, 38,* 201–05.

Dreher, M. J., and Singer, H. (1980). Story grammar instruction unnecessary for intermediate grade students. *Reading Teacher, 34,* 261–68.

Dunkin, M. J., and Biddle, B. J. (1974). *The study of teaching.* New York: Holt, Rinehart and Winston.

Durkin, D. D. (1966). *Children who read early.* New York: Teachers College Press.

Durkin, D. D. (1977). Facts about pre–first grade reading. In L. O. Ollila (Ed.), *The kindergarten child and reading.* Newark, DE: International Reading Association.

Durkin, D. D. (1983). *Teaching them to read.* Boston: Allyn and Bacon.

Durkin, D. D. (1978–79). What classroom observation reveals about reading comprehension instruction. *Reading Research Quarterly, 14,* 481–533.

Dwyer, C. A. (1973). Sex differences in reading: an evaluation of current theories. *Review of Educational Research, 43,* 455–67.

Dykstra, R. (1968). Summary of the second grade phase of the Cooperative Research Program in primary reading instruction. *Reading Research Quarterly, 4,* 49–70.

Ehri, L. C. (1978). Beginning reading from a psycholinguistic perspective: amalgamation of word identification. In F. B. Murray (Ed.), *The recognition of words.* Newark, DE: International Reading Association.

Ehri, L. C. (1979). Linguistic insight: threshold of reading acquisition. In T. G. Waller and G. E. MacKinnon (Eds.), *Reading research: advances in theory and practice.* New York: Academic Press.

Ehri, L. C. (1983). Summaries and critique of five studies related to letter name knowledge and learning to read. In L. M. Gentile, M. L. Kamil, and J. S. Blanchard (Eds.), *Reading research revisited.* Columbus, OH: Charles E. Merrill.

Ekwall, E. E., and Shanker, J. L. (1983). *Diagnosis and remediation of the disabled reader.* Boston: Allyn and Bacon.

Englemann, S., and Bruner, E. C. (1974). *Distar reading I: an instructional system.* Chicago: Science Research Associates.

Finn, P. (1985). *Helping children to learn to read.* New York: Random House.

Fisher, C. W., Filby, N. N., Marliave, R., Cahen, L. S., Dishaw, M. M., Moore, J. E., and Berliner, D. C. (1978). *Beginning teacher evaluation study.* Technical report, V-1. San Francisco: Far West Laboratory.

Flavell, J. (1976). Metacognitive aspects of problem solving. In L. B. Resnick (Ed.), *The nature of intelligence.* Hillsdale, NJ: Erlbaum.

Forrest-Pressley, D. L., and Waller, T. G. (1984)). *Cognition, metacognition and reading.* New York: Springer-Verlag.

Fox, R., and Routh, D. K. (1976). Phonemic analysis and synthesis as word attack skills. *Journal of Education Psychology, 68,* 70–74.

Gagne, R. M. (1970). *The conditions of learning.* New York: Holt, Rinehart and Winston.

Gates, A. I. (1937). The necessary mental age for beginning reading. *Elementary School Journal, 37,* 497–508.

Gates, A. I. (1961). Sex differences in reading ability. *Elementary School Journal, 51,* 431–34.

Gentile, L. M. (1983). A critique of Mabel V. Morphett and Carleton Washburne's study: When should children begin to read? In L. M. Gentile, M. L. Kamil, and J. S. Blanchard, *Reading research revisited.* Columbus, OH: Charles E. Merrill.

Gibson, E. J., and Levin, H. (1975). *The psychology of reading.* Cambridge, MA: MIT Press.

Goldstein, D. M. (1976). Cognitive linguistic functioning and learning to read in preschoolers. *Journal of Educational Psychology, 68,* 680–88.

Goodman, K. S. (1967). Reading: a psycholinguistic guessing game. *Journal of Reading Specialist, 4,* 126–35.

Goodman, K. S. (1984). Unity in reading. In A. C. Purvis and O. Niles (Eds.), *Becoming readers in a complex society.* Chicago: University of Chicago Press.

Goodman, K. S., and Goodman, Y. M. (1979). Learning to read is natural. In L. B. Resnick and P. A. Weaver (Eds.), *Theory and practice of early reading,* Vol. 2. Hillsdale, NJ: Erlbaum.

Gough, P., Juel, C., and Roper/Schneider, D. (1983). Code and cipher: a two-stage conception of initial reading acquisition. In J. A. Niles and L. A. Harris (Eds.), *Searches for meaning in reading/language processing and instruction.* Thirty-second yearbook of the National Reading Conference. Rochester, NY: National Reading Conference.

Gray, W. S. (1960). Reading. In C. W. Harris (Ed.), *Encyclopedia of educational research.* New York: Macmillan.

Greany, V. (1980). Factors related to amount and type of leisure time reading. *Reading Research Quarterly, 15,* 337–57.

Groff, P. (1975). Reading ability and auditory discrimination: are they related? *Reading Teacher, 28,* 742–47.

Guttman, W., Levin, J. R., and Pressley, M. (1977). Pictures, partial pictures and young children's oral prose learning. *Journal of Education Psychology, 69,* 473–80.

Hansen, C., and Lovitt, T. (1977). An applied behavior analysis approach to reading comprehension. In J. T. Guthrie (Ed.), *Cognition, curriculum and comprehension.* Newark, DE: International Reading Association.

Hansen, J. (1981). The effects of inference training and practice on young children's reading comprehension. *Reading Research Quarterly, 16,* 391–417.

Harris, A. J., and Sipay, E. R. (1979). *How to teach reading: a competency-based program.* New York: Longman.

Harste, J. C., Burke, C. L., and Woodward, V. A. (1982). Children's language and world: initial encounters with print. In J. Langer and M. Smith-Burke (Eds.), *Bridging the gap: reader meets author.* Newark, DE: International Reading Association.

Harste, J. C., Woodward, V., and Burke, C. L. (1984). *Language stories and literacy lessons.* Portsmouth, NH: Heinemann.

Hartley, J., and Davis, I. K. (1976). Preinstructional strategies: the role of pretests, behavioral objectives, overviews and advance organizers. *Review of Education Research, 46,* 239–65.

Helfgott, J. (1976). Phonemic segmentation and blending skills of kindergarten children: implications for beginning reading acquisition. *Contemporary Educational Psychology, 1,* 157–69.

Holdaway, D. (1979). *The foundations of literacy.* New York: Ashton Scholastic.

Holdaway, D. (1982). Shared book experience: teaching reading using favorite books. *Theory Into Practice, 21,* 293–300.

Holden, M. H., and MacGintie, W. H. (1972). Children's conceptions of word boundaries in speech and print. *Journal of Educational Psychology, 63,* 551–57.

Holmes, J. A. (1970). The substrata-factor theory of reading: some experimental evidence. In H. Singer and R. B. Ruddell (Eds.), *Theoretical models and process of reading.* Newark, DE: International Reading Association.

Holmes, J. A., and Singer, H. (1964). Theoretical models and trends toward some basic research in reading. *Review in Education Research, 34,* 127–255.

Huttenlocker, J. (1964). Children's language: word-phrase relationship. *Science, 143,* 264–65.

Jackson, N. E., and Biemeller, A. J. (1985). Letter, word and text reading times of precocious and average readers. *Child Development, 56,* 196–206.

Johnson, D. D. (1973–74). Sex differences in reading across cultures. *Reading Research Quarterly, 9,* 67–86.

Johnson, D. D., and Baumann, J. F. (1984). Word identification. In P. D. Pearson (Ed.), *Handbook of reading research.* New York: Longman.

Justman, J. (1965). Academic aptitude and reading test scores if disadvantaged children showing varying degree of mobility. *Journal of Educational Measurement, 2,* 151–55.

Kamil, M. L., Langer, J. A., and Shanahan, T. (1985). *Understanding reading and writing research.* Boston: Allyn and Bacon.

Kantor, K. J., Kirby, D. R., and Goetz, J. P. (1981). Research in context: ethnographic studies in English education. *Research in the Teaching of English, 4,* 293–304.

Kean, M., Summers, A., Ravietz, M., and Farber, I. (1979). *What works in reading.* Philadelphia: School District of Philadelphia.

Kottmeyer, W. (1947). Readiness for reading. *Elementary English, 24,* 355–60.

LaBerge, D., and Samuels, S. J. (1974). Towards a theory of automatic information processing in reading. *Cognitive Psychology, 6,* 293–323.

Lapp, D., and Flood, J. (1983). *Teaching reading to every child.* New York: Macmillan.

Lass, B. (1982). Portrait of my son as an early reader. *Reading Teacher, 36,* 20–28.

Lesgold, A. M., and Curtis, M. E. (1981). Learning to read words efficiently. In A. M. Lesgold and C. A. Perfetti (Eds.), *Interactive processes in reading.* Hillsdale, NJ: Erlbaum.

Lesgold, A. M., and Resnick, L. B. (1982). How reading difficulties develop: perspective from a longitudinal study. In J. P. Das, R. F. Mulcahy, and A. E. Wall (Eds.), *Theory and research in learning disabilities.* New York: Plenum.

Levin, J. R., and Pressley, M. (1981). Improving children's prose comprehension: selected strategies that seem to succeed. In C. M. Santa and B. L. Hayes (Eds.), *Children's prose comprehension: research and practice*. Newark, DE: International Reading Association.

Liberman, I. Y. (1973). Segmentation of the spoken word and reading acquisition. *Bulletin of the Orton Society, 23*, 65–77.

Liberman, I. Y., Shankweiler, D., Fisher, F. W., and Carter, B. (1974). Explicit phoneme and syllable segmentation in the young child. *Journal of Experimental Child Psychology, 18*, 201–12.

Lohnes, P. R., and Gray, M. M. (1972). Intelligence and the cooperative reading studies. *Reading Research Quarterly, 7*, 466–67.

Lyon, R. (1977). Auditory-perceptual training: the state of the art. *Journal of Learning Disabilities, 10*, 564–72.

McKee, P. Brezeniski, J. E., and Harrison, A. L. (1966). *The effectiveness of teaching reading in kindergarten*. Cooperative Research Project No. 5–0381. Denver, CO: Denver Public Schools and Colorado State Department of Education.

Mandler, J. M., and Johnson, N. S. (1977). Remembrance of things passed: story structure and recall. *Cognitive Psychology, 9*, 111–51.

Mason, J. (1984). A schema-theoretic view of the reading process as a basis for comprehension instruction. In G. G. Duffy, L. R. Roehler, and J. Mason (Eds.), *Comprehension instruction: perspectives and suggestions*. New York: Longman.

Mason, J. (1980). When do children begin to read: an exploration of four year old children's letter and word reading competencies. *Reading Research Quarterly, 15*, 203–27.

Mason, J., and Osborne, J. (1982). *When do children begin "reading to learn"? a survey in grades two through five*. Urbana. University of Illinois, Center for the Study of Reading.

Masonheimer, P. E., Drum, P. A., and Ehri, L. C. (1984). Does environmental print identification lead children into word reading? *Journal of Reading Behavior, 14*, 257–71.

Mattingly, I. G. (1972). Reading, the linguistic process and linguistic awareness. In J. F. Kavanagh and I. G. Mattingly (Eds.), *Language by ear and by eye: the relationships between speech and reading*. Cambridge, MA: MIT Press.

Morphett, M. V., and Washburne, C. (1983). When should children begin to read? *Elementary School Journal, 31*, 496–503. Reprinted in L. M. Gentile, M. L. Kamil, and J. S. Blanchard (Eds.), *Reading research revisited*. Columbus, OH: Charles E. Merrill.

Morrow, L. M. (1984). Reading stories to young children: effects of story structure and traditional questioning strategies on comprehension. *Journal of Reading Behavior, 16*, 273–88.

Muehl, S., and DiNello, M. C. (1976). Early first grade skills related to subsequent reading performance: a seven year follow-up. *Journal of Reading Behavior, 8*, 67–81.

Muehl, S., and Kremenak, S. (1966). Ability to match information within and between auditory and visual sense modalities and subsequent reading achievement. *Journal of Educational Psychology, 57*, 230–39.

Murphy, R. T., and Appel, L. R. (1984). *Evaluation of the writing to read instructional system, 1982–1984*. Princeton, NJ: Educational Testing Service.

Nurss, J. R. (1979). Assessment of readiness. In T. G. Waller and G. E. Mackinnon, *Reading research: advances in theory and practice*. New York: Academic Press.

Nurss, L., Hough, R., and Goodson, M. (1981). Prereading language development in two day care centers. *Journal of Reading Behavior, 13*, 23–31.

Paradis, E. E., and Peterson, J. (1975). Readiness training implications from research. *Reading Teacher, 28*, 445–48.

Paul, R. (1976). Invented spelling in kindergarten. *Young Children, 32*, 95–200.

Perfetti, C., and Beck, I. (1982). Learning to read depends on phonetic knowledge and vice versa. Presented at the National Reading Conference, Clearwater, Florida.

Pflaum, S. W., Walberg, H. J., Kargianes, M. L., and Racher, S. P. (1980). Reading instruction: a quantitative method. *Educational Researcher, 9*, 12–18.

Polk, C., and Goldstein, D. (1980). Early reading and concrete operations. *Journal of Psychology, 106*, 111–16.

Railsback, C. E. (1970). Consonant substitution in word attack. *Reading Teacher, 23*, 432–35.

Read, C. (1971). Preschool children's knowledge of English phonology. *Harvard Educational Review, 41*, 1–34.

Reed, D. W. (1965). A theory of language speech and writing. *Elementary English, 42*, 845–51.

Rice, D. R., Doan, R. L., and Brown, S. J. (1981). The effects of pictures on reading comprehension, speed and interest of second grade students. *Reading Improvement, 18*, 308–12.

Richek, M. A. (1977–78). Readiness skills that predict initial word learning using two different methods of instruction. *Reading Research Quarterly, 13*, 200–22.

Robinson, H. M. (1963). Vocabulary: speaking, listening, reading and writing. In H. A. Robinson (Ed.), *Reading and the language arts*. Chicago: University of Chicago Press.

Rose, T. L., and Furr, P. M. (1984). Negative effects of illustrations as word cues. *Journal of Learning Disabilities, 17*, 334–37.

Rosenshine, B., and Stevens, R. (1984). Classroom instruction in reading. In P. D. Pearson (Ed.), *Handbook of reading research*. New York: Longman.

Rozin, P., Bressman, B., and Taft, M. (1974). Do children understand the basic relationship between speech and writing? The mow-motorcycle text. *Journal of Reading Behavior, 6*, 327–34.

Rumelhart, D. E. (1977). Toward an interactive model of reading. In S. Dornic (Ed.), *Attention and performance*. Hillsdale, NJ: Erlbaum.

Rumelhart, D. E. (1978). Understanding and summarizing brief stories. In D. LaBerge and J. Samuels (Eds.), *Basic processes in reading: perception and comprehension*. Hillsdale, NJ: Erlbaum.

Ryan, E. B., McNamara, S. R., and Kenney, M. (1977). Lexical awareness and reading performance among beginning readers. *Journal of Reading Behavior, 9*, 399–400.

St. John, N. H. (1970). Desegregation and minority group performance. *Review of Educational Research, 40,* 111–34.

Sampson, M. R., and Briggs, L. D. (1981). What does research say about beginning reading? *Reading Horizons, 21,* 114–18.

Samuels, S. J. (1967). Attentional process in reading: the effects of pictures on the acquisition of reading response. *Journal of Educational Psychology, 50,* 337–42.

Samuels, S. J. (1985). Automaticity and repeated reading. In J. Osborn, P. T. Wilson and R. C. Anderson (Eds.), *Reading education: foundations for a literate America.* Lexington, MA: Lexington Books.

Samuels, S. J. (1981). Characteristics of exemplary reading programs. In T. J. Guthrie (Ed.), *Comprehension and teaching: research reviews.* Newark, DE: International Reading Association.

Samuels, S. J., and LaBerge, D. (1983). A critique of a theory of automaticity in reading: looking back: a retrospective analysis of LaBerge-Samuels reading model. In L. M. Gentile, M. L. Kamil, and J. S. Blanchard (Eds.), *Reading research revisited.* Columbus, OH: Charles E. Merrill.

Satz, P., and Fletcher, J. M. (1979). Early screening tests: some uses and abuses. *Journal of Learning Disabilities, 12,* 56–60.

Searfoss, L. W., and Readence, J. C. (1985). *Helping children to read.* Englewood Cliffs, NJ: Prentice-Hall.

Shannon, P. (1983). The use of commercial reading materials in American elementary schools. *Reading Research Quarterly, 19,* 68–85.

Singer, H. (1983). A critique of Jack Holmes' study: The sub-strata factor theory of reading and its history and conceptual relationship to interaction theory. In L. M. Gentile, M. L. Kamil, and J. S. Blanchard (Eds.), *Reading research revisited.* Columbus, OH: Charles E. Merrill.

Singer, H., and Ruddell, R. B. (Eds.) (1976). *Theoretical models and processes of reading.* Newark, DE: International Reading Association.

Singer, II. S., Samuels, J., and Spiroff, J. (1973–74). The effects of pictures on contextual conditions on learning responses to printed words. *Reading Research Quarterly, 9,* 555–67.

Slobin, D. I. (1966). Abstract of Soviet studies in child language. In F. Smith and G. A. Miller (Eds.), *The genesis of language.* Cambridge, MA: MIT Press.

Smith, F. (1978). *Understanding reading: a psycholinguistic analysis of reading and learning to read.* New York: Holt, Rinehart and Winston.

Soars, R. S. (1973). *Follow-through classroom process, measurement and pupil growth (1970–71): final report.* Gainesville. College of Education, University of Florida.

Spache, E. (1976). *Reading activities for child involvement.* Boston: Allyn and Bacon.

Speer, O. B., and Lamb, G. S. (1976). First grade reading ability and fluency in naming verbal symbols. *Reading Teacher, 29,* 572–76.

Stallings, J. A., and Kaskowitz, D. (1974). *Follow-through classroom observation evaluation, 1972–73.* Menlo Park, CA: Stanford Research Institute.

Stebbins, L. B., St. Pierre, R. G., Proper, E. C., Anderson, R. B., and Cerva, T. R.

(1977). *Education as experimentation: a planned variation model, Vol. IV-A: an evaluation of follow-through*. Cambridge, MA: Abt Associates.

Stein, N. L., and Glenn, C. G. (1982). Children's concept of time: story schemata and prose processing. In W. Friedman (Ed.), *The developmental psychology of time*. New York: Academic Press.

Sutton, M. H. (1969). Children who learned to read in kindergarten: a longitudinal study. *Reading Teacher, 22*, 595–602, 683.

Teale, W. H. (1978). Positive environments for learning to read: what studies of early readers tell us. *Language Arts, 55*, 922–32.

Templeton, S. (1980). Young children invent words: developing concepts of "word-ness." *Reading Teacher, 33*, 454–59.

Thorndyke, P. (1977). Cognitive structures in comprehension and memory of narrative discourse. *Cognitive Psychology, 9*, 77–110.

Torrey, J. W. (1979). Reading that comes naturally: the early reader. In T. G. Waller and G. E. MacKinnon, *Reading research: advances in theory and practice*. New York: Academic Press.

Tremans-Ziremba, M., Michayluk, J., and Taylor, L. (1980). Examination of some predictors of reading achievement in grade 4 children. *Reading Improvement, 17*, 264.

Vukelich, C., and Golden, J. (1984). Early writing: development and teaching strategies. *Young Children, 39*, 3–8.

Walberg, H. J., and Tsai, S. (1985). Correlates of reading achievement and attitude: a national assessment study. *Journal of Educational Research, 78*, 159–67.

Walberg, H. J., and Tsai, S. (1984). Reading achievement and diminishing returns to time. *Journal of Educational Psychology, 76*, 442–51.

Walker, G. H., and Kuerbitz, I. E. (1979). Reading to preschoolers as an aid to successful beginning reading. *Reading Improvement, 16*, 149–54.

Weaver, P., and Shonkoff, F. (1978). *Research within reach: a research-guided response to concerns of reading educators*. Washington, DC: U.S. Department of Health, Education and Welfare.

Weber, R. (1970). A linguistic analysis of first-grade reading errors. *Reading Research Quarterly, 5*, 427–51.

Whaley, J. F. (1981). Readers' expectations for story structure. *Reading Research Quarterly, 17*, 90–114.

Wiley, D. E. (1976). Another hour, another day: quality of schooling, a potent path for policy. In W. J. Sewel, R. M. Hauser, and D. L. Featherman (Eds.), *Schooling and achievement in American society*. New York: Academic Press.

Williams, J. P. (1985). The case for explicit decoding instruction. In J. Osborne, P. T. Wilson, and R. C. Anderson (Eds.), *Reading education: foundations for a literate America*. Lexington, MA: Lexington Books.

Yopp, H. K., and Singer, H. (1984). Are metacognitive and metalinguistic abilities necessary for beginning reading instruction. In J. A. Niles and L. A. Harris (Eds.), *Changing perspectives on research in reading and language processing and instruction*. Rochester, NY: National Reading Conference.

CHAPTER 6

Research on Science Education for Young Children

GEORGE FORMAN
MELISSA KADEN
University of Massachusetts

Science is often compared to art as work is compared to play. Yet for the young child, play can be pre-science if we take a broader, developmental perspective. For children, "science" is a reflective attitude toward an object of interest, even during play. When so defined, one can not easily identify science within narrow boundaries such as those defining chemistry, botany, and biology. These subjects are organized bodies of knowledge. To the young child, tearing two flowers apart to compare their insides is science, but certainly not botany.

The "scientific" child of age four to seven searches for answers to interesting questions. The child takes the attitude that the thing observed must be worked over and tinkered with to yield information. Why do I sometimes have two shadows? What makes the water puddle disappear on a sunny day? The scientific child appreciates that she or he needs to ask, compare, and keep track, to render new information. The new information concerns the relations among the single events.

A playful mode helps scientific observation, but the balance rests more on truth than fancy. The scientific attitude seeks out the difference between what could be and what is, between what is sought and what is known. Children gradually develop a belief in some constraints on the physical world, some way to avoid magical thinking. They learn that objects do not fall up; water in communicating vessels cannot maintain two different levels. Without a belief in some general limits, there can be no science, no interesting questions (Karmiloff-Smith & Inhelder, 1974). The scientific attitude, then, recognizes that something about the physical world is constant and then seeks to discover if a particular event is somehow governed by this constant. Why does this object (for example, a balloon) move up rather than down? If the water in this U-shaped flask maintains two uneven levels, does the water really pour all the way through?

We have chosen this definition of science because we are more concerned with the child as scientist than with child science. But this does not mean that our process approach gives us license to talk about just any subject. Some subjects, such as levers, heat, or weight, are richer domains for scientific questions. Therefore we will present research that covers both the scientific process in general and the most likely places to find children using scientific thought.

THEORY

An informed approach to science teaching requires a set of theories to guide our judgments in the classroom. These theories fall into at least three categories. We need a theory of development in order to judge when it is reasonable to expect that a child can understand a particular system of facts, such as an ecosystem or seasons of the year. We need a theory of learning to discern the difference between superficial and deep learning. And we need a theory of instruction to assure that the children understand what is being asked.

Developmental Theory

Developmental theory guides our assumptions about what children can do in particular age ranges. Theories of development vary in their usefulness for science education. A broad theory, such as Piaget's, divides human development into only four stages. This means that the primary use of Piaget's stage theory would deal with identifying which concepts require inferential reasoning and which do not. The shift from "I know this because I have seen it before," to "I know this because it can't be otherwise," comes around age six or seven years. Granted that this shift to concrete operational thinking is profound, one cannot build a science curriculum on this milestone alone.

Other theorists have gone further to refine our understanding of development within the four stages identified by Piaget. Robbie Case (1985) has done a great deal of detailed work to organize research into a theory of development that could help a teacher rank-order tasks in difficulty. Tasks that have more variables to coordinate and more demands on memory are proportionately more difficult. Kurt Fischer (1980) also refines Piaget's stages, as does Forman (1981). Forman divides the stage from age two to seven into six substages. These substages plot the child's growing understanding that physical variation can be continuous rather than just "on" or "off." For science education, the use of variables is essential.

Learning Theory

Theories of learning attempt to explain the process by which children progress from not knowing to knowing. The theories of the 1960s have not been that helpful for science education because everything was reduced to reinforcement. The axiom was: break the task into parts and reward correct answers for each part. But this theory does not give a teacher much help in figuring out the sequencing of parts, nor is it necessarily that effective.

Current learning theory relies much more on the competence of the child to figure out the problem. Piaget's equilibration theory assumes that children have an intrinsic need not to contradict themselves. Granting this, learning occurs when children first sense that a contradiction has occurred, and second, when children construct a new way of looking at the concept in order to eliminate the contradiction. Reinforcement in this theory is reinterpreted as the felt satisfaction in knowing that a new perspective has eliminated the contradiction.

Other theories of learning look meticulously at the strategies children use to solve a problem. Karmiloff-Smith and Inhelder (1974) asked children to use a fulcrum to balance long blocks with hidden weights. Children initially used misleading cues, such as the visual symmetry of the block, but gradually constructed a new "theory" of what makes blocks balance. Karmiloff-Smith and Inhelder then built a learning theory based on a microanalysis of each move the child makes. These descriptions of problem-solving behavior have yielded many helpful suggestions for teachers. A microanalysis can help the teacher understand what common errors occur when a child deals with a particular task and what sequence of errors are *necessary* for the child to make in the course of his or her construction of valid knowledge.

Instructional Theory

Instructional theory specifies what the teacher is supposed to do to maximize learning. Ideally, instructional theory flows from a theory of development and learning. Some theories state that the teacher's main role is to present tasks sequenced in increasing difficulty. Other theories place most of the responsibility on the symbols and media used to activate familiar concepts in new contexts. Developmental and learning theories that place most of the responsibility within the child's competence to sense his or her own problems prescribe a primarily supportive role for the teacher.

Each of these theoretical positions can be discerned in the research that follows. Science education for young children has meant (1) presenting a well-researched set of concepts in a sequence of increasing difficulty, (2) searching for more powerful metaphors and symbols to help children understand the concepts, and (3) immersing the child in a rich problem-solving environment that encourages the child to reflect upon his or her own thinking.

RESEARCH

General Concepts

We can look at research from several perspectives. This first section describes what children understand about broad concepts of science, such as causality and conservation. We go to the second section for more specific concepts such as heat, levers, the earth, and other subjects more recognizable as science. One can see the developmental questions here. What can the child of a certain age understand? The research in the third section covers methods of teaching. This research has both a learning theory and instructional theory base. Learning theory is often instantiated in a method of instruction.

Causality.   A child needs to understand that nonrandom events have causes. We should not take this principle for granted when working with young children. Children often do not know that something out there needs to be explained. For example, in a classroom activity for three- and four-year-olds, Forman and Hill (1984) gave children three separate wheels that had sliding weights inside. The weights could be adjusted so that the wheel, of which half of the rim was brown and half green, always rolled to a stop with the green side up. The wheels would even rock backwards sometimes to end up green. We were sure that three separate wheels, all rolling to a stop with the same color up, would create interest in children to figure out why. The children saw nothing here that needed to be explained, and just shrugged their shoulders when we asked, "Why do they all turn up green each time?" From the child's perspective, it was: why shouldn't they turn up green each time? Not until age six or seven do children begin to understand that a recurring pattern requires an explanation (Piaget, 1975b).

Some situations more clearly engender in the child a sense of causation. A moving ball bumping into a stationary ball sets the passive ball in motion. Children as young as three years have an intuitive understanding that the first ball must physically hit the second. That is, they show surprise when the task is rigged so that the passive ball shoots out when the first ball stops short of hitting it. Yet when asked to explain the cause, children until age four will nevertheless conclude that the first ball caused the second to more. Until age four children rely more on sequence than contiguity to explain these simple events (Bullock & Gelman, 1979).

This reliance on sequence, of course, will have to be refined as children learn more. Sequence is sometimes misleading, such as rainfall that *follows* the first sprouts in spring. In many cases the discovery of a cause requires a careful check on the covariation between two events. Often the only true test is to withhold a suspected cause to see if the effect follows anyway. The use of negative information is particularly hard for children under seven (Keil, 1979, p. 66). How many children would think to tell the rooster not to crow in order to test the sun's obedience?

Children are often expected to see causation in no more than a sequence of pictures. Here we have removed children from the physical world and left them with rather impoverished representations of that world. In a study by Schmidt and Paris (1977), children, by age five, were able to find the antecedent to a consequence shown in pictures, such as a tree falling to the ground. By age six children also could ignore distractors in the causal sequence, pictures that did not depict a continuation of a causal chain of events. But we should not assume that reading a causal chain from a sequence of pictures is an easy task for young children.

Causal explanations for living things differ markedly from explanations for physical systems. Living beings have internal energy, volition, and purpose; billiard balls, rolling rocks, and shooting stars do not. An early set of reasons children give to explain an event is to assume that the objects are animate and alive: the ball stops because it is tired. Much is known about animistic thinking in young children (Berzonsky, 1974). Wolfinger (1982) went a step further to see if school science instruction could reduce the amount of animistic thinking in children from five to seven. After five hours of instruction on things that are alive versus those that are not alive, children were able to consistently classify objects without making animistic errors. The ability to make these distinctions did not demand concrete operational thinking. But children who were not in the stage of concrete operations still confused physical force with volition (for example, a light object floats because the water bumps it up). This study bears out the complexity of the causation concept.

Functional Relations

It is reasonable to expect four-year-olds to anticipate the functional relation between events. The harder I throw the ball against the floor, the higher it will bounce. The faster I run to Herbie's house, the less I will feel like playing when I arrive. Children can figure out whether two events covary in a direct functional relation (harder throw equals higher bounce) or inverse functional relation (more speed equals less energy).

Children pass through several substages as they construct functional relations. At first, young children around three or four consider only the end points of a variable (Piaget, 1975a). If the water is not coming out of the faucet fast enough, open the faucet *all* the way. If the bucket is too heavy to be knocked over, empty *all* of the sand from it (see Forman & Hill, 1984). The child behaves as if variables are *all* or *none* rather than continua of change (see also Shaw & Pittenger, 1979).

If a child thinks in *all* or *none* terms, it will be very difficult to teach a concept that involves two factors that each change by degrees, such as, a bean sprout grows poorly in the shade, grows fine in morning sun, but dies in the blazing noonday sun. It is difficult for young children to treat shade, morning sun, and noonday sun as three points on a single continuum. And since they do not, it is unlikely that four- or five-year-olds will speculate about what will happen to the bean sprout at intensities between shade, morning sun, and noontime sun, and not at all about intensities of light less than shade.

Conservation

A fundamental scientific principle is that matter does not decrease or increase with a change in its position. This principle, called the conservation of matter, is one concept that distinguishes science from magic. In magic, matter can decrease to nothing with a change in position, and reappear elsewhere. Even in the first year children show surprise at magic tricks that change an object's form by sleight of hand (Bower, 1974). Conservation of an object's form begins early.

Early Science

It takes five or six more years for the child to understand conservation of quantity. By age six or seven, children learn that some transformations leave the amount of matter unchanged. Now conservation has taken on a higher level of understanding involving a logic of exact compensations. For example, the amount must be the same because what the clay loses from the top as it is flattened is exactly compensated for by what it gains in length after the flattening.

The child's progress through the various types of conservation (matter, space, area, volume, and weight) are common knowledge to the modern-day teacher. The mistake has generally been to teach conservation by directly using the often cited research tasks. But conservation is fundamental to almost every science concept and should not be taught directly as a lesson unto itself. Educators would do better to treat conservation as a general cognitive structure. Used this way, conservation becomes a tool to help teachers understand why a child may be having trouble with some specific concept (see Pinard, 1981). We will occasionally identify the hidden presence of the conservation structure as we shift now to specific science concepts.

Science Concepts

Heat. Scientifically speaking, heat is more than a hot surface to avoid. Even toddlers prefer the cool grass to the hot pavement when walking barefoot in the park. It takes a while longer for children to understand that heat has a source that is independent of the object. For instance, heat can be transferred from a hot fire to a cold potato. If the potato is now hot, it has not always been hot, nor will it continue to stay hot in a cool room. By age four most children know the difference between "I am hot" and "The sun makes me hot." By age six, children understand in a wide array of cases that heat is transferred between two objects. They still may think that a cold liquid cools a hot object but does not itself warm up. Here we have a case of overconservation or, better said, an incomplete understanding of total conservation of heat (Albert, 1978). A more complete understanding of heat comes as children are required to reflect on heat and to measure it systematically.

As an interesting aside to the case of measurement, it is true that some liquids, like sulfur, do not cool at a constant rate. If a chart is made of the degrees changed per second, there would be a plateau along the curve. This means that the temperature change "stalls" for some seconds and then continues to drop. For six- and seven-year-olds, these plateaus have no significance (Tinker, 1983). For an older student, who assumes that liquids placed in a constant environment will cool at a constant rate, the plateaus are phenomena that need to be explained. The felt sense of a problem is an important aspect of scientific thinking and something that teachers should look for in children.

Levers. Children lift, pry, kick, and use a wide class of levers in everyday situations. To what extent can children sufficiently reflect on a new class of levers in order to use them effectively? Forman, Fosnot, Goldhaber, and Edwards (1982) presented children with a roof-building task that required a cantilevered construction with blocks. To make the roof, children had to place smaller blocks on the top left of a longer block, balanced and extended to the right of its fulcrum. Thus placed, the smaller blocks served as counterweights to allow the longer block to be cantilevered beyond the fulcrum by more than one half of its length.

The four-year-olds found it difficult to invent a system of support that called for putting small blocks on the *top* of a long block. Ordinarily, when one wants a block to be supported, one puts blocks underneath. In fact, blocks placed on top usually cause a structure to collapse. The cantilevered structure is difficult because the child has to see that preventing the left end from going up has the reciprocal effect of preventing the right end from going down. The cognitive demands for these reciprocal relations seem to be beyond the average four-year-old. Remember, the solution called for the use of counterweights. Before age two, most children can figure out that a push on the left side of a lever makes the right side go up (Case, 1985). But pushing on a lever is not the same as establishing a self-sustaining system of support. By age seven, children will invent the cantilevered structure, once they see that other solutions are impossible.

Beyond this particular task, the scientific attitude toward a task often calls for a recognition of what is impossible. The whole idea of something being impossible only makes sense when the child accepts certain absolute constraints of the medium in which she or he is working. For example, a wooden beam on a fulcrum cannot go up on one end without at the same time going down on the other. The system has the structure of an inverse functional relation. Once the child accepts the structure of these constraints, problem solving progresses more efficiently.

Weight.   Certainly children at a young age know the terms *heavy* and *light,* and even in infancy know how to adjust their own effort when lifting objects of different weight (Mounoud & Hauert, 1982). The task is more complicated when one asks a child to make two things equal in weight. This task is the beginning of measuring one weight with a standard.

Siegler (1981) has carefully plotted the child's developing understanding of balancing two side of a beam. The beam can hold different numbers of weights at different hook positions from the fulcrum. At first, children predict that the beam side with the greater number of weights will always go down, ignoring the distance from fulcrum. This rule characterizes children's understanding at approximately five years of age. In the next stage children think that the distance from the fulcrum has an effect, but can only handle cases where the number of weights on each side is equal. When the side with the lesser number goes down because they are placed at a sufficient distance from the fulcrum, even seven-year-olds have difficulty understanding this. It takes a few more years for children to coordinate both distance and number. The highest level, relating two relations (for example, L1 times N1 is related to L2 times N2), does not appear until age thirteen or later.

There are easier ways to deal with weight. Children as young as three-and-a-half are able to make a beam strike a bell by placing the heavier of two weights on the side opposite the bell (Case, 1985). When the task has a clearly defined goal, children can often reveal knowledge that is obscured in the "noisy" everyday world. That is, the context of the problem determines if the children use their knowledge appropriately (see Donaldson, 1978).

In yet a different context, children can balance a long block on a fulcrum by age three if all they have to do is position the block at its visual center. But when the block has hidden weights and the balance point is off-center, even four-year-olds assume that it is a "bad block" (Forman, Fosnot, Goldhaber, & Edwards, 1982). It takes a number of years for children to realize that the laws of nature apply to all objects and one cannot exempt an object as if it were a contrary little being. So once again we see that science depends on the assumption that there is an objective set of laws that are stable enough to be discovered and reliable enough to be measured.

Length.   Part of teaching science to young children can be teaching them to use the tools of science. In many situations it is important to measure the linear distance between two points. Is this archway tall enough for my toy truck to go under? Will these two tables match corner to corner? Is my bicycle seat farther from the ground than your bicycle seat? It is not always possible to put two objects end to end. A go-between must be invented.

In a study by Phillips (1982), children were asked to invent a way to use a small stick to compare the heights of two separated towers. Only 6 percent of the first graders could devise the method of laying down the small stick several times to "mark off" the height of the towers. However, 22 percent of these children could use a stick either longer than the tower or the same length as the tower to make an accurate conclusion.

Measuring with a small standard unit is not an easy task. The child must place the trailing edge of the standard unit flush with the beginning edge of the measured object. Then with each laying down of the standard, the trailing edge of the new placement must be placed exactly on the spot that was the leading edge on the previous placement. In addition to all of this, the child must remember how many times this placement is reiterated.

Teachers have several fundamentally different ways of teaching measurement. Many opt to break the task down into small components. For example, first ask the child to find objects in the room that are just as tall as the standard. Then give the child objects that are slightly shorter than the standard, so the child can just put a thumb on the ruler to show how tall the object is. Eventually, give the child objects taller than the standard, but at a whole number multiple to the standard. And so forth.

This technique is common in school texts and training studies (Smith, Trueblood, & Szabo, 1981). However, other options exist. One could ask what is measurement of linear distance in general, rather than specifically. In general, linear measurement takes a continuous length and digitizes it into equal parts. If one begins with this holistic definition, a first lesson in measurement could look quite different from the one stated above.

From a holistic perspective, the teacher would first orient the child to the possibiliy that a continuous length can be digitized by some simple operation. For example, a water spot on a bicycle wheel digitizes the length of sidewalk along which the bike traveled. Then the teacher gradually works to the concept of equal intervals and on to standard intervals by other activities that unitize continuous space.

These two approaches involve very different assumptions about learning. In the first approach, the task is broken down into parts that themselves lose the general objective of unitizing a linear distance. In the second, this objective is preserved, but simplified. The first approach assumes that learning is bottom-up (specific to general), the second, that learning is top-down (general to specific). The general to specific, in the second case, begins with an undifferentiated whole and moves to a differentiated whole. In the first case, the specific to general begins with parts separated from wholes then moves to build the whole from the parts. There is a great deal of passion about the best way to teach: compare Sternberg (1979) to Gallwey (1974).

Earth and heaven. Teachers are tempted to teach young children about the earth and the heavens. Columbus's ship, Galileo's telescope, and Newton's apple are part of early science folklore. However, what does research tell us about what children really understand about the earth and heavens? Who among us has thought through the significance of Newton's apple? Certainly we should not say that Newton "discovered" gravity, as if he had never noticed that object fall to the earth. We must make Newton sound rather dim when we tell children that Newton discovered gravity. So what did he do that was significant? He realized that the laws of falling apples were the same as the laws of the orbiting moon, in spite of the fact that the apple falls and the moon appears not to fall. Newton's genius was in reframing the question. We don't need to explain what medium holds up the moon—we need to explain why the moon does not fly out into greater space.

Children are interested in gravity and construct the complex relations of objects, earth, and space in a series of stages. Using structured interviews, Nussbaum and Novak (1976) found that second-grade children hold a variety of beliefs about gravity. These beliefs range from primitive to accurate. At the first stage, children believe that the earth is flat and all objects fall toward that surface. Later children do believe in a round earth, but the objects on the South Pole fall away from earth toward some greater surface in the southern universe. Then children progress to higher levels, where they understand that all objects fall toward the earth, but get confused if asked about objects falling into a hole dug all the way through the earth. At this stage, they think that objects falling into holes fall in a basically southern direction, even though objects just above the surface of the South Pole would fall toward the earth. Finally, children understand that all objects fall toward the center of the earth. If two holes with a common mouth are dug in Canada, one a perfect radius to the earth's center, one parallel to the north-south axis, these children know an object would free-fall down the radius hole. In a follow-up study, Sneider and Pulos (1983) found a statistical relation between children's knowledge of the earth's shape and the earth's gravity.

Both of these studies used some ingenious questions as tools to measure concept development. For example, Nussbaum and Novak (1976) asked children to consider what would happen to water in an open flask if it were taken from the North Pole to the South Pole. Many children thought the water would "spill" out of the top of the bottle. Sneider and Pulos (1983) asked children where would Superman(woman) look with X-ray vision to see far-off countries like China or India. These questions themselves are worth our attention. They can be the beginning of discussions among children that eventually lead to greater understanding.

Time.   How much can we expect young children to understand about time? Temporal concepts such as *before* and *after, tomorrow* and *yesterday,* are easy. These concepts require only that children "position" two points in time. There is no need to judge the magnitude of the interval between the events (duration). Temporal sequence requires only qualitative comparisons, much as little versus large and inside versus outside are qualitative comparisons. In fact, there is evidence that children first learn spatial contrasts, such as *near* versus *far* and *long* versus *short,* then extend these terms to temporal relations (Clark, 1973). Children as young as five can reason that if A came before B and B came before C, then in effect A has preceded C (Fajardo & Schaeffer, 1982). These qualitative relations are important precursors to quantitative relations, but they do not make the cognitive demands contained in the latter.

To make a quantitative temporal relation, the child must realize that the interval between, say, one and two o'clock is the same as that between two and three o'clock. Children who understand only the sequence may not fully appreciate that the intervals are equal. Parenthetically, this same problem with equal intervals characterizes the child's initial mistakes in unitizing linear distance.

A five-year-old knows that waiting ten minutes takes more patience than waiting five minutes. But this same ability to relate time to personal effort causes some difficulty. The same child will also think that a fast-turning wheel that spins for five minutes has taken less time than a faucet that slowly drips for five minutes. Children only gradually learn to objectify time independent of subjective experience (Piaget, 1969; Acredolo & Schmid, 1981).

Given that subjective experience has such a strong effect on time judgments in young children, one wonders what they think of curriculum units on the four seasons, the calendar, and the historic past. How can a five-year-old understand that autumn is no particular day, but an interval within a larger interval that repeats itself but is never the same? An unassuming remark about the "colors of winter" will be reduced to a literal meaning by the average kindergarten child (Winner, 1982). Time concepts have both literary and scientific applications and none of them is obvious to the young child.

Gears.   Gears, like levers and balance beams, involve the physics of rigid objects. When one gear turns clockwise, the connecting gear turns counterclockwise. But did you know that four gears arranged in a circle can turn freely, while three or five gears in a circle cannot? Metz (1985) and Metz and Boder (1985) have done extensive work on children's understanding of how gears change direction in various configurations.

Children pass through many levels in understanding the transmission of force in gears. These levels can be treated as rather intact, but incomplete, mental models. The first level is called a perceptual non sequitur: "Because these and these are the same size and these and these match, that's why"; "because that one is round." In the second level, the children focus on the site of applied force: " 'Cause the handle's there." At the third level, the children attend more to their own action on the knob: "Because I'd have my hand here, and I'd turn it around like that."

In higher levels, children around age six begin to pay particular attention to how the gears are touching or not touching. The factor of connectedness is further modified to bring in the relevance of gear teeth. Here they begin to talk about how one tooth pushes against another and that the gears are interlocking. The attention to gear teeth will eventually allow children to think about relative speed of different sized gears.

It is not until around eight or nine that children begin to consider the configuration of the several gears as a system. Until children take this more comprehensive perspective, they will not be able to explain why, say, three gears connected in a closed loop will jam. The shift at this higher level is one of trying to explain the possibility of all gears turning. Children before this shift try to explain only why one particular gear moves. Herein Metz and Boder (1985) have identified a charming example of how form determines function, an important principle in science.

In summary, children understand the transmission of movement in stages that begin with (1) focusing on some salient feature with no particular functional relavance, (2) noting the site of the action, (3) commenting on oneself as agent at a site, (4) recognizing that the gears must be connected, (5) understanding that the configuration makes a difference, to emphasizing that the gears have teeth that mesh rather than just touch. The emphasis on gear teeth allows them to think freely about sticking yet moving. The point is that the "conceptual object" changes with development. They first think that some perceptual feature (color, gear size) is relevant, then the location of the knob, then what is touching, and finally the conceptual object becomes the configuration of interlocking gears as a whole, which leads them toward the construction of "jamming" (that is, one wheel cannot turn in two directions at the same time).

Work such as these studies by Metz is extremely important to science education for young children. The more we know about children's construction of what they accept as explanations, the better prepared we will be to counter with well-chosen examples. Using developmental levels in this fashion can move children toward a more complete understanding of physical events (see Forman & Fosnot, 1982).

Life and death. As mentioned earlier, it would be an overstatement to say we teach biology, as subject matter, to young children. However, individual concepts, such as living versus not living, have proven to be interesting and teachable concepts. Children pass through stages in their understanding of what is alive. This usually begins with movement as an important criterion, particularly movement that has no visible source external to the object. Movement that varies its path creates the illusion of "aliveness" more than linear movement. Later in development, children need to see purposive movement (for example, a moving dot that avoids obstacles) before they call a thing alive (Silverman, 1982).

As children mature, their criteria for attributing life to an object become more subtle. Turkle (1984) cites examples of a seven-year-old who thinks that Merlin, a computer toy that plays tic-tac-toe, is alive because it cheats ("and if you cheat you're alive"). A playmate, age six, insists that Merlin does not know if it cheats, and it won't know if you break it, so therefore it is not alive. These concepts of what is alive are pushed to almost absurd limits in modern times with toys that behave "intelligently." The criterion of self-reflective consciousness seems advanced for a six-year-old but could well represent the sophistication that has resulted from interaction with the computer or what Turkle calls the "evocative object."

Other concepts from the life sciences include death and illness. How much can we expect children to understand about these rather intangible concepts? White, Elsom, and Prawat (1978) determined that children under ten years of age understand the irrevocability, cessation of body process, and universality of death. But the universality of death could not be understood by children incapable of making inferences based on logical necessity (concrete operational thinking).

Illness is particularly intangible, since causes are frequently unobservable agents, such as germs. Kester and Paterson (1980) interviewed children from four to seven. The younger children overextended the germ theory and thought that scraped knees and toothaches are contagious. Explanations for why people get sick relied heavily on immanent justice (for example, "because she was naughty"). Even when they had some notion about the transmission of germs, they were confused about the role of physical proximity. These researchers suggest that parents emphasize the physical causes of illness to alleviate the child's fear that illness is a consequence of being bad.

Instructional Techniques

There is less good empirical research on instructional techniques than one might imagine. Most of the research comes in the form of observations and measurements of what children do. In the absence of proper control groups, one can reason equally well that the children would have done better *without* the instruction. We have tried to find studies that make an attempt to compare instructional techniques rather than just observe a single technique. The research falls into two categories arranged by the following questions. Can conflict inducement lead to meaningful learning? How important is physical manipulation of materials?

Conflict inducement. All teachers relish a subject that can yield surprises that get the student thinking. Most science lessons have the potential for surprise. An unexpected event often causes the attentive student to rethink his or her assumptions about some class of events. For example, a child may assume that physical contact is necessary for one object to transmit force to another. Yet a ball striking only the first ball in a row of balls moves only the last ball in the row. This surprise can cause children to rethink their assumptions about how the force is transferred even in the simpler cases of one ball hitting a single ball (Piaget, 1974).

In exciting research described by Inhelder, Sinclair, and Bovet (1974), children were led to contradict themselves as they tried to decide if two rows are the same length just because they have the same number of elements. Interestingly enough, the teachers never gave explicit feedback. The child constructed the correct set of concepts as the only way to reduce conflict. Gallagher and Reid (1981) give a nice summary of research on conflict inducement and the use of countersuggestion as an instructional device.

Perhaps the most recent and promising application of teaching via conflict comes from work at the University of Delaware. The general design of the research is to place two children together who hold different views about conservation. One child says the clay has the same amount after it is rolled out flat, the other child says the amount is less. The consistent finding in these studies is that the nonconserving child yields to the logic of the conserver's justifications. The change in the direction of conservation occurs independently of who is more vocal or physically dominant (Murray, 1972; Ames & Murray, 1982; Smith & Murray, 1985).

The important fact here is that there seems to exist almost an aesthetic appeal in the more logical answer to which young children bow. The power of logical consistency has to be explained by some mechanism other than external reinforcement or acquiescence to an authority: the children are peers. These studies give credibility to teachers who believe that students working in small groups can often progress on their own. Let us add that the group project needs sufficient structure to give the students something to debate and something to submit to logic.

Cooper (1977) was more interested in just what are the communication skills that effective groups use to solve problems together. She had three-and-a-half- to four-and-a-half-year olds work in pairs to find which two blocks were weight-identical, even though many of these same-sized blocks were unequal in weight. She listened to them as they used a pan balance to find the matched pair. She found that the effective pairs, often the older children, used more attention-focusing statements, questions, directives, accurate labels, accurate use of nonverbal responding (gestures), and sensitivity to the requests of the partner. Some of the younger children did well on this task, but they were distinguished only by the absence of irrelevant comments—a general measure of task orientation. Contrary to common expectation, praising the partner was seldom used by any child between the ages of three and a half and four and a half and was not necessary for success in pair problem solving.

Manipulation.   Despite the rhetorical support for "hands-on" science curricula, teachers often resist using them. In their concern to meet a quota of concepts each year, teachers are tempted to stage demonstrations didactically supplemented only by readings and worksheets. Educators need to be convinced by research that the activity-based curricula are worth the extra effort. Several reviews of the literature have concluded that the effort is worthwhile.

Bredderman (1982) has reviewed the research since 1967 on the value of activity-based science curricula compared to the more didactic textbook curricula. Children in the hands-on science programs outperformed the control groups on measures of creativity, language development, attitudes toward science, and science content. The strongest gains were made in process skills such as observing, measuring, interpreting data, inferring, and graphing. There was also strong evidence for advances in reading readiness (see also Renner, 1973).

Shymansky, Kyle, and Alport (1982) reviewed research that compared activity-based science with read-and-recite. They looked at the ESS (Elementary Science Study), SCIS (Science Curriculum Improvement Study), and SAPA (Science—A Process Approach). These activity-based units lead to higher scores, compared to those of control groups, on everything from academic achievement, to preference for science lessons, to performance on math and language. The message seems clear that activity-based science curricula not only improve performance on science-related measures, but also generalize to reading and math. More corroborating evidence comes from Janus (1977), MacBeth (1974), and Judge (1975). Nevertheless, none of these three science curricula is used by more than 3 percent of classes for children in kindergarten through third grade in U.S. schools (Directorate, 1980).

Most of these studies, given their pretest/post-test design, do not tell us now activity-based units work, even though we know that this approach works. The research typically does not analyze the minute-to-minute processes by which children learn in different instructional settings. As a model of process analysis, Kuhn (1972, 1974) followed how children learn to isolate variables in a science activity. She found that children, when given a chance to ask their own questions, do better than children who are asked these identical questions by a teacher. She reasons that when children ask their own questions, they do so because they have, at that point, identified what information is needed and how the answer relates to a growing understanding of related facts. On the other hand, when children are given identical questions, they fail to relate their own answers to each other because the series of questions came from the teacher and not from a framework being built by the child. Studies of this nature should increase our understanding of how activity-based education works rather than simply confirming our belief that it works. Herein lies a great challenge, since the phrases "hands on" and "learning by doing" are the most misunderstood yet most commonly used axioms of early education (Forman & Fosnot, 1982).

Educational Technology

Any chapter that purports to review the recent developments in science education has to include the role of the microcomputer. Despite this mandate, two problems exist. The amount of controlled research is sparse and the research tally for work with young children is downright meager. Much of this research is more on the order of software field testing rather than systematic attempts to isolate the effective variables.

Software for science education falls into three categories. First are skill builders, second are simulated worlds, and third are real-world interfaces. Examples of the first are the program Nomad (Minnesota Education Computing Consortium), which develops map-reading skills, and the Early Childhood Learning Program (Educational Activities), which helps children think about the four directions of the compass. These programs are slightly more than drill and practice because they at least use a strategy-game format.

In the simulated-world category, a good example is the Bill Budge Pinball Construction Set (Electronic Arts). This program allows children to build their own pinball environments on the computer screen using only a joystick. Children can experiment with making spaces that give the ball good play. They can even increase or decrease Newtonian parameters such as gravity, elasticity, speed, and kick (see Greenfield, 1984, p. 119). Rocky's Boots (The Learning Company) is a simulated electric circuit board that allows children to explore different configurations of on/off switches. This program teaches children the logic of conjunction and disjunction as they relate to current flow. We found only one study on its effectiveness (Piestrup, 1982b), but the program is widely distributed and used in many schools, primarily with children over ten years of age.

In the third category, the real-world interface, AtariLab (Ataria and Dickinson College) makes a thermometer that interfaces with a computer and displays a chart of changing temperature. The student can even change the scale of the chart to see how the same thermal event can look moderate or extreme, depending on the scale of the chart.

The success of early science computer programs is best known to the teachers who use them. The research on skills, simulations, and interfaces with the real world includes mostly descriptive pieces. Most of the controlled research has measured the benefits of computer programming itself (see Pea, 1983, 1985) and the benefits of computers for high school and college science students (DiSessa, 1985; Brown, 1982). There is even more software and research on math education through computers (Burns & Bozeman, 1981; Piestrup, 1982a), but this chapter does not cover math.

Many cognitive scientists make valid arguments for the value of descriptive research. The best way to understand the young child is to get a "cognitive trace" of his or her problem-solving strategies (Brown, 1984). The computer can present problems to a child, can record the child's attempts, and then present the patterns of those attempts to the child. The theory is that once the child begins to see a pattern in his or her errors, then the child can begin to construct new and more successful strategies to the problem close at hand. Once we take such an individualized approach to the study of learning, the value of averaging scores across children diminishes. To make an analogy, you don't need to measure the height of 100 plants to see the effect of a new nutrient if instead you can trace the microcybernetics by which the nutrient and cell assemblies interact within a single plant. No doubt the computer itself will make it possible to gain a richer understanding of the individual child and to conduct research with new methods.

Instead of just dropping this topic with a promissory note, we will share a few observations from our own lab at the University of Massachusetts on two new technologies we have found useful for teaching science concepts. The first is a product by Milton Bradley, a robot construction set called Robotix. Children can build machines in any configuration they want and then remotely operate the small motors to move the machines. This activity does not involve a computer but does require some challenging concepts of how to sequence the on-line commands to the robots and how to make the robot stable.

Our best activity to date is getting children to design a moving machine that has enough leverage, torque, mass, and a low enough center of gravity to push an opposing child's machine off a table top. We are not pleased that the context is competitive, but we are pleased to find that children do work together to build better machines. And in the process of making a better machine, they discover principles of physics in a real-world context. One eight-year-old child even discovered that if he made one motor turn another motor, he would get twice the speed (and therefore twice the impact) of a limb driven by only one machine. We have also designed a six-motor robot that two children must command cooperatively. Each child individually controls only three of the six motors. Here we have noticed that children create an explicit nomenclature of machine parts and actions as they try to make the robot behave in an intelligent manner. These robots qualify as good examples of new educational technology that give children reasons to invent scientific principles and a scientific language.

Video is the second technology we have found useful. Video technology is not so new, but is a highly underutilized, educational technology for early science education. At the University of Massachusetts, Forman, Fosnot, Goldhaber, and Edwards (1982) investigated the power of instant video replay to help children from ages four to eight construct a theory about balance. The task, using long blocks on a fulcrum, has been described in a previous section. Regarding video feedback, children profited only when the instant replay was freeze-framed just prior to placing a block on the fulcrum. With this freeze-framed feedback, children began to reflect more on their reasons for particular placements. Freeze frames after a block had already been placed or just a continuous replay of an attempt, did not improve reflective thought. The effects were significant for only the older group of children. Obviously, video equipment can be used in schools in more ways than documenting the class play. Children can learn to reflect on their own theories about physical principles through well-designed video replay.

GAPS IN RESEARCH

The research on curriculum models has been fairly extensive, perhaps as a result of the passion that generated such studies in the late sixties. SCIS, S-APA, and ESS have had their proponents and detractors. The gap in research comes from the very magnitude of the independent variable, an entire curriculum package. How much can we understand about the effectiveness of teaching when our unit of analysis is so large? We end up with conclusions that sound like this: one year of schooling at Franklin Elementary improved problem-solving skills. How will that information help the teachers at Jefferson redesign their curriculum? Research should be conducted on a level of specificity that is applicable to other schools.

Research on developmental stages has also been fairly extensive, but mostly in a limited number of domains. These domains have been researched in recent studies because the methods of measurement have already been worked out. For example, we know now that children pass through fairly defined stages in understanding the conservation of weight, how to establish equilibrium on a balance beam, and how not to confuse speed with duration. Much more developmental research needs to be done on the many other science domains that children find interesting, but the methods of measurement will have to be worked out anew. One fine example is Rheta deVries' work at the University of Houston. She painstakingly studies the child's growing understanding of shadows. What about developmental research on rain, the calendar, sound waves, bubbles, and animal tracks? We may know from past experience the appropriate age to present a unit to a child, but practical knowledge is not enough. An understanding of theoretical stages will help us to make sensitive responses to individual children and to recognize when a child is on the brink of an important advance.

As a counterpoise to developmental stages, consider the literature on cognitive styles. There is currently a bevy of cognitive styles that describe what sounds like "brain personalities." There are children who characteristically zoom in on details versus those who live in a global world of wholes (Coates, 1974; Hoffman, 1979). There are children who deal with complexity by transforming it into a stationary pattern versus those who make that same complexity sensible by transforming it into a narrative flow of events (Gardner, 1983). There are some children who look to people as primary sources of knowledge versus those who are more oriented to objects (Jennings, 1975; Voyat, 1978). Little research has dealt with the interaction between cognitive style and teaching strategies. What teacher has not said, "If I just knew how Lucy thinks!"

Lastly, the authors of this chapter had to struggle with the poverty of good research on the use of computers in early science education. We need to let research confirm or dispel our reservations about computers for young children. Our intuitions say that young children need to touch and manipulate real objects in science activities, yet none of us would object to young children taking photographs on a nature walk or keeping a frequency count of flora and fauna. The computer has even greater potential for displaying representations of things we have seen and want to reflect on later. The computer also has the potential to display not only the objects we see, but more important, a picture of our own thinking (Forman, 1985). A computer display of our thoughts should make us more aware of our biases and assumptions about the "objects" that we see. We need a whole new category of research to determine the educational value of the symbol systems that computers have made available to young science students for the first time in history.

REFERENCES

Acredolo, C., and Schmid, J. (1981). The understanding of relative speeds, distances, and durations of movement. *Developmental Psychology, 17*, 490–93.

Albert, E. (1978). The development of the concept of heat in children. *Science Education, 62*, 389–99.

Ames, G., and Murray, F. H. (1982). When two wrongs make a right: Promoting cognitive change by social conflict. *Developmental Psychology, 18*, 894–97.

Berzonsky, M. D. (1974). Reflectivity, internality, and animistic thinking. *Child Development, 45*, 785–89.

Bower, T.G.R. (1974). *Development in Infancy*. San Francisco: W. H. Freeman.

Bredderman, T. (1982). Activity science—The evidence shows it matters. *Science and Children, 20*, 39–41.

Brown, J. S. (1982). *Intelligent Tutoring Systems*. New York: Academic Press.

Brown, J. S. (1984). Process versus product: A perspective on tools for communal and informal electronic learning. In Report from the Learning Lab, *Education in the Electronic Age*. New York: Educational Broadcasting Corporation.

Bullock, M., and Gelman, R. (1979). Preschool children's assumptions about cause and effect: Temporal ordering. *Child Development, 50*, 89–96.

Burns, P. K., and Bozeman, W. C. (1981). Computer-assisted instruction and mathematics achievement. *Educational Technology, 21*, 32–39.

Case, R. (1985). *Intellectual Development, Birth to Adulthood*. New York: Academic Press.

Clark, H. H. (1973). Space, time, semantics, and the child. In F. E. Moore (Ed.), *Cognitive Development and the Acquisition of Language*. New York: Academic Press.

Coates, S. (1974). Sex differences in the field dependence-independence between the ages of 3 and 6. *Perceptual and Motor Skills, 39*, 1307–10.

Cooper, C. R. (1977). Collaboration in Children: Dyadic interaction skills in problem solving. Presented at the biennial meeting of the Society for Research in Child Development, New Orleans.

DeVries, R. (May, 1985). Personal communication.

Directorate for Science Education (1980). *Science Education Databook*. Washington, DC: National Science Foundation.

DiSessa, A. (1985). Learning about knowing. In E. Klein (Ed.), *Children and Computers*. San Francisco: Jossey-Bass.

Donaldson, M. (1978). *The Child's Mind*. Glasgow: Fontana.

Fajardo, D. M., and Schaeffer, B. (1982). Temporal inferences by young children. *Developmental Psychology, 18*, 600–07.

Fischer, K. W. (1980). A theory of cognitive development: The control and construction of hierarchies of skills. *Psychological Review, 87*, 477–531.

Forman, G. (1981). The power of negative thinking: Equilibration in the preschool. In I. E. Sigel, D. M. Brodzinsky, and R. M. Golinkoff (Eds.), *New Directions in Piagetian Theory and Practice*. Hillsdale, NJ: Erlbaum, 145–53.

Forman, G., and Fosnot, C. (1982). The use of Piaget's constructivism in early children education programs. In B. Spodek (Ed.), *Handbook of Research in Early Childhood Education*. New York: Free Press, 185–214.

Forman, G., Fosnot, C., Goldhaber, J., and Edwards, C. (1982). The use of stopped-action video replay to heighten theory testing in young children solving balancing tasks. Final Report to the National Institute of Education, Grant NIE G-81-0095.

Forman, G., and Hill, F. (1984). *Constructive Play: Applying Piaget in the Preschool*. Menlo Park, CA: Addison-Wesley.

Gallagher, J. M., and Reid, D. K. (1981). *The Learning Theory of Piaget and Inhelder*. Monterey, CA: Brooks/Cole.

Gallwey, W. T. (1974). *The Inner Game of Tennis*. New York: Random House.

Gardner, H. (1983). *Frames of Mind: The Theory of Multiple Intelligences*. New York: Basic Books.

Greenfield, P. (1984). *Mind and Media*. Cambridge, MA: Harvard University Press.

Hoffman, M. (1979). Field independence-dependence, social orientation and preference for praise or conflict in young children. Ph.D. diss., University of Massachusetts, Amherst.

Inhelder, B., Sinclair, H., and Bovet, M. (1974). *Learning and the Development of Cognition*. Cambridge, MA: Harvard University Press.

Janus, L. H. (1977). Activity oriented science: It is really that good? *Science and Children*, April.

Jennings, K. (1975). People versus object orientation, social behavior, and intellectual abilities in preschool children. *Developmental Psychology, 11*, 511–19.

Judge, J. (1975). Observational skills of children in Montessori and S-APA classes. *Journal of Research in Science Teaching, 12*, 407–13.

Karmiloff-Smith, A., and Inhelder, B. (1974). If you want to get ahead, get a theory. *Cognition, 3*, 195–212.

Keil, F. C. (1979). *Semantic and Conceptual Development, An Ontological Perspective*. Cambridge, MA: Harvard University Press.

Kester, M., and Paterson, C. (1980). Children's conceptions of the cause of illness, Understanding of contagion and use of immanent justice. *Child Development, 51*, 839–46.

Kuhn, D. (1974). Inducing development experimentally: Comments on a research paradigm. *Developmental Psychology, 10*, 590–600.

Kuhn, D. (1972). Mechanism of change in the development of cognitive structures. *Child Development, 43*, 833–44.

MacBeth, D. R. (1974). The extent to which pupils manipulate materials and attainment of process skills in elementary school science. *Journal of Research in Science Teaching, 11*, 45–51.

Metz, K. (1985). The development of children's problem solving in a gears task: a problem space perspective, *Cognitive Science, 9*, 431–71.

Metz, K., and Boder, A. (1985). The development of children's explanations of movement in gears: Changing and expanding attributions of meanings. Presented at the 15th annual symposium of the Jean Piaget Society, Philadelphia.

Mounoud, P., and Hauert, C. (1982). Development of sensorimotor organization in young children: Grasping and lifting objects. In G. Forman (Ed.), *Action and Thought*. New York: Academic Press.

Murray, F. B. (1972). Acquisition of conservation through social interaction. *Developmental Psychology, 6*, 1–6.

Nussbaum, J., and Novak, J. D. (1976). An assessment of children's concepts of the Earth utilizing structured interviews. *Science Education, 60*, 535–50.

Pea, R. (1985). Integrating human and computer intelligence. In E. Klein (Ed.), *Children and Computers*. San Francisco: Jossey-Bass.

Pea, R. (1983). Logo programming and problem solving. In *Chameleon in the classroom: Developing roles for computers*. Tech. Rep. No. 22. New York: Bank Street College of Education, Center for Children and Technology, 25–33.

Phillips, D. G. (1982). What research says: Measurement or mimicry. *Science and Children, 20*, 32–34.

Piaget, J. (1969). *The Child's Conception of Time*. London: Routledge and Kegan Paul.

Piaget, J. (1975a). *The Equilibration of Cognitive Structures*. New York: Viking.

Piaget, J. (1975b). *The Origin of the Idea of Chance in Children*. New York: W. W. Norton.

Piaget, J. (1974). *Understanding Causality*. New York: W. W. Norton.

Piestrup, A. M. (1982a). Early learning of logic and geometry using microcomputers. Final Report. Portola Valley, CA: Learning Company.

Piestrup, A. M. (1982b). Young children use computer graphics. ERIC Document 224564.

Pinard, A. (1981). *The Conservation of Conservation: The Child's Acquisition of a Fundamental Concept*. Chicago: University of Chicago Press.

Renner, J. W. (1973). An evaluation of the Science Curriculum Improvement Study. *School Science and Mathematics, 73*, 291–318.

Schmidt, C. R., and Paris, S. G. (1970). Children's understanding of causal sequence. Presented at the biennial meeting of the Society for Research in Child Development, New Orleans.

Shaw, R., and Pittenger, J. (1979). Perceiving change. In H. I. Pick, Jr., and E. Saltzman (Eds.), *Modes of Perceiving and Processing Information*. Hillsdale, NJ: Lawrence Erlbaum, 187–204.

Shymansky, J. A., Kyle, W. C., and Alport, J. M. (1982). How effective were the hands-on science programs of yesterday? *Science and Children, 20*, 14–15.

Siegler, R. S. (1981). Development sequences within and between concepts. *Monographs of the Society for Research in Child Development, 46*, (Whole No. 189).

Silverman, P. (1983). The development of the concept "alive" as seen in patterns of movement. Presented at the 13th annual symposium of the Jean Piaget Society, Philadelphia.

Smith, D. C., and Murray, F. B. (1985). Necessity in nonconservers' reasoning. Presented at the 15th annual symposium of the Jean Piaget Society, Philadelphia.

Smith, S., Trueblood, C., and Szabo, M. (1981). Conservation of length and instruction in linear measurement in young children. *Journal of Research in Science Teaching, 18*, 61–68.

Sneider, C., and Pulos, S. (1983). Children's cosmographies: Understanding the Earth's shape and gravity. *Science Education, 67*, 205–21.

Sternberg, R. (1979). The nature of mental abilities. *American Psychologist, 34*, 214–30.

Tinker, R. (1983). Personal conversation. University of Massachusetts at Amherst.

Turkle, S. (1984). *The Second Self: Computers and the Human Spirit*. New York: Simon and Schuster.

Voyat, G. (1978). Cognitive and social development: A new perspective. In J. Glick and K. Alison Clarke-Stewart, *The Development of Social Understanding*. New York: Gardner, 11–24.

White, E., Elsom, B., and Prawat, R. (1978). Children's conception of death. *Child Development, 49*, 307–10.

Winner, E. (1982). *Invented Worlds: The Psychology of the Arts*. Cambridge, MA: Harvard University Press.

Wolfinger, D. (1982). Effect of science teaching on the young child's concept of Piagetian physical causality: Animism and dynamism. *Journal of Research in Science Teaching, 19*, 595–602.

CHAPTER 7

Early Mathematics Education

ALBERTA M. CASTANEDA
The University of Texas

Mathematics is a multiple field. If we consider only those strands that commonly are included in elementary school curricula, its content is as diverse as arithmetic, geometry (space and logical thinking), and probability. Because one of the most common problems of children who are not succeeding in mathematics is weakness in basic number facts (Russell & Ginsburg, 1984), this chapter will be limited to arithmetic. Many of the illustrations used in the chapter are taken from the learning of number facts because much of early mathematics education is devoted to them.

Decisions about mathematics curricula are based on explicit or implicit assumptions about young children as learners and mathematics as subject matter to be learned. These assumptions will be examined below.

The characteristic of young children that has the greatest significance for their learning, and thus for those who take responsibility for their school programs, is that they are highly dependent on information that is available directly to them through their sensory, kinesthetic, or proprioceptive receptors, that is, on primary information. Only as primary information is acquired and organized and associated with labels (spoken words, gestures, signed words or phrases) can secondary information be acquired.

The ability to acquire information from sources such as spoken, signed, or written words, and thus about classes of phenomena that are distant in time or space, or without perceivable examples, is not a general one. Its functioning depends upon the reception of any language used for specific instruction.

Mathematics does not exist in the real world. No mathematical concept has a concrete, perceptible referent. No number has weight, color, smell, texture, or any perceptible attribute and no number operation produces any perceptible change. Coupling this absence of perceivable attributes of mathematics with the need of young children for tangible information illustrates the basic problem of attempting to teach mathematics to young children and the need for seeking perceptible, real-world, analogies to at least some mathematics concepts as an entree to mathematics.

For example, collections of three objects provide an analogy to the number 3. Some of the attributes of the number 3 are that it is an odd number, a prime number, greater than 2, two less than 5, the sum of $1 + 2$, the difference between 5 and 8, and a factor of all whole numbers whose digits sum to a multiple of three. None of these attributes is perceptible as such.

A collection of three objects, if the objects are of appropriate size, however, does have perceptible attributes. These are as follows: (1) when one object is placed in each hand, one object is left over, (2) when one object is picked up from the table, two objects are left on the table, (3) when the members of the collection are placed in one-to-one correspondence with those of a set of five objects, the collection of three is exhausted when two members of the larger collection are left unpaired, (4) the number in the collection remains the same when the three objects are placed in a container, when evenly spaced across a table top, when held in the palm of the hand, or when arranged with two of the objects together and the other apart, with all in view.

None of these statements contains information from mathematics or about the number 3. Rather, they contain information about the numerousness or "manyness" of collections of three objects. They are valid statements about the real-world performance of collections of three objects; their validity is publicly verifiable. They belong to premathematics and are useful in early mathematics education because they provide information analogous to some specific aspects of the cardinal or the ordinal property of the number 3, and because information supporting their validity is available as primary information, provided the objects are movable, small enough to be moved and small enough for the collection to be perceived as an entity.

Children learn to trust their perception and cognition as they work with objects and learn from sets of objects under a teacher's guidance. They learn to trust their cognition further as they transfer that information to numbers and number operations. The young child's need for perceptible information and the characteristics of mathematics as a subject matter have been honored both in content and manner of thinking.

THEORETICAL BASES

Judgments about what mathematics is or what the desired outcomes of mathematics education should be, rather than the learning characteristics of young children, control most conventional programs in early mathematics.

Mathematics, arithmetic specifically, can be seen as a set of skills or as a set of relations with significant effects on curriculum and instruction. Burton (1984) notes that curriculum and instruction can be chosen to emphasize the content (the facts and skills) or the processes (the manner of thinking) associated with mathematics.

If arithmetic is a set of computational skills, acquisition of skills must be the objective of mathematics education, with memory and practice the mode of instruction. Decisions about which skills to include in programs for young children should be made on the basis of the mature skill desired.

In most programs for young children, goals of mathematics instruction are stated as skills. Some examples of the earliest skill objectives are that children will be able to

> *identify,* from two sets, the set with more members
> *order* sets of objects as to quantity
> *rote count* to 5, 10, or beyond
> *take a count* to determine the number of objects in a collection
> *identify, or name* and form numerals through 5, 10, or beyond
> *recall,* or use counters to find sums to an appropriate number.

Typically, subtraction facts, place value, and the addition and subtraction algorithms follow.

In most conventional programs the skills mentioned above are taught as memory tasks and children can succeed in all of them without understanding the words used. Rote counting requires the memorization of a sequence of names. Writing numerals requires the memorization of a sequence of physical actions. Rational counting and using counters to find sums are taught as a memorized sequence of physical actions to be used with the memorized sequence of names. The recall of sums requires memorizing sequences of three number names (as: "Two plus two equals four").

Counting is a mainstay in early mathematics education. Parents model the counting order of number names to their infants and express delight when their child says, "One, two, three." "The baby can count," they announce proudly. In daycare settings, preschools, and kindergartens three-, four-, and five-year-old children daily count the boys present, the girls present, the children present, the number of children who are buying lunch, the days of the month that have passed. They may count the days left until the chickens hatch and the days that have passed since the eggs went in the incubator, the colors on the American flag, the children who prefer Fluffy, Spot, George, or Pig as the name for the new hamster, the hamster's eyes, ears, nostrils, feet, toes on a front foot, toes on a back foot, teeth, and so forth. The counting almost invariably starts with "one" and proceeds in increments of one. The children almost never see or hear adults use any other method to find "how many." Our children are taught to count, and they are taught to count from 1.

When children can count, name, and form numerals, say, to 5, they are deemed ready for addition with sums to 5. For many children this begins in kindergarten, for some earlier and for some in first grade.

Many, perhaps most, American children are introduced to addition, as in "three plus two is how many?" when the only information they have about 3, 2, and 5 is that these numbers are expressed as the words following "two," "one," and "four" in the counting jingle. Lacking information about the numbers or even about the quantities associated with each, the children can not think about what a sum might be and so they are shown how to manipulate counters to "get the answer." Similarly, they are introduced to subtraction equations, and if missing addends are included in their program they are shown another "how to get the answer." In actual practice, for each example the children name numbers, count, and write a numeral.

From the beginning, mathematical thought processes, such as finding, hypothesizing about, and testing patterns, as well as engaging in deductive reasoning, are sacrificed to the hope that with practice the number facts will be acquired. Repeated practice with meaningless symbols teaches children that mathematics is not a subject that can be thought about, in which they can use what they already know, but rather is made up of arbitrary and isolated associations. Conventional early mathematics programs are based on the assumption that mathematics is a set of skills.

Seeing arithmetic as a skill subject places emphasis on the content of arithmetic. Seeing arithmetic as a set of relations places the emphasis on processes. When arithmetic is taught as a set of relations, the desired outcomes include computational skill, but the development of that skill is seen as an outgrowth of what the children know about and how they use the relations between symbolic meanings. From this point of view, the first goal of instruction must be to teach the meaning of the symbols of arithmetic, such as numerals, operational signs, equality and inequality signs. The counting order of the number names, the simple sums and differences, grow out of these first meanings. Later skills, such as expanded notation and employing algorithms, grow out of meanings and relations that build on earlier meanings and relations.

A main question for educators who think of mathematics or arithmetic as a set of relations is how and where to begin teaching about entities and relations between entities that have no physical existence. To consider that problem, the following section will contrast association theory with constructivism (or constructionism) and meaning theory.

In the "learning" of arithmetic skills, such as the addition facts, those who see learning as a matter of building bonds between or associating one thing or symbol with another, can be contrasted with those who want each learner to construct, not simply to remember or apprehend the facts. The first, associationists, subscribe to association theory; the latter, constructivists or constructionists, subscribe to construction theory.

Association theory in arithmetic was articulated by Thorndike in 1922. From the associationist point of view, the essential task in learning the addition facts is to associate 4 and 2 with 6 and in that way to "know" the addition fact. The instruction that results from this point of view gives the learner practice in completing equations and reinforcement, that is, a judgment about the correctness or incorrectness of the associations displayed by the learner.

Conventional early mathematics education teaches addition facts according to association theory despite the use of counters. Children do use counters to find sums, but the objective is for them to remember sums and to become less dependent on counters. Other methods common in conventional programs such as drill with flash cards, games that reward quick recall, and timed tests are all aimed at building and testing for associations.

In contrast to associationism is constructivism or constructionism. In Piagetian theory the construction is said to be of logicomathematical knowledge. Kamii distinguishes between the three kinds of knowledge defined by Piagetian theory in this way:

> The fact that a ball bounces when it is dropped is observable (physical knowledge). The fact that a ball is not appreciated in the living room is also observable (social knowledge). But logico-mathematical knowledge consists of relationships, which are not observable. Although four balls are observable, the "four-ness" is not. (Kamii, with DeClark, p. 67)

Piaget and those who apply his theory to mathematics instruction speak of "reflective abstraction" as the process through which logicomathematical knowledge is constructed. Simple or "empirical" abstraction describes the process of attending to and apprehending some attribute of an object. Reflective abstraction seems at once to be more active and more contemplative because what is being abstracted—a relationship—is theorized as not physically existing. Kamii explains, "The similarity or difference between one chip and another does not exist *in* one chip or the other, nor anywhere else in external reality. This relationship exists only in the minds of those who can create it between the objects" (p. 9).

Clearly, a relationship—for example, "is taller than"—does not exist as an attribute of either object, nor does it have concrete existence at all; but to say that it does not exist except in a mind ignores the fact that, at least when two objects can be juxtaposed with one end of each on a common baseline and the opposite end of each can be seen relative to the other, one presentation of the relationship is perceptible and is open to public inspection and discussion. "Is taller than" is not a mathematical relationship but it is a relationship between two objects. The somewhat analogous mathematical relationship "is greater than" cannot be made perceptible but, as Kamii says, it does exist as an abstraction in the mind.

There are implications for curricula in seeing all relations between entities as abstractions that cannot be empirically perceived. Kamii includes all relations in logicomathematical knowledge and emphasizes that logico-mathematical knowledge cannot be transmitted to the child either through direct instruction or by the child's inspection of the real world. The conclusion is that each child, autonomously, must cognitively construct all relations.

We have noted the contrast between the theoretical positions that consider mathematics or arithmetic as a set of skills versus a set of relations, and between association and construction as the best mode of learning mathematics or arithmetic. Another theoretical contrast should be drawn between association and meaning theories (Baroody, 1985). In association theory the task is simply the building of bonds. In meaning theory the need to associate spoken names with numerals and sums with pairs of addends is not denied, but the emphasis is on building the bonds through meaning of the symbols being associated. In meaning theory children use general principles or relations to establish and perhaps to recall some sums. Brownell was the first modern mathematics educator to champion this point of view, and his statement that mathematics should be considered more a matter of intelligence and less of memory is often quoted (Brownell, 1922). In meaning theory, "Learning mathematics—including mastery of the number combinations—is viewed as a slow, protracted process. Children are not expected by meaning theory to imitate immediately the skill or knowledge of adults. In other words, the child's psychological readiness for learning is considered" (Baroody, 1985, p. 85).

Psychological readiness for learning is an important and controversial aspect of early mathematics education. Perhaps two main streams of thought are stage theory and nonstage theory. Stage theory, like that of Piaget, describes children's broad cognitive abilities at difference ages. Nonstage theory considers more specific aspects of a child's readiness for specific learning. The first has been described in many places; the latter can emphasize the skills, concepts, or language the child has developed. In meaning theory the primary emphasis is on the child's concepts and language.

Aspects of meaning theory and construction theory can be combined when one distinguishes between premathematics and mathematics and when early mathematics instruction begins with premathematics. The distinction has the following implications for early mathematics education. First, the content of premathematics becomes an important part of early mathematics education. Second, because different relations exist in premathematics and mathematics, there is proper language to associate with each. A change of language can be used to cue the children that a change in meaning has occurred and that the teacher is asking the children to move from the world of objects where their sensory perceptions function to the world of numbers where they must depend on what they know.

Third, the distinction changes the role of manipulatives. In premathematics, concrete materials or manipulatives are not mere answer-finders. They are sources of information about the attributes of sets of objects of known number and the results of actions upon them, and the relations between sets of objects of the same or different number.

Fourth, through the materials and tasks they provide, the language they model, and the questions they ask, teachers can have an active role in giving the children the opportunity to acquire, from objects and sets of objects, information as relevant as possible to the first mathematical concepts and skills of counting, adding, and subtracting. Because the children come to addition and subtraction with information they can use in thinking about sums and differences, the children have less need for manipulatives as mindless answer-finding devices.

Fifth, beginning with premathematics reduces the need for memory tasks in early mathematics education. In premathematics where their perception functions, children can be active learners as they find and use patterns and draw conclusions, as they acquire information from the real world, and as they combine information in the development of mathematical concepts and form the basis for skill development.

Anyone who considers mathematics a set of relations will have difficulty accepting early children mathematics curricula based on association theory. If mathematics is seen as a set of relations, then it is not necessary to memorize the names of numerals, how to form numerals, the counting order of number names, and basic number facts. Such drills imply that mathematics involves skills that are unrelated to each other and to what the child already knows.

RESEARCH BASES

The general method of the first studies reviewed in this section is to observe, describe, and analyze how children approach or perform arithmetic tasks and how children's performance changes over time. Given that children are so consistently taught not just how to count, but also *to* count, it is not surprising that their behavior often includes counting. And so, counting is a mainstay of research and curriculum in early mathematics education. How early and through what process young children learn to count and their use of counting in solving addition and subtraction equations are two areas that have received concerted attention in recent research. This research is not curriculum research, but I will review a limited selection of studies to consider their usefulness for making curriculum decisions.

Gelman and Gallistel (1978) analyzed counting behavior and identified these five principles of counting: (1) putting one number name to one object, (2) using a stable order or counting names, (3) reporting the last name used as the number of objects, (4) the application of counting to sets of mixed objects, and (5) appreciation of the irrelevance of the order in which the objects are counted. They reported that while many two- and three-year-olds do not count reliably beyond 3 or 4, they typically use only number words in counting (though they sometimes use the words out of arithmetic order), and they do follow several of the above principles. Gelman and Gallistel concluded from watching young children count frequently, spontaneously, and apparently with pleasure, that children acquire their representations of numerosity through counting.

Fuson, Richards, and Briars (1982) found that while many prekindergarten children can produce a significant segment of the counting order of number words beginning with "one," they cannot readily count-on, beginning with other numbers. However, many kindergarten children can count-on from number words other than "one." Fuson and colleagues further report finding five levels of elaboration as children acquire the counting order of number names. At the first level, the "string" level, the sequence of names is produced always from 1 and the words may be undifferentiated. At the "unbreakable chain" level, the sequence of names is always produced from 1, but the words are differentiated. At the "breakable chain" level, the children can begin counting from numbers other than 1 and the notion of one number falling between two others is begun. At the "numerable chain" level, the children can count-on, meaning they can begin counting at a number other than 1 and know (1) when they have counted-on some number of steps or (2) how many steps they have counted to get to a second number. At the "bidirectional chain" level the children can count up or down quickly from any number and can shift direction (up or down) easily. Children's movement to the last level makes it possible for them to use counting in solving addition and subtraction equations.

Houlihan and Ginsburg (1981) found that, generally, first graders add by counting and most frequently by counting-on from the larger addend and counting from 1 starting with the first addend, while second graders use both counting and noncounting methods, with counting-on as their favored counting method.

Secada, Fuson, and Hall (1983) hypothesized and tested the validity of three skills as requisites to a child's changing from counting-all to counting-on. They concluded that the following can be considered subskills of counting-on: (1) the ability to produce the correct sequence of counting words from numbers other than 1, (2) the ability to shift from the cardinal to the counting meaning of the first addend, and (3) the ability to begin the count of the second addend with the counting word following the name of the first addend.

Heibert (1982) reports that first-grade children's approach to and success with word problems differs depending on the location of the unknown for problems in addition or subtraction. His first-grade subjects used small cubes to model the action in the problem. They used them most often when the unknown was the sum or the difference, and least frequently when the unknown was the first addend or the minuend. Heibert concludes that "the similarity of behavior on a pair of addition/subtraction problems with the unknown in the same position supports the hypothesis that the position of the unknown is a critical factor in determining whether children will model a problem situation" (p. 345).

Carpenter and Moser (1984) and Fuson (1984) identified and labeled ways in which children use counting in addition or subtraction. Carpenter and Moser conclude that from first through third grade modeling strategies are replaced by "more sophisticated counting strategies" (p. 179).

Only a few studies have been reviewed, and of those studies only selected findings have been reported here. Let us consider the applicability of those findings to classroom practice with young children. Gelman and Gallistel's conclusion that young children obtain "representations of numerosity by counting" (1978, p. 243) should not lead educators to conclude that there is anything natural, developmental, or necessary about counting in the acquisition of early number concepts. To do so would ignore the fact that our children are taught to count from a very early age and are enthusiastically rewarded for counting.

It should be remembered, also, that when Fuson et al. identified five ordered levels in children's acquisition of the counting order of number names, those children had been taught to count first with a rote jingle. The existence of the first level, the "string" level at which the words are not differentiated, should not be interpreted to suggest that children's development of counting skill must begin with a mindless repetition of a jingle or that instruction in counting must begin with rote counting. The finding suggests to me that the teaching of counting might be postponed until children have acquired enough information about the cardinality of sets of one through five, ten, or some number of objects so that the counting order of number names can be taught as a rational reflection of the meaning of the words used.

It is highly likely that Heibert's (1982) subjects, who used objects more often to demonstrate addition and subtraction problems when the unknown was the sum or the minuend, had always been shown addition and subtraction equations as two numbers linked by an arithmetic operation sign (plus or minus) on the left side of the equality sign and the unknown on the right. They probably had been taught how to use counters to solve such equations. It is not surprising that they were more likely to model with objects and were more successful in solving examples with the two actions in which they had been rehearsed. We should not conclude that unknowns in other positions are naturally more difficult for children to think or to learn about.

In a review of articles (Carpenter & Moser, 1984; Baroody, 1984; Fuson, 1984) relative to children's use of counting in subtraction, Cobb comments:

> The most needed curricular innovation is, in my opinion, to encourage children to talk with each other and with teacher about mathematics—their mathematics. Such interactions might sustain the beliefs that it is acceptable to think about mathematics and that mathematics involves understanding and the gaining of insights rather than finding ways to give the impression that one is behaving "appropriately." (1985, p. 144)

Research on children's counting behavior continues to direct teacher's attention to skill development. For example, when Secada, Fuson, and Hall (1983) tentatively identify three subskills of counting-on and Carpenter and Moser characterize counting methods as "more sophisticated" than modeling methods, these findings can be interpreted to suggest that instructional goals should be structured around what children can do rather than what they know, and to reinforce the traditional tendency to begin early mathematics education with memory tasks.

The findings of Baroody, Ginsburg, and Waxman (1983) suggest an opposite conclusion. In a game setting that placed a value on quick response, they gave first, second, and third graders addition and subtraction examples on separate cards ordered so as to allow the use of commutativity, the inverse relation between addition and subtraction, and a plus-one progression in their solutions. They found that commutativity was the principle most often used. However, I find the final paragraph of the report more interesting than the primary findings of the study. The authors report that a number of the children seem to have interpreted looking at the examples already solved as cheating, despite the fact that the examiners explicitly told them that it was all right to figure out the answers any way they could. The children had somehow been taught that arithmetic was not a subject to be thought about but one to be remembered, and that process was not as important as answers.

We should remember research that analyzes children's approaches to or the methods they use in arithmetic tasks does not measure "innate" mathematical ability uninfluenced by teaching. Even at the age of two or three, performance is based on some formal or informal instruction. By the end of first grade most children have experienced at least two, possibly three, years of planned, concerted instruction heavily weighted toward skill practice. The behavior or sequence of behaviors might have been quite different with different instruction.

Another kind of research in early mathematics education is to test, carry out a specified kind of instruction (a treatment), and retest, looking for change in behavior or comparing the behavior of the children under the treatment condition with that of children whose instruction has not been altered. This kind of curriculum research is fraught with difficulty. It often must be carried out with only a few subjects, making it subject to the vagaries of individual differences and attrition. It is most convincing when it is carried out over a period of years because a change in behavior at the end of even a full year of instruction is unlikely to persist when the children return to conventional mathematics education. It requires planning, instruction, and evaluation instruments. However, if change in classroom practice is to be made, such studies must be carried out. One such study is Kamii, with DeClark (1985). The study, of two years' duration, consisted of the teaching and evaluation of a first-grade mathematics curriculum, based on Piagetian theory. The program was conceptualized and supervised by Kamii and carried out in DeClark's first-grade classroom.

One of the strengths of the program is that it was devised and taught with clear general goals for education and firm beliefs about how young children learn. Kamii believes that the development of autonomy, moral and intellectual, is the aim of education and that logicomathematical knowledge must be constructed by each learner. She argues that group games and real-life situations provide the best format for early arithmetic instruction because they encourage autonomous logicomathematical thinking. Thus the program was "taught" totally through group games and real-life situations.

Worksheets were not used because Kamii felt that if children have memorized sums, they can readily fill in answers. Further, she condemns worksheets that require the entry of a sum because (1) the necessity of forming the numeral interferes with children's possibility of remembering the sum, (2) they encourage children to work in a "mindless, mechanical way," such as using counters rather than using what they know to think about the sum, (3) they fail to reinforce children's autonomy because the teacher is in control of what sums are to be done and which answers are correct, and (4) they discourage social interaction among the children.

The program attempted only to teach addition. Place value and subtraction were considered as objectives, but were discarded. One reason for not including subtraction was the success that the children in the first year of the program had with subtraction without instruction. The second reason was that in development "all actions, perception and cognition first function positively" (p. 98), and that addition is positive, while subtraction is negative. Kamii cites research to support the above proposition, but its application to the reported behavior seems tenuous to me. It may be that children see real-life additive action as positive and subtractive action as negative, but it seems to be stretching a point to consider the number operations of addition and subtraction as having positive and negative connotations.

The goal was to teach the children to construct sums. Within that goal, there were five specific objectives, ordered according to the success of the program's first-year children with certain tasks. The objectives were: (1) adding addends up to 4, (2) adding addends up to 6, (3) adding doubles, such as $2 + 2$, $3 + 3$, up to $10 + 10$, (4) set partitioning of sums already known, and of 10, and (5) thinking about 6, 7, 8, and 9 as $5 + 1$, $5 + 2$, $5 + 3$, and $5 + 4$, and add addends up to 10.

Addition examples with missing addends were not included. They were considered inappropriate for first-grade children because "addition is natural for them, and they cannot make the hierarchical relationship necessary to *read it into the equation*" (p. 81). The latter part of the statement, I believe, means that the children cannot read addition into an equation such as $3 + \underline{\hspace{1cm}} = 5$. To my mind, such sweeping statements as "addition is natural to young children," and they "cannot make the hierarchical relationship necessary," weaken the value of this book in which Kamii displays, as she has elsewhere, valid and keen insight into the problems of conventional early mathematics instruction. However, it certainly is true that as missing addends are usually taught they are difficult for young children.

Three bodies of data are presented in the evaluation of the program: one from the performance of the first group of experimental children at spaced intervals during 1980–81 (their year in the program); and one from the performance of the experimental and another group of first-grade children at the end of 1980–81 and again after 1981–82. The data report the percentage of correct responses made within two seconds by each group of children to items that are reported as addition expressions, such as $4 + 1$.

The twenty-four children in the program the first year were shown two dice marked with numerals and asked, "how many points would you have if you got those numbers?" (p. 232). Their performance on twenty-eight combinations of dice faces in October 1980, January, April, and June 1981, is the first body of data reported. The use of dice controlled for size of addend, limited to six. Although the testing was done as described, the items were tabulated as addition expressions such as "2 + 2" or "4 + 1." However, they are not addition problems, for the children were asked about points rather than a sum and there was apparently no use of the word or the symbol "plus" in the evaluation items.

Except for seven of the items, the percentage of correct immediate answers increased arithmetically with each successive test. For all items, the percentages rose from October to June. These data were interpreted as showing that throughout the year the children learned sums with no direct instruction or worksheets.

Similar data were gathered from the performance of the program's children (twenty-four the first year and twenty-one the second) versus a control group of like-aged children (twelve in an ungraded primary room the first year and twenty in a first-grade room the second year). The data, gathered at the end of 1980–81 and 1981–82, are reported as percentages of correct responses to forty-two items, apparently including the combinations reported in the ongoing evaluation of the program in its first year and other items that included an addend greater than six. I am not sure how the additional items were presented, but Kamii summarizes the findings at the end of the first year thus:

> [O]ur children did slightly better on certain items and slightly worse on others, but did not differ on the whole from the "control" group. More specifically, the two groups did equally well with the easy sums, the "control" group did slightly better on the more difficult ones involving addends up to 6, and the "experimental" group did slightly better with addends larger than 6. (p. 233)

Two problems confound this finding. First, if the dice were used to test the control group, that would seem unfair. While their mathematics program is not described, one may assume that they had been learning that "5 plus 2 is equal to 7," not that "5" on one die and "2" on the other yielded seven points or moves in a game. Second, DeClark did all of the testing in 1981 alone and Kamii acknowledges this as a problem, since DeClark was familiar with the experimental children and not with the control group.

At the end of the second year, the same items were again administered and Kamii summarizes the findings: "There were no differences between the two groups on four easy items (2 + 2, 5 + 1, 1 + 10, 10 + 10), but the control group had higher percentages on all the others" (p. 237). These results are explained with references to differences between the two groups of children. Kamii states that the children in the program the second year included "three low-level children . . . who did not blossom as the low-level children had done during the first year." It also included one underaged child, and fewer "very 'sharp' children" than did the children in the program the first year (p. 237). She notes that while the "control group was uniformly strong in 1982 (except for one child who frequently counted on fingers), the experimental group could be divided into two subgroups—the higher-level two-thirds (14/21) and the others (7/21)" (p. 237). The "difference between the control and experimental groups" in June 1982 "can thus be said to have been produced mainly by the low-level children" (p. 239). That explanation will not convince many skeptics that the program is worthy of consideration for general use.

The positive parts of the evaluation lie not in the percentages of correct responses but in the evidence that the children in the program used what they knew to figure out or to reason many answers, whereas the control children seemed to rely on memory only.

The formal evaluation of this experiment does have problems. First, the measure chosen was not compatible with the most valued outcomes of the program. Second, it is not clear what the children were shown or asked, and what was quantified, when comparative data were gathered at the end of the school year. Third, as has been mentioned, the use of dice for both groups and DeClark's conducting all of the 1981 testing could be unfair to the control group. Fourth, insufficient care was taken to test for or to cope with differences between the experimental and control groups even in the second year when a comparison was anticipated. Fifth, the mathematics programs of the control groups are not described.

Notwithstanding such objections, the curriculum and instruction used in this study is radically different from conventional early mathematics education, which usually includes more content than can be learned by many first graders. Many educators believe that we hurry our children to the recognition and use of written symbols. This program alleviated both of those problems. The evidence it offers of its subjects' knowledge of relationships between numbers and "sums" of numbers and their ability and predisposition to use that knowledge gives it value beyond the formal evaluation results.

Evaluation of programs not based on skill development is difficult. As long as evaluations are carried out with standard achievemant tests or measures such as that used in the Kamii-DeClark study just reviewed, it will be difficult to demonstrate the value of alternative early mathematics education programs based on the view that mathematics is a set of relations and that meaning is important in early mathematics learning.

Implications

Research has not given us unequivocal guidance for classroom practice. There are no clear-cut results to unsettle those who see arithmetic or mathematics as a set of skills and who feel that a good beginning is to teach young children the names of the symbols and how to write them, to count, and to add and subtract by memorizing equations. Educators who feel that conventional early mathematics education is inappropriate for young children and contrary to the discipline of mathematics or arithmetic can find a body of theory and opinion to support that position, and can attribute the unsatisfactory performance of many secondary students to such training. However, it is hard to prove the superiority of alternative curricula and methods.

Longitudinal curriculum studies are needed, of perhaps five or more years' duration. Mathematics education research studies should clearly state desired outcomes, should employ content and methodology appropriate to early mathematics education, and should use evaluation methods consistent with the outcomes desired.

SUMMARY

One may view mathematics as a set of skills or a set of relations, as something to learn to do or something to learn about. The position that mathematics is a set of skills and that acquiring those skills can best be developed through the building of associations leads to instruction that emphasizes drill and practice. If one sees mathematics as a set of relations that cannot be transmitted through direct instruction or the child's inspection of the real world, one advocates a learning environment that fosters general cognitive development and the construction or invention of relationships. If one sees mathematics as a set of relations in which learning the meaning of symbols—that is, of numerals, operational signs, equality and inequality signs—and the relations between those meanings is the desired outcome, one supports early mathematics education that teaches information about the real-world analogies to the mathematical meanings and the association of proper language with real-world phenomena.

REFERENCES

Baroody, A. J., Ginsburg, H. P., and Waxman, B. (1983). Children's use of mathematical structure. *Journal for Research in Mathematics Education, 14,* 156–68.

Baroody, A. J. (1985). Mastery of basic number combinations: Internalization of relationships or facts? *Journal for Research in Mathematics, 16,* 83–98.

Brownell, W. A. (1935). Psychological considerations in the learning and the teaching of arithmetic. In *The teaching of arithmetic* (10th Yearbook of the National Council of Teachers of Mathematics), pp. 1–31. New York: Bureau of Publications, Teachers College, Columbia University.

Burton, L. (1984). Mathematical thinking: The struggle for meaning. *Journal for Research in Mathematics Education, 15,* 25–49.

Carpenter, T. P., and Moser, J. M. (1984). The acquisition of addition and subtraction concepts in grades one through three. *Journal for Research in Mathematics Education, 15,* 179–202.

Cobb, P. (1985). A reaction to three early number papers. *Journal for Research in Mathematics Education, 16,* 141–45.

Fuson, K. C. (1984). *Journal for Research in Mathematics Education, 15,* 214–25.

Fuson, K. C., Richards, J., & Briars, D. J. (1982). The acquisition and elaboration of the number word sequence. In C. S. Brainerd (Ed.), *Children's logical and mathematical cognition,* pp. 33–92. New York: Springer-Verlag.

Gelman, R., and Gallistel, C. R. (1978). *The child's understanding of number.* Cambridge, MA: Harvard University Press.

Hiebert, J. (1982). The position of the unknown set and children's solutions of verbal arithmetic problems. *Journal for Research in Mathematics Education, 13,* 341–49.

Houlihan, D. M., & Ginsburg, H. P. (1981). The addition methods of first- and second-grade children. *Journal for Research in Mathematics Education, 12,* 95–106.

Kamii, C. K., with DeClark, G. (1985). *Young children reinvent arithmetic.* New York: Teachers College Press.

Russell, R., & Ginsburg, H. P. (1984). Cognitive analysis of children's mathematics difficulties. *Cognition and Instruction, 1,* 217–44.

Secada, W. G., Fuson, K. C., & Hall, J. W. (1983). The transition from counting-all to counting-on in addition. *Journal for Research in Mathematics Education, 14,* 47–57.

Thorndike, E. L. (1922). *The psychology of arithmetic.* New York: Macmillan.

ANNOTATED BIBLIOGRAPHY

Brainerd, C. J. (Ed.) (1982). *Children's logical and mathematical cognition*. New York: Springer-Verlag.
    The first chapter, "Conservation-nonconservation: Alternative explanations," and the second, "The acquisition and elaboration of the number word sequence," will be of interest to teachers of young children.
Bryant, P. (1974). *Perception and understanding in young children*. New York: Basic Books, Inc.
    This book offers studies that support alternatives to Piagetian explanations of young children's behavior in areas including size, number, and invariance.
Dienes, Z. P. (1973). *Mathematics through the senses, games, dance and art*. Windsor, Berks, UK: NFER Publishing Company.
    A series of games designed to bring mathematics together with other disciplines such as physical education, dance, music and art. For example, movement through space is used as a way to study the properties of space and thus to begin the study of geometry.
Donaldson, M. (1978). *Children's minds*. New York: Norton.
    Shows how a simple change in language can change the performance of children on some Piagetian tasks.
Furth, H. G., and Wachs, H. (1974). *Thinking goes to school: Piaget's theory in practice*. New York: Oxford University Press.
    This book is not specific to mathematics but it describes many activities used in a school program planned to develop "thinking" human beings.
Gelman, R., and Gallistel, C. R. (1978). *The child's understanding of number*. Cambridge, MA: Harvard University Press.
    A book of great influence that reports on young children's counting abilities and what they know about numbers and the reasoning they can do about numbers.
Kamii, C. K. (1982). *Number in preschool and kindergarten: educational implications of Piaget's theory*. Washington, DC: National Association for the Education of Young Children.
    Includes chapters on the nature of numbers, objectives for "teaching"number, principles of teaching and the use of situations in school to "teach" number. It also includes some group games.
Kamii, C. K., with DeClark, G. (1985). *Young children reinvent arithmetic*. New York: Teachers College Press
    A statement of the rationale for, and a description of and evaluation of an alternative first-grade mathematics program taught totally through group games and real-life situations.
Kamii, C., & DeVries, R. (1980). *Group games in early education*. Washington, DC: National Association for the Education of Young Children.
    The games listed include games for early mathematics.
Payne, J. S. (Ed.) (1974). *Mathematics in early childhood education* (37th National Council of Mathematics Teachers yearbook). Reston, VA: National Council of Teachers of Mathematics.
    A golden oldie, this book includes chapters of activities in several areas of mathematics, other chapters of theory, and research as of that date.

CHAPTER 8

The Visual Arts

CAROL SEEFELDT
University of Maryland

Art seems to belong to young children. Wherever groups of children gather, whether at home or at school, there are art activities. Children intent on scribbling designs on paper with large chunky crayons, engrossed in spreading bright-colored tempera paint over large sheets of newsprint, or patting, pushing, and pounding moist clay, are seen across the nation in Head Start classrooms, child care centers, private nursery schools, public kindergartens, and primary classrooms. These years are described as "a golden age of creativity, a time when every child sparkles with artistry" (Gardner, 1982, p. 86).

From the very beginnings of early childhood education, art has held an honored position. In the late 1800s, the Froebelian kindergarten, which first introduced children to a variety of art activities, began a long tradition of including art in the curriculum. Even during the 1960s, when emphasis was placed on cognitive and academic skill development, art activities did not lose their revered place in the preschool/primary curriculum.

Art and young children are a natural combination. Uninhibited children, anxious to explore their environment, to experiment with materials, to understand their world, and to communicate ideas and feelings, find making art an intriguing and gratifying experience (Winner, 1982). Teachers of young children seem to enjoy children's art nearly as much as the children. Any teacher who is in child growth and development, anxious to provide an optimum educational environment for children, and concerned about each individual child, sees art as an integral part of the program, and finds the theories of art congruent with ideas about how children grow, develop, and learn.

THEORIES OF CHILDREN'S ART

A number of theories have been used to explain the art of children. Among these are the developmental, cognitive, psychoanalytic, perceptual, and perceptual-delineation theories. Each of these has influenced the teaching of art to young children, and each is useful in explaining the nature of children's art.

Developmental Theories

Although other theories of art have been used to direct practice and explain children's art, and are endorsed by teachers, the developmental theory may be among the most widely accepted. Early childhood educators view their role as providers of materials and builders of an environment in which children can grow through exploration and experimentation: "Prepare a secure environment which offers art activities suited to the developmental needs and levels of the children. Advice on matters of technique have no place in the art of children. Indeed, it is likely to affect their development adversely. Given the right environment and offered the right experiences, the creative expression of children will flourish" (Ebbeck & Ebbeck, 1974, p. 88). And, "The role of the teacher in art activities is to create an environment that fosters optimum growth, a setting that is challenging and stimulating" (Leeper, Skipper, & Witherspoon, 1979, p. 339).

Thus, the developmental theory, which suggests that direct instruction or any interference with children's personal expression is inappropriate, has received wide acceptance. As early as 1885 Ebenezer Cooke drew attention to the successive stages of development found in children's drawings and advanced the theory that children drew in accordance with their general development. Since that time, the developmental stages found in children's drawings have been well established and documented. There is general agreement, even among those who advocate a variety of other theories, that children's drawings do follow a general pattern of progression.

Drawings by children appear to progress through the following stages:

1. The use of circular, ovoid, and sticklike representations of people and things, during the early preschool years.
2. The creation and representation of people and things, by around age four or five.
3. The creation and repetition of basic representational formulas, including representations of space and motion, during the early primary grades.
4. An increasing degree of visual correspondence, during the elementary grades.
5. The shape, color, and spatial location of objects, during the upper elementary years.
6. A type of realism in adolescence.

The work of Lowenfeld did much to foster the acceptance of the developmental theory of art. In *Creative and Mental Growth* (1947) he categorized the stages in children's art as:

1. Scribbling, ages 2–4. The first stages of self-expression.
2. Preschematic, ages 4–7. The first representational attempts.
3. Schematic, ages 7–9. Achievement of a form concept.
4. Gang Stage, ages 9–11. The dawning of realism.
5. The Stage of Reasoning, ages 11–13. Pseudo-realistic stage.

Lowenfeld described these stages as the unfolding of a genetic program. Each of the stages is believed to be a part of the natural and normal aspects of human growth and development. Children, he claimed, must pass through one stage before they can achieve another. Changes in the level of stages are contingent upon changes and growth in the child's total development—that is, their affective, intellectual, social, and physical growth. The form and content of a child's drawing is believed to be totally dependent on the particular stage of social, emotional or intellectual development. Children's maturation, their experiences as well as their values, are believed to be represented in their art. No external teaching could assist a child in moving from one stage to another.

Reflecting the naturalistic, neo-Rousseauian point of view, the developmental theory has received endorsement from many early children educators. Early children teacher training is based heavily on theories of child development. Teachers still try to follow the tradition of Froebel, who saw the teacher as a "gardener," one who brings forth what the child possesses, rather than as an instructor. Therefore, they have logically incorporated the developmental theory of art into their thinking and practice.

Developmental theorists do advocate the role of the teacher as that of a guide (Lowenfeld, 1974; Kellog, 1969, Read, 1943). Read writes, "the logical role of the teacher is one of a guide, attendant, inspirer, psychic, midwife" (1943, p. 206). Lowenfeld states, "Generally speaking, the activity of self-expression cannot be taught. Any application of an external standard, whether of technique or form, immediately induces inhibitions and frustrates the whole aim. No proper stimulation of the child's creative activity can be given without a thorough knowledge of what changes can be expected as various developmental stages in the child's subjective relationship to an environment" (1947, p. 12).

These theories directed early childhood art activities until the 1960s. The entire climate during the sixties focused on change and reform in curriculum and the practice of education. Bruner attacked the concept of maturation and readiness by arguing "that any subject can be taught effectively in some intellectually honest form to any child at any stage of development" (1960, p. 33). Others also challenged the developmentalists by suggesting that developmental theory doesn't recognize the impact of instruction on development (Ausubel & Sullivan, 1970). For example, a child may well be ready to incorporate baselines into her work, but does not do so because she has not been effectively taught.

Nevertheless, educators still embrace the developmental theories of art, and use Lowenfeld's work as their guide: "Because of Lowenfeld's humanness, his sense of social justice, and his role as a social engineer, his ideas have new meaning. . . . someone with his orientation is now needed to redirect art education toward a greater concern for the individual and social ends and move it away from the excess of concern with the cognitive goals and discipline centeredness" (McWhinnie, 1971, p. 11).

The Cognitive Theory

That children draw what they know rather than what they see (Luguet, 1913) is an assumption that best expresses the cognitive theory of art. The cognitive theory accepts the idea that children's art develops along predictable, predetermined maturational lines, but bases this development on children's cognition. "To little children, drawing is a language—a form of cognitive expression—and its purpose is not primarily esthetic" (Goodenough, 1926, p. 14). Goodenough and others advocating the cognitive theory of art believe that explanations of children's art must go beyond the fields of simple visual imagery and eye-hand coordination and take into account the higher thought processes.

Drawings by children, then, are not dependent on the general developmental level of the child, but rather represent concept formation. Distortions of size and shape, inaccuracies, and perplexing images found in children's drawings are believed to be the result of their lack of understanding and knowledge of the world around them. As children gain in understanding, grow, and have more experiences, they increase their fund of concepts; likewise, their drawings and paintings increase in detail, complexity, and accuracy.

Goodenough believed that children's ability to form concepts is an intellectual ability, requiring that children recognize similarities and differences among a group of objects or ideas (1926). If children can make these distinctions, and are able to recognize instances of a class when they confront it, they have attained a concept of that class (Goodenough & Harris, 1963). "The child's drawing of any object will reveal the discriminations that he has made about that object as belonging to a class, that is, a concept. In particular, it is hypothesized that this concept of a frequently experienced object, such as a human being, becomes a useful index to the growing complexity of his concepts" (Goodenough, 1926, p. 35).

By analyzing the amount of detail and realism that appears in children's drawings, Harris (Goodenough & Harris, 1963) demonstrates that one can indeed obtain an index of a child's intellectual maturity simply by asking the child to draw a picture of a man and then evaluating that drawing on a set of specified criteria. A survey of the research on the validity of the Goodenough-Harris Draw-A-Man Test (1963) suggests that it is a useful measure of nonverbal intelligence and can yield stable assessments of intelligence. Correlations of the Goodenough-Harris test with a variety of other intelligence tests, including the Stanford-Binet, the Wechsler Intelligence Scale for Children, and the Primary Mental Abilities Tests range from correlations of .55 to 180 and support the concept that children draw what they know (Center for Health Statistics, 1970).

The U.S. National Center for Health Statistics (1970) studied over 7,000 children between the ages of six and eleven. The Goodenough-Harris Draw-A-Man Test (1963) was used as the measure of intelligence. Although this study was concerned with the analysis of intellectual maturity of noninstitutionalized children in the United States, it did validate the theory that children, with increased maturation, experiences and more complete concepts, draw with progressively more detail and realism (CHS, 1970).

On the other hand, there is evidence to suggest that the Draw-A-Man Test is extremely sensitive to a number of variables that can serve to influence scores, such as color of drawing tool, type of paper, and conditions of the testing situation (McWhinnie, 1971). Medinnus, Bobbitt, and Hullett (1966) believe that scores on the test can be altered by simple experiences, such as having children complete a puzzle of a man prior to drawing the man. Thus, there is evidence that leads to questioning the relationships between a child's drawing and his or her intellectual ability.

Yet the idea that children's art is correlated with cognitive functioning continues to receive wide support. Piaget and Inhelder (1969) related children's art to their ability to understand the permanent existence of objects. Unless children understand that objects have a permanent existence, children have no imagery through which they can evoke the past and anticipate the future in the absence of present objects.

Children, according to Piaget (1955), must be able to evoke what is absent or past in order to think about it, and this evocation requires a symbol to stand for what is not here and now. Representation is the means by which human beings organize their experiences of the world in order to understand it further. Such representation requires symbols, and imagery is one way of symbolizing the world, with language being another.

Representation gradually becomes not only imagery but rather images that inhere within certain relationships, including spatial ones, which are increasingly understood and reproduced in the child's expressions (Brearley, 1970). Adopting terms originally used by Luquet (1913), Piaget (1955) calls the stages of children's understanding of pictorial space synthetic incapacity, intellectual realism, and visual realism. Synthetic incapacity is the stage found during the preschool years and is characterized by partial and fragmented images. The "inaccuracies" that occur in children's art during this stage are believed to be caused by the fact that children neglect spatial relationships of proportion, distance, orientation, and perspective; this neglect results in a failure to synthesize image elements.

The second stage, intellectual realism, is one in which children draw what they know. Children who draw a dog with four legs to one side do so because they know a dog has four legs, rather than the two they can see. The third state, visual realism, appears around the age of nine or ten, and is characterized by drawings indicating that children now know more. This "more" consists of an understanding of the relationship of objects to their spatial coordinates, not just an increase in concepts.

Brearley (1970) claims that these stages are a matter of development, but development related to at least two types of experiences. One type of experience is sensorimotor. The other brings content to children's expressions. "Children need experience with materials to acquire skill in using various media, but there are other sorts of experiences which are crucial, for they are the experiences which give content to children's expressions" (Brearley, 1970, p. 40). To the cognitive theorists, development and maturation in relation to experiences direct children's art. Conditions favorable to stimulating children's art are seen as a combination of the proper tools and materials, the time to gain skill in the use of them, and a wide spectrum of experiences. For Brearley, these experiences should be provided to children sequentially, related to the developmental level of each child, and juxtaposed in such a way as to lead children to greater depths of understanding.

The Psychoanalytic Theory

Children do not draw what they know, rather they draw what they feel. Their art comes from *deep down inside* (Cole, 1966). Firmly based on the concept of an unconscious—a type of mental activity that people are not even aware of—this theory of child art postulates a relationship between children's psychological development and their art. Children's art products are believed to reflect their emotions and are expressions of deep, unconscious feelings instead of reflections of their conscious knowledge, general development, or concept development.

According to this theory, children draw themselves as large circles with sticks that represent arms and legs not because they are unaware of shoulders, necks, or stomachs, but because the circle represents a force deep within a child as a symbol for the womb, the breast, or some other emotionally potent object. The progression from a circle to realistic representation is explained as a growth process. As children grow, their conscious thoughts suppress the powerful force of the unconscious, and they are able to draw and paint more realistically.

Psychoanalytic thought has greatly influenced early childhood educators. The contributions of Anna Freud (1955), Lois B. Murphy (1960), and Katherine B. Read (1976) contributed to early childhood educators' acceptance of the psychoanalytic theories of art. A number of practices in early childhood stem from these theories. The use of finger paints, clay, and free-flowing tempera paint are based, at least in part, on the idea that these materials allow children to release inner feelings and emotions, and do not restrict them as small crayons, pencils, or other tools might.

Alschuler's and Hattwick's work (1947), based on the psychoanalytic theories of art, held that children's art is a reflection of the unconscious and is a preverbal mode of expression. Alschuler and Hattwick studied preschool children's easel paintings and concluded that children's painting styles were correlated with personality traits in the following ways:

1. Children who have strong emotional lives also tend to exhibit strong preferences for certain colors and express themselves with color and mass, rather than line and form.
2. Children who focus on line and form rather than on color, show greater self-control, more concern with external stimuli, and higher reasoning behavior.
3. Children who favor predominantly warm colors tend to be free in their behavior and display warm, affectionate relations; they are sympathetic with others, cooperative in play, and make relatively good adjustments.
4. Those who consistently focus on cool colors tend to be restrained and repressed in their inner feelings.

Children's treatment of space was also analyzed, and believed to be a sample of their use of the total environment. The relationship between children's personalities and the use of colors and various painting procedures such as overpainting, making of crosses, long strokes, color placement and use was also explored (Alschuler & Hattwick, 1947).

This study is now dated, and may be methodologically flawed. Nevertheless, more recent research suggests a relationship between drawing and painting styles and personality. Lewis and Livson (1980) hypothesize that there is a difference in performance on the Goodenough Draw-A-Man Test based on personality characteristics of children. Those children who are socially secure, and comfortable with themselves in facing the challenges of their worlds find greater pleasure in conventional tasks and perform higher on traditional intelligence tests than those who are considered shy. Shy and withdrawn children seemed to score higher on the Draw-A-Man Test than on conventional I.Q. tests, leading authors to conclude that "the solitude of the graphic test may ameliorate damaging interpersonal effects, thereby permitting higher achievement" (Lewis & Livon, 1980, p. 11).

Reichenberg (1950) concluded that psychological state is related to artistic production. When positive-toned affective states were experimentally induced, children's drawings were given higher ratings by judges. Brittain (1970) also found that children's artistic production could be influenced by affective or psychological treatments. Brittain (1970) manipulated children's block building by criticizing attempts. Children receiving negatively critical treatment produced drawings that were rated as constricted and impoverished. On the other hand, children who received warm positive support for their block building, produced drawings that were described as expansive and elaborate.

Gardner (1969) in a study of over 2,000 boys, demonstrated that there were significant differences in drawings of boys from various cultures and groups, and between those who were rated as high or low on hostility measures. Burns and Kaufman (1970) concluded that children's psychological state can be deduced from their drawings. They categorized children's drawings of families in terms of significance of objects, position on the page, omissions, barriers, and force fields, and believed they could use these in their diagnosis of psychological disorders.

Nevertheless, other researchers find little relationship between children's psychological state and drawings. Manzalla (1963) explored the relationship between children's drawings and personality, postulating that children's feelings of self influence their art work. He found no significant differences in children's art work that could be attributed to their emotional state. Lingren (1971) attempted to identify emotional indicators in human figure drawings of children who were rated as shy and aggressive. Ninety-seven pairs of children, ages five to twelve, were matched for age, sex, and I.Q. No significant differences appeared to characterize drawings of children who were rated as shy or aggressive.

The Toronto Board of Education conducted a large-scale study of children's drawings of their classrooms (Rogers & Wright, 1971). A taxonomic approach led to the conclusion that children's drawings, as a whole, are measures of skill execution and are more reliable as predictors of drawing intelligence than they are of mood, attitude, or personality.

Given the conflicting research on the validity of the psychoanalytic theory of child art, the conclusions of Alschuler and Hattwick (1947) seem to have at least marginal validity. From their study of personality and children's paintings, they concluded that art could possibly be useful as one source of data that might *indicate* behavior patterns or personality; however, they warned that children's art cannot be used with any degree of confidence to *predict* behavior or personality (Alshuler & Hattwick, 1947).

The Perceptual Theories

Children draw what they see, not what they feel or know (Arnheim, 1974). The Gestaltists believe that children do not see objects as the sum of observed parts; rather they see perceptual wholes or total images structured by the brain on the basis of retinal impressions. For the Gestaltists, perception is an active process. The brain acts on incoming visual perceptions according to laws of perception (McWhinnie, 1985a). These include the need of the organism to achieve completeness, closure or unity; regularity, continuity or rhythm; and balance, similarity, or symmetry. "The perceiver works on his sensations; he makes something with the sensory excitations focused in his eyes and transmitted to his brain. It is a mistake to believe that human perceiving is completely like the action of a camera; . . . our brains organize and restructure the electrochemical impulses received from our eyes" (Feldman, 1970, pp. 152–53).

Arnheim (1974) believes seeing is a visual judgment, although he accepts the role of intelligence in perception (McWhinnie, 1985). "The oldest, and even now most widespread explanation of children's drawings, is that since children are not drawing what they are assumed to see, some mental activity other than perception is responsible for the modification. It is evident that children limit themselves to representing the overall qualities of objects, such as the straightness of legs, the roundness of a head, the symmetry of the human body. These are facts of generalized knowledge, hence the theory according to which the child draws what he knows rather than what he sees" (Arnheim, 1974, p. 128).

Thus young children draw a person as a head (the circle) with arms attached, not because this is the only thing they know about people, but because this is all that is seen as necessary to represent a human being. Freeman (1980) tested this hypothesis. Preschool children were given a predrawn head and trunk and asked to add arms. The reasoning was that if the circles which children usually draw represent a head only, then children should add arms to the head on this task. If these circles are a head and trunk fused, then children should add arms to the trunk.

When the predrawn head was smaller than, or the same size as the trunk, children drew the arms correctly from the trunk. If the head was larger than the trunk, they would draw the arms from the head. These findings led Freeman to conclude that children know that arms come from trunks, not heads. The circles children drew to represent the human body are not simply heads without trunks—rather, they are undifferentiated head-trunk units.

Further evidence for this theory was found in Golomb's (1973) study. Children between the ages of three and eleven were administered a variety of tasks involving the representation of a human being. She found that children are quite capable of achieving a higher degree of realism, but they do not choose to do so.

Arnheim (1974) explains why children's drawings do not include all they see by the process of representation. He claims that the child, in attempting to recreate a perceived object on a two-dimensional sheet of paper, must use ingenuity. He states,

> Thus, seeing the shape of the human head means seeing its roundness. Obviously, roundness is not a tangible perceptual thing. It is not materialized in any one head, or in any number of heads. There are shapes, such as circles or spheres, that represent roundness to perfection. Even these shapes stand for roundness rather than being it, and a head is neither a circle nor a sphere. In other words, if I want to represent the roundness of an object, such as a head, I can use the shapes actually given it, but must find or invent a shape that will satisfactorily embody the visual generality "roundness" in the world of tangible things. If the child makes a circle stand for a head, that circle is not given to him in the object. It is a genuine invention, an impressive achievement, at which the child arrives only after laborious experimentation. (Arnheim, 1974, p. 31)

Knowledge of perception and Gestalt psychology seem necessary to understand Arnheim's theory fully. Eisner (1972) states that Arnheim's views are useful for thinking about the relationship between drawing and perception, relating as they do to a variety of theoretical frameworks.

In practice, the perceptual theory of art has led to the design of instructional programs. These programs have as their goal the improvement of children's visual discrimination. McFee (1972) states that the body of research suggests that visual training helps children to see more details and significant relationships as they respond to their environment, both visually and cognitively. Gibson (1969) concludes that aspects of visual perception may be improved under appropriate learning conditions involving practice and reinforcement. Others (Kendler, 1956; Nelson, 1967; Rennels, 1970; Salome & Reeves, 1972; Salome & Szeto, 1976) also present evidence that visual perceptual skills of young children are amenable to training and guided experience.

The Perceptual-Delineation Theory

In *Preparation for Art,* June King McFee advances yet another theory of art. McFee (1972) bases her theory on concepts from the behavioral sciences and claims that art is based on several factors, rather than just one. The factors she identifies are:

1. The readiness of the child. This includes the child's physical development, intelligence, perceptual development, response sets, and cultural dispositions acquired.
2. The psychological environment in which children work. This includes the degree of threat or support in this environment and the number and intensity of rewards or punishments.
3. Information handling. This factor is affected by children's ability to handle detail, their intelligence, ability to handle asymmetrical detail, and the categories they possess for organizing details.
4. Delineation skills. This includes children's ability to manipulate media, their creative ability, and ability to design qualities of form.

McFee (1970) believes art education is a multifaceted phenomenon. She identifies the content of art as drawing, painting, sculpture, and claims that art education is design in its broad ramifications—it is art as historical impact; it is art criticism; it is also cultural communication. In order to teach art, a person must have a highly developed understanding of both the individual and the culture, and how both are related to the process of learning. This curriculum is built on the premise that a culture, an environment, has a very definite effect on the artistic achievements of children. McFee claims that today's society, because of its complexity as well as mobility, has placed children from many different subcultural groups in the same classrooms. She believes that the teacher should help children find avenues of maintaining their own subculture through art. Eisner believes that McFee's theory, based on four broad factors that would affect nearly any human activity, is "comprehensive and useful as a theory of child art— indeed artistic learning in general—for it is reasonable to assume that these four factors will need to be taken into account" (Eisner, 1972, p. 93).

ART RESEARCH: IMPLICATIONS FOR TEACHING

Art education presents a fertile field for researchers (McWhinnie, 1985). In the past, many art educators held the position that research on children's art was inappropriate. D'Amico (1966) wrote that researching the art of young children is not only inappropriate, but irrelevant. If children's art is the result of emotional feelings, the probing of researchers would destroy the unique characteristics of art, and would be devoid of any meaning. The findings of research into children's art are "devoid of any real relationship to creative behavior or understanding of children's art" (Burns & Kaufman, 1970, p. 30).

Thus, splintered by a variety of theoretical bases, and hampered by the belief that research could impede children's natural and creative expression, research in art education has been piecemeal, with few longitudinal, comprehensive reports or advanced investigations bringing together research and theory. However, two longitudinal studies of import are available. Harvard's Project Zero is one such study of children's participation in a range of art activities. Gardner (1982) concludes that through this work, "we have been moving toward an understanding of the drawings, songs, and metaphors created by young children" (p. 87). Another long-term study of children's art is that of Brittain at Cornell University. Brittain (1979), having analyzed observations of children engaged in art activities and children's comments and reactions to the teaching environment, concluded that "more questions were raised than answered" (p. 231).

In addition to these two major studies, other research has been conducted and does influence teaching practices. Studies are available supporting the idea that art is valuable as a content area that can contribute to the growth of children; these studies support specific techniques for teaching art, selecting goals, media, planning and motivating artistic expression.

Art is Basic

Art is a valuable activity for young children. Related to children's visual perception, concept formation, and emotions, art holds tremendous power in the curriculum. Art is no longer considered a "frill" in our schools (Lansing, 1981).

Nevertheless, rising costs, accountability, and new priorities dictate that school systems must re-examine agendas and expenditures. Under this pressure, art often becomes the first subject to be eliminated from the curriculum. "In a world dominated, sometimes obsessed by utilitarian needs, teachers of the arts are often forced into defensive positions" (Reid, 1979).

Research supports the value of art for children. There is a growing "body of information with highly significant results attesting to the relationship between participation in art activities and learning in many areas" (Cohen & Gainer, 1976, p. 208). The program *Learning to Read Through the*

Arts documents the relationship between children's participation in art activities and achievement in reading. The project, which consisted of three consecutive programs, involved children who were initially at least two years below expected reading levels. After participating in the project, where reading was taught in the context of art activities, children were found to make significant gains in reading scores, as well as showing increased enthusiasm for and application to academic learning in general. These program directors concluded that it is "possible to effectively teach reading in a program of instruction primarily focused upon the arts" (Conant, 1973).

The California Achievement Test (Reading) was administered to all children on a pre/post-basis, and an exceptionally significant reading score gain of 8.4 months over a four-month chronological period was determined. Similar results were reported from a study called *Arts IMPACT* (Interdisciplinary Model Program in the Arts for Children and Teachers). Conducted in five states, this study concluded that education is made more effective for both teachers and children when arts are utilized (Arts IMPACT, 1975). Still another project is described in *All the Arts for Every Child,* a part of the Arts in General Education Project, which reports that children's self-concept and academic achievement can be enhanced through participation in the arts.

Mills (1973) postulated that art education could play an important role in reading by helping children to differentiate between letters and words, and analyzed the effectiveness of art instruction on reading readiness. He used a classical paradigm of control and treatment groups, randomly selected, and both pre- and post-testing on the Metropolitan Reading Readiness Test. The treatment consisted of ten art lessons for ten consecutive days. During the treatment, the main objective was to attempt to influence the treatment group to include more details in their drawings. The procedures consisted of questioning and making statements concerning the topic of the art lesson. Results indicated that children who received the art training achieved significantly higher scores on five subtests of the Metropolitan Reading Readiness Test. These findings, according to Mills, suggest that children's reading development can be improved through art lessons that stress inclusion of details.

Art has been shown to increase children's language concepts. Green and Hasselbring (1981) introduced visual arts concepts to hearing impaired children and concluded that "the linkage of visual art activities to language development objectives produces a highly effective tool for teaching language concepts to young students who are prelinguistically and profoundly hearing impaired" (p. 36). Green and Hasselbring believe that if their brief introduction of art activities can influence the achievement of hearing-impaired children, it follows that the acquisition of objectives in other areas, such as math or science may also be enhanced through similar methods. General objectives geared to using imagination and memory, generalizing information and making associations, making independent decisions, expressing original ideas and developing flexibility, should reflect even greater gains over longer periods of time. The development of these skills during the transition from preoperational thinking to concrete operational thinking could have a significant impact on later intellectual and academic success. (1981, p. 36)

Forseth (1980) demonstrated that, in fact, experiences with art can lead to achievement in mathematics. Introduction of art activities were found to influence children's attitudes toward math, as well as having a positive effect on children's growth in logico-mathematic modes of thinking.

Drawing is believed especially effective in influencing children's cognitive development. A demonstration that drawing aids the formation of mental representations, and hence gives children more freedom for thought, has been documented by Lansing (1981). Drawing is considered to be an important educational activity that helps children learn and remember. These abilities can be useful in the learning of spelling, reading, mathematics, and the other subjects of the school.

The primary value of art education for young children, however, is believed to stem from the fact that children need to experience art and be introduced to the content of art. Dewey (1934) saw creating art as one form of experience that helps the growing organism recognize that it is alive, to make it possible for a person to identify the uniqueness of life. Because of this, art is intrinsically valuable, and "should not be subverted to serve other means" (Eisner, 1972, p. 5). To dilute art education, or to justify its place in the curriculum for young children on the grounds that it fosters reading or mathematics achievement, is to dilute and destroy its power and serves to rob children of the most important contributions of art, those that only art can provide" (Eisner, 1972, p. 5).

Art is basic. Its value lies in the contributions it makes to the individual's experience with and understanding of the world. The visual arts are necessary to introduce children to an awareness of color, form, line, shape, and texture in their environment and in art works. Children need to understand the content of art, to create and produce art, and to appreciate the art of others. No other subject matter can meet these needs.

Research on Planning for Art: Selecting Goals

For many early childhood educators, the idea of selecting goals and objectives for art instruction is inappropriate. When art is viewed as a creative, spontaneous expression based on a child's growth and development, identifying the behavior that could result from artistic experiences and expression seems totally uncalled for.

Nevertheless, objectives do have a place in art education for the young. They serve to focus teachers' attention on the content of art, and enable them to view art as a body of knowledge. Thus, selecting objectives can protect children's opportunity to experience art for art's sake. Further, objectives permit teachers to become aware of all the potential learning that can stem from experiences in the visual arts, as well as lead to evaluation of children's progress in the arts.

The National Art Education Association's major objectives (below) can be used as a guide for early childhood educators.

All children should be able to:

1. see and feel visual relationships,
2. make art,
3. study works of art, and
4. critically evaluate art (NEA, 1973).

Schwartz and Douglas (1967) found that children as young as four could achieve these art objectives: understanding that art is a means of nonverbal communication; that the art product is the result of an idea of the artist; that the artist uses what she or he sees, thinks, and feels to create art; and that there is a great variety of materials available to the contemporary artist.

State departments of education are another source of objectives for teaching art. *A Guide to Art in Florida's Schools: Bulletin 77* introduces the general objectives of art education which lead children to see and feel visual relationships, produce works of art, know and understand art objectives, and develop the skills of critiquing art. The guide separates each of these general goals into specific objectives. Examples of specific objectives are the following: The child will be able to mix the primary colors to make secondary colors, will be able to make a design out of an arrangement of three colors using repetition, pattern, and line forces, and will be able to use the emotional connotations of colors and shapes to convey a specific mood or feeling.

Demonstrating how objectives are determined through observing and assessing children's entering skills, the Southwest Regional Laboratory (1969) has developed a year-long kindergarten art program. As an early step in the project, children's entering skills in two areas were observed and assessed. These were psychomotor skills, such as holding a pencil, tearing a piece of paper along a line, or copying a shape or line, and knowledge of colors, shapes, textures, and lines. The results of observing and assessing children's skills then led them to the development of objectives for the *Kindergarten Art Program* (KAP). Skills that children had already mastered were decreased in importance, and other objectives were focused on those skills that few children had obtained, as well as those found to be most difficult.

Eisner recognizes the value of objectives in avoiding fuzzy thinking: "Since most objectives describe the ways in which students are to behave or the competencies they are to display after working through a curriculum, the careful statement of such objectives mitigates against the fuzzy thinking and language that too often makes goals in the field appear like slogans" (1972, p. 154).

Nevertheless, Eisner suggests that another type of objective be utilized to guide children's experiences in the visual arts. These are the expressive objectives, which do not describe the behavior or product that a child is to display or construct, rather, they describe the encounter a child is to have (p. 156). The major aim of instructional objectives, the development of specific skills, negate children's determining their own expression, and place emphasis on the end product and the development of specific skills, rather than the process. When this occurs, many important outcomes of the art experience can be lost. Thinking in terms of expressive objectives enables teachers to plan and think clearly about the aims of their art program, and at the same time, intentionally encourages children to "expand and explore their ideas, images, and feelings through the use of the skills in their repertoire" (p. 157).

Motivation

Although young children are believed to be in a period of growth characterized by uninhibited and spontaneous creativity, it doesn't take long before teachers hear the plaintive, ever so familiar "I can't draw, show me." Often by the time children reach kindergarten and the primary grades, their art becomes stereotypic, and their ability to express themselves freely through the visual arts is stunted. Linderman and Herberholz (1974) believe that motivational experiences will enable children to retain their original approach to art and negate the belief that they "can't draw." Linderman and Herberholz classify motivational techniques designed to "wind up the mainspring" of motivation into three main categories:

1. Artistic motivation, which includes all of those things that increase perceptual awareness, aesthetic sensitivity, and skills with art media.
2. Intellectual motivations, which have as their aim the development

and enrichment of children's concepts for natural objects and those made by people.

3. Imaginative motivations, which help children develop their imagination, inventiveness, and originality.

Eisner (1970) noted that the amount of detail and ingenuity displayed in children's art work after they have had an opportunity to role play is greater than when they are exposed to other motivational procedures. He claims that role playing, such as acting like a wave crashing upon a shore or a bird lofting through the sky, tends to increase the presence of certain artistically valued components in children's work.

Calling motivation a set variable, McWhinnie (1971) demonstrated how motivational experiences do influence the aesthetic quality of children's drawings. Groups of children were asked to draw trees. They made a first drawing after being asked simply to "draw a tree." Another was completed after children had been shown pictures and paintings of trees and had discussed them. In over 90 percent of the cases, the first drawings of trees were stereotypic "lollipop trees" whereas the second were far more differentiated and complete.

Schwartz and Douglas (1967) motivated four-year-old children through the use of art objectives. They shared ceramic works with the four-year-olds, discussing the techniques the artists used to make the pieces and identified other materials that could have been used to make the same thing. Children's own clay products increased in complexity in a number of ways. After the children had examined various ceramic pieces and participated in the discussion of their works, their attention span when they worked with clay increased, and their products increased in dimensionality, complexity, and detail. In addition, children who received this form of motivation made significant increases in verbal language and verbalizations about their own work.

Praise has often been thought of as a tool for motivation. Nevertheless, praise can serve to stifle children's creativity. Brophy (1981) reviews the research on teacher praise, and points out that when used as a reinforcer for children under the age of seven or eight years, praise constitutes "guidance from an authority figure and feedback indicating that one is pleasing that authority figure" (p. 19). Children under seven or eight are very oriented toward pleasing adults and have what Kohlberg (1969) calls a "good girl, good boy" sense of morality. When teachers praise art work, saying "I like that," "Isn't this beautiful?" "This is the best painting I've ever seen," children may be trapped into trying to please a teacher, the authority figure, rather than into developing their own tastes and preferences.

Reinforcements have also been shown to increase young children's creative responses (Fallon & Goetz, 1975; Goetz & Baer, 1971; Goetz & Solloman, 1972). The number of paint forms used by preschool children were increased through the use of descriptive reinforcers. Kratochwill et al. (1980), increased the diversity of children's responses in easel painting through the use of reinforcers. Because of the criticism that reinforcement might adversely affect children's creativity, children were deliberately not judged by the reinforcement, nor told what to paint. The reinforcement was kept in the form of a discussion of the qualities of the paintings, and children did learn to produce more varied types of paintings as a result of the treatment.

The use of motivational techniques with young children offers a fruitful area for research. How different motivational techniques influence children's art, how the teacher might use these to increase children's artistic concepts and expressions, are questions of interest. Questions about the role of praise, and in fact, what constitutes praise and reinforcement, are still unanswered.

Selecting Media

Each of the theories of art offers teachers guidelines for the selection of materials and media for children's work in the visual arts. The psychoanalytic theorists, such as Alschuler and Hattwick (1947) would endorse the use of free-flowing tempera paint, finger paints, and clay that would give children the opportunity to express feelings and emotions directly, without being constrained by small paintbrushes or other tools. Those endorsing other theories of art believe other types of media are more appropriate. Arnheim (1954) believed that the fluid paints and wide brushes recommended for nursery school children could actually hinder children's expressions of their experiences and restrict their artistic potential. The broad brushes might prevent children from clarifying their observations of reality and from creating order out of these observations.

Lowenfeld (1947) also believed that liquid paints and large brushes, as well as finger paints, were inappropriate for children. Children who are just learning to use tools need to be encouraged in the use of tools. They should have the opportunity to work with tools and media that permit them to gain control of, rather than to simply mess around with, media. Lowenfeld (1947) suggested that the most appropriate materials for children would be crayons and plain paper.

Early childhood educators, however, favor the use of a variety of materials and media—so much so in fact, that they may judge the quality of an art program by the number of, and variety of, media supplied to children. "The more media they provide, the better they think they are; the more varieties of media their children experience, the better they assume the learning to be. Most teachers are on a perpetual hunt, not only for more media, but also for new ones" (Barkan, 1966, p. 426).

Instead of being preoccupied with introducing children to many new and varied media, teachers might strive to better understand their role and the complexities involved in artistic learning. Eisner (1974) believes that when teachers do not understand the goals and objectives of an art program, they haven't the vaguest idea of the skills that can be developed with the simple tools of paint, crayons, paper, and clay. Therefore, they have no alternative but to continually introduce children to new media.

Children continually faced with new media are never able to gain control over, or develop skill in, the use of any one medium. Nor are they able to discover and explore the opportunities present in any one medium. Visitors to the Far East note that very young children cut wood block prints well in advance of those cut by much older children in the United States. Asian children are introduced to block carving early in life, and are allowed to continue developing skill and proficiency with the tools of this medium. Children in the United States usually only experience wood cutting in the fifth or sixth grade, as they cut wood, or some other materials, to create a block-print holiday card. Unless children have the opportunity to gain experience with a medium over time, they will find it difficult to achieve the skills required to use that medium as a means of artistic expression.

Studies suggest that media do have an influence over children's artistic expression. Investigations of children's drawings completed with either a pencil or crayon lead to the conclusion that tools do influence drawing ability. Badri (1967), studying rural children, believed that lack of experience with pencils would inhibit their drawing; he found that children's initial experience with pencils were related to later drawings. Children who had previously used pencils did complete figure drawings that had a greater differentiation of form than those without such experience. Figure drawings in pencil and crayon and personality correlates were investigated by Koppit (1967). She compared the drawings made with pencils and those made with crayons and found little differences between the two when scored with the Goodenough-Harris Draw-A-Man Test. She did, however, find significant correlations between the medium used and the emotional factors present when the drawings were scored using the Machover Scale, a scale of emotional indicators. Crayon drawings were believed to contain more emotional factors than those completed with pencil.

Salome (1967) conducted an analysis of kindergarten children's drawings using colored pencils and crayons, and found no significant differences in the amount of detail children included in their drawings, whether the drawing was in either pencil or crayon. Most of the children delineated larger shapes in their crayon drawings than in their pencil drawings, and the

202 The Early Childhood Curriculum

majority of them filled more space on a piece of 12″ × 18″ paper when drawing with crayon than with pencil. The lines children produced using crayons were more definite, bolder, freer, and heavier than those produced in the pencil drawings. Salome concluded that children can draw with both pencils and crayons and questioned the theory of meeting children's developmental needs by providing them with large crayons for drawing. Children's paintings completed with the traditional wide paintbrush and those with finer, pointed brushes were analyzed using the Lantz Easel Age Scale. Understandably, paintings executed with narrow brushes invariably included more detail, design, and complexity than those done with wide brushes (Seefeldt, 1973). Griffin, Highberger, and Cunningham (1981) compared paintings completed on horizontal and vertical surfaces. They concluded, "On the practical level, this study can be applied directly to the teaching of painting in the preschool. It is evident that the use of tables as a painting surface facilitated the use of more advanced hand positions during painting tasks than did the use of easels" (p. 45). With this information the teacher can provide more opportunity for children to paint by removing easels, which take up a great deal of room and only permit painting by a few children at a time.

Brittain (1979) observed the use of materials in nursery schools and concluded that "it was difficult for teachers to explain why they were using certain materials, but it was much easier for them to talk about art in general ways" (p. 98). Brittain recommended decreased emphasis on the new and different, with more thoughtful choices of media and materials to meet the developmental and artistic needs of children.

The Role of the Teacher

The role of the art teacher has also been widely debated. Those endorsing the psychoanalytic or child development theories of art believe that the teacher's role should be passive, should be that of a provider of materials, a guide, and an encourager. Acting as a true "gardener," the teacher, according to these theories, provides the motivation and psychological climate required for children's growth. "We concluded that there is no need for any formal teaching of the procedures of painting to any nursery school child; . . . no child acted as if he or she were inhibited from lack of instruction on how to hold the brush, how to mix the paint, or how to plan or execute the painting" (Brittain, 1979, p. 159).

As early as 1946, however, research demontrated that children's artistic expression could be improved when teachers assumed a more active role. Dubin, in an early and classical study (1946), worked with nursery school children. She identified a series of stages in the literature frequently used to describe children's art, and placed children's paintings into these previously identified categories. Dubin identified the particular stages at which children in the experimental group were working. Through a program designed around the discussion about their work and questions of a variety of types, she was able to move these children up to the next stage of painting. Dubin concluded that the simple technique of discussing children's art products could increase artistic development.

Rand (1973) employed more direct teaching techniques designed to improve children's ability to copy forms. Rand postulated that, theoretically, copying requires at least two abilities: visual analysis and use of the drawing rule. First, Rand implemented two training methods designed to improve preschool children's ability to analyze figures and to use drawing rules; she then analyzed the effects of these training procedures on children's ability to discriminate figures and to copy them. Training in how to use drawing rules resulted in improved copying accuracy, but did not improve discrimination ability. Training in visual analysis resulted in improved ability to discriminate figures, but not in improved copying. Improvement in figure discrimination was related to a decrease in ability to copy with accuracy. Rand concluded that using rules of drawing is essential and that adequate visual analysis is a necessary, but not sufficient, prerequisite to the production of adequate copies.

Specific instruction was found to increase first-grade children's ability to draw a simple figure (Nelson & Flannery, 1967). The most effective instructions directed children to pay attention to the shape of the figure instead of to the total figure. Children receiving no instruction tended to draw a less differentiated and more global perception of the figure-ground relationship. Asking children to criticize their own work was somewhat productive, but was not useful as a specific task instruction. Two types of instruction, repeated practice and attention to the proportions of the shape copied, produced lower scores on children's drawing tests. Nelson and Flannery (1967) concluded that the drawing behavior of children is cognitive in nature, rather than simply sensorimotor, since specific task instruction proved most effective in increasing drawing ability.

Salome and Reeves (1972) conducted two pilot studies to determine the effects of perceptual training on children's ability to draw. The first study consisted of practice in visual discrimination, and the second of drawing lines of varied direction and shapes including contour, direction changes in angles, peaks of curvature, and lines due to abrupt color changes. The results, as measured by scores on the Early Childhood Embedded Figures Tests and other drawing tests, indicated that the training did effect greater differentiation in children's drawings of a truck, and appeared to be a significant factor in explaining the experimental group's higher level of performance on the ECEFT. The authors suggest that in view of the significance of their findings, continued investigations are in order.

Examining the effects of a training program on visual perception, Seefeldt (1979) randomly assigned five-year-olds to three groups. A series of lessons, designed to teach concepts of texture, were given to the first and second groups. These children were taught to recognize the textures of rough and smooth, to discuss texture in the art of others, and to incorporate texture into their own drawings. Children in one of the treatment groups received lessons of approximately fifteen minutes in length for ten consecutive days. These were conducted by a doctoral student in early childhood education. The other group received one lesson per week, for thirty minutes, conducted by the school's art teacher. The third group received no treatment. Children in the two treatment groups gained significantly in their ability to incorporate texture in their art work, and to discuss texture in their work, as well as in the works of others.

Taylor and Trujillo (1973) arranged a prototype environment, designed to stimulate children's multisensory cognitive system as well as to offer children training in the use of discovery techniques and questioning strategies. The four-year-olds who participated in the study showed gains in the overall aesthetic quality of their art products. Taylor and Trujillo concluded that the environment contributed to significant changes in the quality of tempera paintings for the experimental groups and gains in concept formation. There was, however, no measurable gain in children's ability to make critical aesthetic judgments.

Research on teaching strategies gives the overall impression that the adult can determine what children are to produce, and implement teaching strategies to achieve the desired results. When goals are predetermined by the adult, and the children are instructed in how to achieve these goals, a variety of teaching strategies seems feasible. The question remains, however, as to the efficacy and efficiency of any of the teaching strategies described by the research. Most of the strategies appear to be designed to answer what Piaget (1969) once described as the "American question," that is, "How can you get children to proceed through normal developmental tasks at a quicker speed?" One may ask whether or not it is efficient, or even ethical, to *teach* children skills, techniques, or responses to the visual arts that will appear naturally as children grow and mature.

The long-range effectiveness of the studies on teaching strategies has not been determined. No longitudinal follow-ups or explorations of the long-range effects of the treatments have been conducted. Nor have children's perceptions of the treatments or teaching strategies been exlored. Then too, the fact that each study reports positive findings may only be due to the bias of the researchers, or to the ever-present Hawthorne effects of participating in a study.

SUMMARY

There is a body of knowledge called art that can and should be passed on to children. Children's participation in the visual arts can benefit their total growth and development, as well as introduce them to the content of art. Theories of art education offer implications for how this body of knowledge can be transmitted to the young, and the research in the field is beginning to offer empirical evidence for the greater validity of some methods of teaching rather than others.

Although each of the theories differs significantly from the others, they are all similar in recognizing developmental stages in children's production of the visual arts. No theory supports a didactic role for the teacher, and none implies that adults should interfere directly in children's free, spontaneous expression of their ideas through art.

Traditionally, art education for the preschool/primary child has been heavily based on the psychoanalytic theories of art or the developmental theories. Teachers endorsing these theories believe that no instruction on their part is required to promote children's growth and learning in the visual arts.

When art is viewed as a response to inner feelings, the program is totally child-centered. To the psychoanalytic theorists, art is a way children can come to know themselves, to recognize and reveal inner feelings not only about themselves, but also about those around them. Teachers are encouraged to be there as a support for children's creative and spontaneous thinking, but not to interrupt this process. No direct instruction is advocated. and the teacher is expected merely to provide a psychologically and physically safe environment, with plenty of free-flowing, unrestrictive materials readily available for children's explorations.

If children's art is a personal affair, a process of individual self-expression, then it is difficult, if not impossible, to suggest teaching methods or techniques. Since no two children would hold the same feelings or have an identical experience, there would be no way to design arbitrarily teaching strategies appropriate for one child, much less a group of children.

Currently, the cognitive theories have had a great influence on art education and research. Art educators who base their work on Piaget's and Inhelder's (1969) are calling for a more active role for the teacher. The teacher is still viewed as a supporter of children's expression and creativity; however, since this expression is viewed as a cognitive process, an understanding of children's thinking is called for.

An understanding of children's thought processes permits teachers to plan for a type of interaction between children and themselves that is geared toward the child's development, and that can foster this development. Once teachers understand children's thinking, they can provide children with alternatives that will expand their frame of reference and can build opportunities for children to act on their environment with their present state of knowledge. Teachers can also supply plentiful opportunities for children to explore and investigate, manipulate, alter, and question (Brittain, 1979). The teacher would use this understanding of children's thinking, coupled with an understanding of the content of art, to promote children's conceptualization as fully as possible (Smith, 1982).

Giving the teacher a more active role would mean that media and materials would be carefully selected to enable children to express specific ideas, feelings, and emotions. Instilling motivation would be a part of the program. Smith (1982) believes that motivation, through the use of direct and indirect experiences, is a necessary role of the teacher in order to fulfill the cognitive needs of children: "Teachers need to help children select developmentally appropriate objects and events as subjects and to help them expand their range of responses to these experiences. Direct, as well as indirect experiences of objects, events, and works of art are needed in the classroom" (p. 310).

The perceptual theories offer an alternative role for the teacher—that of fostering children's ability to perceive their environment fully. These theories would have the teacher plan for and implement experiences in which children would be asked to observe specific details in their environment, as well as gain experience in translating these observations into concrete art products. Because very young children appear to lack both the necessary physical ability and motor skills to represent their world, as well as the ability to respond to visual configurations, they need time to mature and experience, in order to move in an orderly progression from mastery of the simple to the more complex visual and motor skills. In Smith's words, "It is essential to the creation of meaning with materials for the child to develop a deep and rich understanding of the physical and visual properties of materials. In order for this to take place, opportunities for experimentaion with appropriate materials, over sufficient time, are necessary" (p. 302). The work of researchers and theorists, when coupled with the traditional theories of art, does provide direction for early childhood educators. It seems possible for teachers to draw on these theories, taking whatever is valuable from each, and to examine the research, applying those findings that seem appropriate for specific children and programs. Yet teachers can go beyond this, becoming double specialists; they can draw on both theory and research for their practice. Then, reflecting on the responses of the children, teachers can experiment, change, try again, and contribute theoretically to our understanding of how children experience growth in the visual arts.

REFERENCES

A guide to art in Florida's elementary schools: Bulletin 77 (1969). Tallahassee, FL: State Department of Education.

All the arts for every child: Final report on the arts in general education project in the school district of University City, Mo. (1973). New York: J.D.R. III Fund, Inc.

Alschuler, R., & Hattwick, L. B. (1947). *Painting and personality: A study of young children.* Chicago: University of Chicago Press.

Arnheim, R. (1947). *Art and visual perception.* Berkeley: University of California Press.

Arts IMPACT: Curriculum for change: A summary report (1973). Washington, DC: Office of Education. U.S. Department of Health, Education, and Welfare.

Ausubel, D. P., & Sullivan, E. V. (1970). *Theory and problems of child development.* (2nd Ed.) New York: Grune & Stratton.

Badri, M. B. (1965). Use of figure drawing in measuring the Goodenough Quotient of culturally deprived Sudanese children. *Journal of Psychology, 59,* 333–34.

Barkan, M. (1966). Transition in art education. In E. W. Eisner & D. W. Ecker (Eds.), *Readings in art education.* Waltham, MA: Blaisdell.

Brearley, M. (1970). *The teaching of young children: Some applications of Piaget's theory.* New York: Schocken Books.

Brittain, W. L. (1979). *Creativity, art, and the young child.* New York: Macmillan.

Brophy, J. (1981). Teacher praise: A functional analysis. *Review of Educational Research, 51,* 5–32.

Bruner, J. S. (1960). *The process of education.* New York: Vintage.

Burns, R., & Kaufman, S. H. (1970). *Kinetic family drawings: An introduction to understanding children through kinetic drawings.* New York: Brunner/Mazel.

Cohen, E. P., & Gainer, R. S. (1976). *Art: Another language for learning.* New York: Citation.

Cole, N. R. (1966). *Children's art from deep down inside.* New York: John Day.

D'Amico, V. (1966). Art education today: Millennium or mirage? *Art Education, 7,* 46–53.

Dewey, J. (1934). *Art and experience.* New York: Minton, Balch.

Dubin, E. R. (1946). The effects of training on the tempo of development of graphic representations of preschool children. *Journal of Experimental Education, 15,* 166–73.

Ebbeck, T. N., & Ebbeck, M. A. (1974). *Now we are four.* Columbus, OH: Charles E. Merrill.

Eisner, E. W. (1972). *Educating artistic vision.* New York: Macmillan.

——— (1970). Evaluating children's art. In E. Pappas (Ed.), *Art Education.* New York: Macmillan.

Fallon, M. P., & Coetz, E. M. (1975). The creative teacher: Effects of descriptive social reinforcement upon the drawing technique of three preschool children. *School Application of Learning Theory, 7,* 27–42.

Feldman, E. B. (1970). *Becoming human through art.* Englewood Cliff, NJ: Prentice-Hall.

Foreseth, S. D. (1980). Art activities, attitudes, and achievement in elementary mathematics. *Studies in Art Education, 21,* 22–27.

Freeman, N. (1980). *Strategies of representation in young children.* London: Academic Press.

Freud, A. (1955). *The psychoanalytic treatment of children.* New York: International University Press.

Gardner, H. (1982). *Art, mind and brain.* New York: Basic Books.

――― (1969). A cross cultural comparison of hostility in children's drawings. *Journal of Social Psychology, 19,* 219–92.

Gibson, E. J. (1969). *Principles of perceptual learning and development.* New York: Meredith.

Goetz, E. M., & Bear, D. M. (1971). Social reinforcement of creative block building by young children. In E. A. Ramp & B. L. Hopkins (Eds.), *A new direction for education: Behavioral analysis.* Lawrence: University of Kansas Press.

Goetz, E. M., & Salmonson, M. L. (1972). The effect of general and descriptive reinforcement on creativity in easel painting. In G. Semb (Ed.), *Behavior analysis and education.* Lawrence: University of Kansas Support and Development Center for Follow Through Description of Human Development.

Golomb, G. (1973). Children's representation of the human figure: The effects of models, media, and instruction. *Genetic Psychology Monographs, 87,* 197–251.

Goodenough, F. L. (1926). *Children's drawings as measure of intellectual maturity.* New York: Harcourt, Brace Jovanovich.

Goodenough, F. L., & Harris, D. (1963). *Children's drawings as measures of intellectual maturity.* New York: Harcourt, Brace Jovanovich.

Green, J. C., & Hasselbring, T. S. (1981). The acquisition of language concepts by hearing impaired children through selected aspects of an experimental core art curriculum. *Studies in Art Education, 22,* 32–37.

Griffin, M. E., Highberger, R., & Cunningham, J. L. (1981). Young children's paintings: a comparison of horizontal and vertical painting surfaces. *Studies in Art Education, 23,* 40–46.

Kellog, R. (1969). *Analyzing children's art.* Palo Alto, CA: National Press.

Kohlberg, L. (1969). Stages and sequence: The cognitive developmental approach to socialization. In D. Goslin (Ed.), *Handbook of social theory and personality.* Chicago: Rand McNally.

Koppitz, E. (1967). A comparison of pencil and crayon drawings of young children. *Journal of Clinical Psychology, 72,* 205–07.

Kratochwill, C. E., Rush, J. C., & Kratochwill, T. R. (1980). The effects of descriptive social reinforcement on creative responses in children's easel painting. *Studies in Art Education, 20,* 29–39.

Lansing, K. M. (1981). The effect of drawing on the development of mental representation. *Studies in Art Education, 22,* 15–23.

Leeper, S. L., Skipper, D. S., & Witherspoon, R. L. (1979). *Good schools for young children.* (4th ed.) New York: Macmillan.

Lewis, H. P., & Livson, N. (1981). Cognitive development, personality, and drawing: Their interrelationships in a replicated longitudinal study. *Studies in Art Education, 22,* 8–11.

Lindermann, E. W., & Herbolz, D. W. (1974). *Developing artistic and perceptual awareness*. Dubuque, IA: Wm. C. Brown.

Lingren, R. H. (1971). An attempted replication of emotional indicators in human figure drawings by shy and aggressive children. *Psychological Reports, 29,* 35–38.

Lowenfeld, V. (1947). *Creative and mental growth*. New York: Macmillan.

Luquet, G. H. (1913). *The drawings of a child*. Paris: F. Alcan.

Manzella, D. (1963). The effects of hypnotically induced change in the self image on drawing ability. *Studies in Art Education, 4,* 59–70.

McFee, J. K. (1970). *Preparation for art*. (2nd ed.) Belmont, CA: Wadsworth.

Medinnus, J. R., Bobbitt, D., & Hullet, J. (1966). Effects of training on the Draw-A-Man test. *Journal of Experimental Education, 35,* 62–64.

McWhinnie, H. J. (1963). Lowenfeld revisited. *Creative Crafts,* Fall, 35–37.

———— (1985a). On Rudolph Arnheim's contributions to art education. Paper submitted to *Studies in Art Education*.

———— (1985b). A review of research in the teaching of drawing. Unpublished. College Park: University of Maryland.

———— (1971). Viktor Lowenfeld: Art education for the 1970's. *Studies in Art Education, 4,* 8–13.

Mills, J. C. (1973). The effect of art instruction upon a reading development test: An experimental study with rural Appalachian children. *Studies in Art Education, 14,* 62–64.

Murphy, L. B. (1960). *Personality in young children*. Vols. 1–2. New York: Basic Books.

National Art Education Association (1973). The essentials of a quality school art program: A position statement. *Art Education, 26,* 21–25.

Nelson, T. M., & Flannery, M. E. (1967). Instruction in drawing techniques as a means of utilizing drawing potential of six and seven year olds. *Studies in Art Education, 3,* 58–65.

Piaget, J. (1955). *The child's concept of reality*. London: Routledge & Kegan Paul.

Piaget, J., & Inhelder, B. (1969). *The psychology of the child*. New York: Basic Books.

Rand, C. W. (1973). Copying in drawing: The importance of adequate visual analysis versus the ability to utilize drawing rules. *Child Development, 44,* 47–53.

Read, H. (1943). *Education through art*. New York: Pantheon Books.

Read, K. B. (1976). *The nursery school*. (6th Ed.) Philadelphia: W. B. Saunders Company.

Reichenberg, H. W. (1950). Changes in children's drawings after a gratifying experience. *American Journal of Orthopsychiatry, 23,* 501–17.

Reid, L. A. (1979). Foreword. In K. Swanwick (Ed.) *A basic for music education*. Windsor, Berks: NFER Publishing Company.

Rennels, M. R. (1970). Four methods of teaching spatial tasks to disadvantaged Negroes. *Studies in Art Education, 11,* 51–54.

Rogers, R. S., & Wright, E. N. (1971). A study of children's drawings of their classrooms. *Journal of Educational Research, 64,* 370–74.

Salome, R. A. (1967). A comparative analysis of kindergarten children's drawings in crayon and colored pencil. *Studies in Art Education, 72,* 25–27.

Salome, R. A., & Reeves, D. (1972). Two pilot investigations of perceptual training of four and five year old kindergarten children. *Studies in Art Education, 13,* 3–9.

Salome, R. A., & Szeto, J. W. (1976). The effects of search and practice and perceptual training upon representational tonal drawings. *Studies in Art Education, 18,* 44–55.

Schwartz, J. B., & Douglas, N. J. (1967). *Increasing the awareness of art ideas of culturally deprived kindergarten children through experiences with ceramics.* Washington, DC: Office of Education, U.S. Department of Health, Education, and Welfare.

Seefeldt, C. (1979). The effects of a program designed to increase young children's perception of texture. *Studies in Art Education, 20,* 40–44.

——— (1973). The validity of the exclusive use of the wide paintbrush in the five-year-old kindergarten. *Studies in Art Education, 14,* 48–54.

Smith, N. R. (1982). The visual arts in early childhood education. In B. Spodek (Ed.), *Handbook of research in early childhood education.* New York: Free Press.

Southwest Regional Laboratory (1969). *Kindergarten Arts Program.* Tucson, AZ.

Taylor, P. A., & Trujillo, J. L. (1973). The effects of selected studies on the art products, concept, form and aesthetic judgmental decisions of four year olds. *Studies in Art Education, 14,* 57–63.

Winner, W. (1982). *Invented worlds: The psychology of the arts.* Cambridge, MA: Harvard University Press.

U.S. National Center for Health Statistics (1970). *Intellectual maturity of children as measured by the Goodenough-Harris Draw-A-Man Test.* PHS, Publication no. 100, Series 11, No. 105. Rockville, MD: U.S. Center for Health Statistics.

CHAPTER 9

Early Childhood
Music Education

CLIFFORD D. ALPER
Towson State University

Art and appreciation of art constitute a general capacity or talent of man,
and should be cared for early, at the latest in boyhood. . . . A universal
and comprehensive plan of human education must, therefore, necessarily consider at an early period singing, drawing, painting, and modeling;
it will not leave them to an arbitrary, frivolous whimsicalness, but treat
them as serious objects of the school. Its intention will not be to make
each pupil an artist in some one or all of the arts, but to secure each
human being full and all-sided development, to enable him to see man
in the universality and all-sided energy of his nature, and, particularly,
to enable him to understand and appreciate the products of true art.
—Friedrich Froebel (1782–1852)
The Education of Man

These prophetic, though obviously sexist comments by the German-
born founder of modern early childhood education, Friedrich Froebel, have
important implications for current theories in music education for young
children (see Mark, 1982, p. 96). In nineteenth-century Germany Froebel
was among the first to speak out in favor of children's natural capabilities, in
an era when child passivity and obedience were the rule. With the advantage of hindsight, we can see Froebel's principles as having prevailed,
although the specific methodologies he advocated have now been discarded.
Among the current practices in music education that can be traced to
Froebelian theory, one can cite the ideas of Dalcroze, Orff, and conceptual
education. Kodaly methodology, while not particularly Froebelian, also
plays a vital role in current music education practices, having had considerable impact on education for very young children, as well as that for older
students.

Emile Jaques-Dalcroze (1865–1950), born in Vienna of Swiss parents, advocated using one's entire body as a kind of musical entity, "becoming" the music, so to speak. The term "eurhythmics" is associated with his work, where through the use of their bodies, children increase their understanding by having consistent and increasingly complex experiences with music and movement. At the early childhood level, for example, students might move in new directions or in different ways when a previously unheard section or melodic idea occurs in the music. Or, if dynamics are being emphasized, students might alter their patterns of movement when the volume of sound increases or decreases. Dalcroze techniques thus enable teachers to observe, in behavioral terms, how students respond to musical tasks. In addition, motivation is assured, due to the intensity of psychomotor, cognitive, and affective involvement required. Dalcroze's writings reflect Froebelian thought, particularly Froebel's principle of self-activity, where the objective is to attain fulfillment and self-realization almost simultaneously. How better to achieve this than through Dalcroze's total physical and mental immersion in musical experience?

The *Schulwerk* of the German composer Carl Orff (1895–1982) also has played an important role in music education during the past several years. Orff's system employs experiences using such instruments as metallophones, xylophones, and glockenspiels. Children play these pitched percussion instruments, producing borduns and ostinati for mainly pentatonic songs. This provides musical experiences with a great deal of interest and variety, and even lends a "professional" sound to the music made by children. At the early childhood level, Orff methodology might include instrumental borduns and ostinati with simple nursery rhyme-type songs based entirely upon the pitches *so* and *mi*. A simple song, such as "Rain, Rain, Go Away," sung entirely on *so* and *mi*, becomes a truly aesthetic experience when combined with Orff instruments playing a bordun and one or two ostinati. Indeed, youngsters become real musicians when engaging in these endeavors.

The conceptual approach offers yet another valid way of working with children in music. This system, which came into use in the late 1960s and continues to have current implications, tends to avoid mere singing of songs as a total music education program. Instead, when music is taught, children are exposed not only to the music itself, but also to melody, rhythm, harmony, form, tone color, dynamics, and tempo. For example, in addition to singing a song, children may learn to notice when pitches go up, down, or are repeated, and when pitches move stepwise, or move by leaps. Or, if rhythm is stressed, the children might be exposed to the fact that music always involves rhythm, or that music usually embodies a recurring pulse, called the beat. In order to facilitate comprehension of what is the beat, children might engage in physical movement or instrumental experiences to illustrate and reinforce this concept. Although singing remains an important element in the conceptual approach, as it does in most systems, songs and listening activities must be augmented by an introduction to the elements of music, thus providing comprehensive musical experiences for children.

The music education system devised by the Hungarian composer, Zoltan Kodaly (1882–1967), has had tremendous impact all over the United States. The Kodaly System enables children, even at a very early age, to read and articulate rhythmic and melodic notation, encouraging them to internalize the elements of music and their concomitant skills. The methodology includes so-called stick notation, which leaves out the head part of quarter, eighth, sixteenth, thirty-second, and sixty-fourth notes. Whole and half notes are notated in the usual manner. The teacher shows the children how to assign rhythmic syllables to specific note values according to this notation. For melodic reading experiences, children learn to use the familiar pitch syllables, *do-re-mi-fa-so-la-ti-do*. Extensive listening activities and playing instruments, other than recorders, are not used very often.

The so-called Eclectic Curriculum combines elements of Dalcroze, Orff, and Kodaly, using representative elements from each. Although not looked upon favorably by purists who advocate exclusive use of just one of these methods, usually the one they espouse, the Eclectic Curriculum has proven to be a viable and practical way to combine the most representative components of these various methods.

DALCROZE

Young children, filled with physical energy, react very favorably to Dalcrozian movement activities, especially when introduced to them at an early age. When children feel comfortable with Dalcroze activities, and these are used consistently, gradually increasing in difficulty and complexity, it is possible for children, even when in secondary school, to continue participating in music and movement. It is essential, therefore, to build an atmosphere of trust, confidence, and psychological safety, so that initial hurdles are surmounted, and aesthetic considerations can begin to prevail.

One of the many advantages of the Dalcroze idea is the fact that it becomes no longer necessary to imitate or "be" something (an animal, airplane, robot, etc.) when moving to music. Children instead can react to music in terms of its own components, rather than to extraneous constructs such as stories or pictures. In terms of aesthetic theory, reacting to the integral parts of music (melody, rhythm, tone color, and form) falls into the area of absolute expressionism or absolute formalism. In *absolute expressionism*, one acknowledges the emotive/affective elements in art, but does not conjure up stories or pictures extraneous to the art work, especially if its originator indicated no such intentions. *Absolute formalism*, on the other hand, deals solely with an art work's constituents, which in the case of music would involve rhythm, melody, harmony and counterpoint, form, dynamics, timbre, and tempo. If one prefers to adopt a *referential* view of music, however, one could add all kinds of stories, pictures, and other extramusical factors not really part of the art work itself. The trend today, and one which Dalcroze foreshadowed in his integration of movement-with-music concept, is toward an absolute expressionist way of dealing with the arts in education (Reimer, 1970).

If one accepts absolute expressionism as a desirable and aesthetic way of incorporating music into early childhood education, teachers will gear their activities to the component parts of music itself, regardless of whether it is considered to be "program music" or "absolute music." So, if rhythmic elements are to be presented, children would be asked to respond to basic pulse (beat), then perhaps to the rhythm of the words. Initially, such rhythmic factors should be repetitious enough to enable youngsters to internalize patterns they hear, and to solidify specific ideas about the music in their minds. Listed below are some possibilities for initiating Dalcroze-like activities with young children, using an absolute expressionist point of view as the aesthetic framework.

> *Melody:* Children move in certain ways or directions for: (1) legato (smooth) melody segments, and differently for staccato (detached) melody segments, (2) melody lines that move by steps and those that move by leaps, (3) melody lines that ascend or descend, (4) melody lines that contain repeated notes and changes notes.
>
> *Rhythm:* Children move in certain ways or directions for (1) music with longer or shorter sounds, or silences (rests), (2) groups of longer or shorter sounds, or silences (rests), (3) the recurring pulse (beat), and any changes in that pulse, (4) music that stops suddenly or unexpectedly, and then resumes immediately.
>
> *Harmony:* Children move in certain ways or directions (1) each time underlying chords should be (or are) changed, (2) when two melodies are being sounded simultaneously, (3) when accompaniment patterns (chordal, triadic, oom-pah-pah, etc.) are changed, (4) when a major key is changed to minor, or minor to major.
>
> *Form:* Children move in certain ways or directions (1) when they hear like and unlike phrases in music, (2) when entire sections are repeated, or contrasting sections are introduced, (3) when they hear

melodic sequences (patterns immediately repeated at pitches higher or lower than in their first appearance), (4) when a familiar idea is altered or varied, but is still recognizable as being based upon the original.

Tempo: Children move in certain ways, directions, or at varying speeds (1) when music becomes faster or slower, (2) when selected tempi seem "appropriate" or "inappropriate" to the type of music being played.

Dynamics: Children move in certain ways or directions (1) when music is very loud or very soft, (2) when music gets louder (crescendo) and softer (decrescendo), (3) when selected dynamic levels are "appropriate" or "inappropriate."

Timbre (Tone Color): Children move in certain ways or directions (1) when they hear vocal sounds, then instrumental sounds, (2) when they hear strong contrasts between instruments, such as between flute and double bass or cello, or clarinet and tuba, (3) when they perceive "thin" tone qualities, then "thicker" ones, (4) when they hear male, then female voices, (5) when they hear high-pitched, then low-pitched instruments or voices, (6) when they hear a small group performing, such as a string quartet or woodwind ensemble, then a larger group, such as an orchestra or chorus, (7) when the same melody is played by a different group of instruments.

Although teachers need not adhere solely to a particular philosophical view, their options are increased by thinking in wider aesthetic terms. The tendency for most teachers has been to embrace referentialism when dealing with the arts, mainly because it is easier, or seems easier, to tell stories or evoke pictures of specific things. When adults become comfortable with the intrinsic elements of the arts, however, it can follow naturally that these, when properly presented, can provide important and less subjective opportunities for children. The students themselves draw conclusions as to the music's emotional climate and the moods it conveys. Teachers are freed from making such banal comments to children as: "Is this music happy or sad?" "How does this music make you feel?" and "Major keys signify happiness and minor keys, sadness." Instead, children respond in various ways to music's constituent elements, and eventually draw their own conclusions about feelings or "messages" contained therein. If children, on their own, prefer to adopt a referentialist view, so be it. But also having had experiences with absolute expressionism or formalism provides them with a larger group of viewpoints from which they may select. Does this not support Froebel's still valid plea to let children develop naturally, with minimal interference from adults?

ORFF

Whereas Dalcroze emphasizes movement, Orff deals primarily with instrumental experiences, often combined with song. Dalcroze and Orff have certain philosophical elements in common, however, including an interest in children's gradual development and natural growth processes. In that sense, Dalcroze and Orff are related to each other more than either one is related to Kodaly, despite certain superficial resemblances in methodology between the latter two. Key words to keep in mind with regard to Orff are bordun, ostinato, and rhythmic chant. Borduns, frequently open fifths such as the partial chords C–G or D–A, are repeated consistently, providing a drone to everything else happening in the music. In addition, these borduns supply needed rhythmic consistency to music in which young children participate, facilitating their ability to maintain accuracy. After the bordun is well established—that is, consistent and reasonably accurate—an ostinato can be added, superimposed upon the already sounding bordun(s). Since many songs in Orff methodology are pentatonic, even if children err in their articulation of an ostinato, they cannot really "make a mistake" in pitch, if all inappropriate tone bells or bars on xylophones and metallophones are removed in advance. This constitutes one distinct advantage of using pentatonic material, since harmonic success is virtually assured. At the early childhood level this is of particular importance, for we are not only teaching subject matter, but perhaps more importantly, feelings of self-worth and confidence. Once children have achieved such perceptions of themselves, their learning is vastly improved and expedited.

For an example of an Orff approach, let us take the familiar children's tune, "Rain, Rain, Go Away." Sung only on the syllables *so* and *mi*, this song, with these or other words, is known to children the world over. Researchers have found that the melodic minor third interval—in the key of C, this would be G *(so)* and E *(mi)*—is sung spontaneously by all youngsters, regardless of their race or nationality. Remember your own childhood days, when you sang "Johnny is a baby" *(so-so-mi-la-so-mi)*? Nobody knows for sure why you sang it on just those pitch levels, but on those levels you sang them, nevertheless. After the children's memories of the tune and the words of "Rain, Rain, Go Away" have been refreshed, a bordun consisting of, say, *do* and *so* (C and G) played simultaneously, is sounded on a bass xylophone. If the children's accuracy on this falters, they can be tapped gently on the shoulder in the correct rhythm and tempo, to help bring them up to standard. At this point, "Rain, Rain, Go Away" is sung while the bordun continues to sound. If all goes well up to this point, an ostinato is added, perhaps on a soprano xylophone, metallophone, or glockenspiel. This ostinato might be as simple as C′–E–G

repeated consistently throughout the song, in combination with the bordun. When the song has been sung two or three times, the ostinato can cease, then the bordun, or the reverse. If the children prefer to have a feeling of closure, in the tonal sense, an ostinato can be devised that ends on *do*, thus giving a feeling of finality to the music, especially if the ostinato ceases after everything else has stopped. All this results in a belief by the children that they have made real music, something they probably did not think themselves capable of previously. Their musical accomplishment has led also to psychological well-being, a not inconsiderable achievement, and extremely important for this very young age level.

THE CONCEPTUAL APPROACH

When the Music Educators National Conference in 1967 published *The Study of Music In The Elementary School—A Conceptual Approach* (Gary, 1967), that organization was responding to trends that had intensified during the previous decade. There had been criticism that general music programs encompasses only singing of songs, with occasional listening lessons thrown in. To some extent, these criticisms were well founded, and have since been addressed.

In the excellent scope and sequence chart included with this book, the authors make the following statement:

> The conceptual learnings outlined in the scope and sequence chart require *aural perception* which, in turn, is developed through *listening, kinesthetic rhythmic responses, singing,* and *playing of instruments.* Within a carefully planned musical environment, children will be stimulated through these activities to

Imitate	Differentiate
Explore	Verbalize
Discover	Memorize
Recognize	Recall
Identify	Evaluate

> These processes are essential in the development and clarification of musical concepts (Gary, 1967).

When one considers all ten of these processes, one begins to understand exactly what the conceptual approach encompasses. In many cases, children have been taught merely to memorize, then spew back that exact information, at which time they were considered to "know" the material. However, looking at this list of verbs immediately reveals that memorization is but one of ten activities in which children engage in order to conceptualize, and memorization is not even necessarily the most important among them. The valid assumption in the conceptual approach is that if youngsters have opportunities to engage in many or all of these processes, their ability to internalize increases. It follows, then, that if teachers are interested in providing more conceptually oriented activities, they must allow for more of these experiences to take place. They might ask themselves: "Am I merely a purveyor of information?" "Do I tell a lot, or do I encourage responses and comments from children?" "When I review, do I encourage the children to recall what they can before I 'fill in' any gaps?" "Must my children's responses be only verbal?" "What nonverbal options do children have in my classroom?"

If we return to the concepts of music mentioned earlier in this chapter (melody, rhythm, harmony, etc.), and choose harmony as the example to be dealt with, how might we go about enabling children to conceive of this important aspect of music? One way would be through listening, in which the children, after hearing and singing a song that has become familiar, respond to where the chords should change on an accompanying instrument (autoharp, guitar, or piano). It can be presented to children as a game in which they are asked to raise their hands each time they think the currently used chord should be changed. At first, responses are tentative and reluctant, but this soon improves as they naturally begin to understand the concept and have greater faith in what they hear. Not everyone in the group grasps this immediately, but there usually are enough who do to constitute a nucleus from which the others can be motivated. After many of the children have grasped the idea, they are ready to play the autoharp themselves on a simple one- or two-chord song.[1] Initially, they must be guided carefully by the teacher, who might need to tell them exactly what chords to play. Eventually, however, they should be weaned from this, so that they can begin to decide which of two chords is preferable at any given moment in the song being accompanied. When this freedom is ultimately achieved, and the children feel comfortable with this activity, their aural perception can be extended further by adding tone bells in chords (I, IV, and/or V_7 are the usual chords needed in many children's songs). One group plays these bells while another plays an autoharp, or two at the same time. Not only is this

---

[1]A one-chord song, such as a round, of course does not require chord changes. It is necessary, however, to help children with the motor skills required in strumming the autoharp while holding down the bars. For the youngest children, the teacher should hold down the bars as the child strums.

great fun for youngsters of all ages, but also they are beginning to conceive of harmonic principles, albeit on a simple level. The "fun" element should not be underestimated. As Froebel indicated in his prophetic writings in the last century, children's play activities provide the seeds from which their adulthood springs. If they perceive their learning experiences as "play" or "fun," and teachers can facilitate that perception, so much the better. Only adults make the differentiation between work and play. Since play is children's work, they make no such differentiation, and neither should their teachers.

KODALY

Unlike the Orff system, Kodaly emphasizes music literacy, that is, children's ability to read music notation and to use this skill in various ways, which lead ultimately to comprehensive musical understanding. Early in the program, children learn to read and articulate rhythmic figures through the use of echo clapping and stick notation. The most frequently used notes for early childhood and their rhythmic syllables are given in Figure 9.1, mostly in the Kodaly stick notation, which omits the head part of notes where feasible.

Figure 9.1.   Frequently Used Notes and Their Rhythmic Syllables

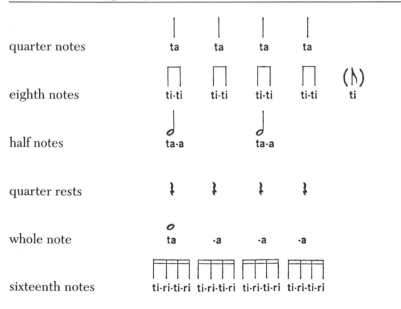

In behavioral terms, echo-clapping experiences enable teachers to observe and evaluate their students' understanding of rhythmic concepts. The teacher claps a simple rhythmic pattern at a consistent tempo (not too fast), say,

Another suitable pattern for clapping might be

where on the rest, either silence with hands to the sides and palms facing the ceiling (preferable), or actually saying the word "rest" is indicated. After children have engaged in many such experiences over weeks and months, including performing these rhythm patterns on classroom percussion instruments, further development and extensions are possible. For example, four patterns, such as those illustrated in Figure 9.2, numbered for quick identification, might be on a chart or chalkboard. (It is always desirable in education to include visual presentations when feasible.) As the teacher claps each pattern, the children determine which one they hear, and indicate their choice by calling out the proper number. Later, they might invent and articulate their own rhythms for other class members' responses. If approximately five minutes of each period are devoted to such rhythm activities, children's ability to read music can become almost second nature.

Figure 9.2.   Four Rhythmic Patterns

(1)   (ta   ta   ta   ta)

(2)   (ta   ta   ti-ti   ta)

(3)   (ta   ta   ta   [rest])

(4)   (ta   [rest]   ta   ta)

In terms of melody experience, the Kodaly system at the outset uses primarily pentatonic songs, that is, songs using only the five tones *do, re, mi, so,* and *la* in varying order. Initially, Kodaly uses *so-mi* songs almost exclusively, with *do, la, fa, re,* and *ti* gradually introduced later, after the children have grasped many of the concepts related to *so* and *mi*. Although seemingly restrictive, the *so-mi* song idea can be applied to literally hundreds of nursery rhymes and children's jingles, enabling them to "set to music" any of their favorites. Let us consider, as an example, "Humpty Dumpty." The entire rhyme is chanted on *so* and *mi,* using Kodaly hand signs. (These signs actually were developed by an Englishman named John Curwen, but have since been integrated into the Kodaly system.) Using hand signs for *so* and *mi* (see Figure 9.3) provides added dimension to the

Figure 9.3.   Kodaly Hand Signs

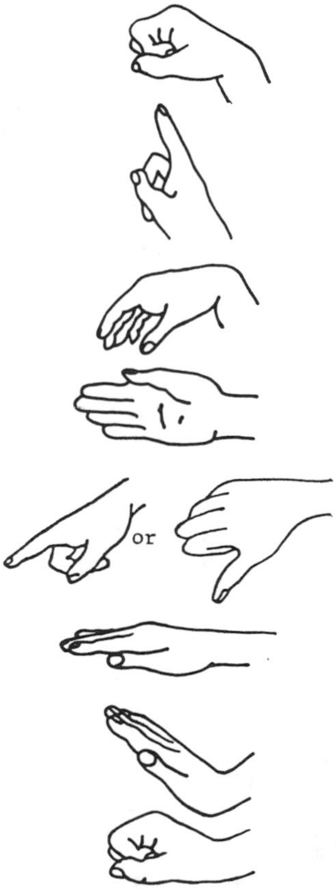

DO' (1')		(above head)
TI (7)		(at forehead level)
LA (6)		(near eye level)
SO (5)		(near chin level)
FA (4)	or	(near shoulder level)
MI (3)		(near chest level)
RE (2)		(just below chest level)
DO (1)		(just above waist level)

simplicity of the rhyme and its "tune." After children have mastered singing while making hand signs—and this usually requires time and effort for them to learn—they can play on pitched percussion instruments such as tone bells, the *so-mi* pattern to accompany their singing of "Humpty Dumpty." Since *so-mi* is part of the "universal chant of childhood," the entire experience can take on an inevitably natural quality for all to enjoy. If, at the early childhood level, one applies Kodaly methodology strictly, *so* and *mi* are used almost exclusively for as long as the first year, after which the other syllables are introduced gradually. If, however, teachers feel that their children are capable and interested, and they usually are, songs using the entire pentatonic scale (*do, re, mi, so,* and *la;* or, in the key of C Major: C, D, E, G, and A) may be used, as well as song materials using any tones of the major and minor keys.

THE ECLECTIC CURRICULUM

The Eclectic Curriculum utilizes elements of Dalcroze, Orff, and Kodaly in ways deemed appropriate for the particular children being taught. For example, Orff-like borduns and ostinati might be played as children sing and others move to the music being performed. There might be included with Kodaly-type activity, such as vocally articulating TA's and TI's, or recorded selections of important music, thus involving children in "listening" experience. Or, a conceptual approach might be included, involving such experiences as listening, singing, instruments, improvisation, physical movement, and skills activities. Goals including rhythm, melody, harmony, form, tempo, dynamics, tone color, and mood would play important roles here.

It is possible that so-called listening activity may be the most important music experience in schools, for most people will become consumers of music (concert and operagoers, record buyers, radio station listeners) rather than professional musicians. If one accepts music listening as an important facet of the school experience, using Kodaly as the sole method would be self-defeating. Teachers usually want to include live and recorded listening experiences with which children can interact (through movement, simultaneous singing and/or playing of instruments, dramatization, and pantomime), in addition to the cognitively oriented activities such as music reading. The so-called affective area, especially in arts education, might very well be equal in importance to the more readily evaluated cognitive domain. For very young children, should the two be separated, or are they not two sides of the same coin? Since one of the objectives of all education is to help students develop insights and to embrace concepts, one can look to the arts whose inherent nature encompasses, and often requires, internalization. If students are expected merely to memorize information, they hardly require education in the arts to do so, for many other fields of endeavor can teach this as well or better. Reimer (1970) sees the intent of art as providing insight, rather than being just informational. If this is indeed the case, the arts can nurture those abilities and attitudes that enable students to develop insights, leading to their interest in seeking out information when needed. For maximum comprehension to take place, should insight precede information, or should the reverse occur? If one agrees with Reimer, and there are reasons to believe his point is well taken, the former is more desirable. If one has insight, finding needed information becomes less difficult. If one merely has information, however, it does not necessarily follow that the uses and import of that information are known to the learner. In other words, developing insights can help one to gain concepts, while information alone may be isolated and out of the learner's mainstream of thought. Ausubel theorized that meaningful reception learning takes place only when ideas and understandings are properly classified hierarchically ("subsumed") by learners in relation to what they already know, thus becoming part of what he calls their cognitive structure (Leonhard, 1965a). In the connections that Ausubel views as essential to meaningful learning and retention, conceptualization and internalization form the core. What better vehicle to accomplish this than education in the arts?

IMPLICATIONS OF RESEARCH

One of the problems with music education research and philosophy is the fact that, until recently, the primary work was done not by music educators, but by psychologists, philosophers, and generalists. "It is the responsibility of music educators themselves to systematize and verify their principles and to develop a theoretical rationale for music education" (Leonhard, 1965b, p. 48). A major response to this suggestion was Bennett Reimer's A Philosophy of Music Education (1970), in which the author offered guidelines based upon aesthetic principles. Although Reimer does not deal specifically with the early childhood level, his commentary has implications for very young children, especially in the area of music listening, in which he advocates absolute expressionism, rather than referentialism or absolute formalism, as the most desirable framework in which to operate. This, however, does not preclude the possibility of utilizing referentialism or formalism on those occasions when they are deemed to be appropriate.

Research on the musical potential of young children indicates that, even at the ages of, say, four or five, they can learn to match pitch, accurately replicate subtraction and melodic patterns (through such experiences as echo clapping and repeating sung patterns), and, for the most part, correctly sing simple songs. Nye states that "writers in the field of music education conclude that early musical experiences must develop musical percepts in order that musical concepts can be acquired" (1979, p. 2). Implied in Nye's statement is that percepts—not only in music but perhaps in all learning—must be presented and received in such a way as to encourage and lead logically to conceptualization. Experiences in music must become, therefore, not isolated or merely entertaining, but integral parts of children's total learning process. If this occurs, the probability of retention and utlization increases considerably.

Nye also advocates, in addition to its being taught in its own right, music as "an integral part of all activities in the educational program— science, social studies, language, health, safety, values, and mathematical concepts" (p. 3). If one accepts this viewpoint as valid, one's anxieties about teaching music simply due to "lack of training" or "not being musically inclined," can be reduced or eliminated. Most teachers of early childhood are not "scientists," "mathematicians," "language experts," "historians," "artists," and "geographers," yet they all teach these subjects, usually free of undue anxiety. Why view music differently?

SINGING

Young children's sense of pitch tends to be variable, according to each individual. Some youngsters match pitches with ease, while others need further experiences and sometimes hard work to "find" themselves in terms of singing.

Nye and Nye offer some useful and valuable guidelines (1985, pp. 9– 19) for dealing with many kinds of musical problems for ages four to eight or nine. For singing, they suggest using tone matching games, singing conversations, and the use of pitch-giving devices (autoharp, bells, piano, and the like) to help assure proper ranges for young children.

A good rule to remember is that those pitches right on the lines and spaces of the treble staff usually are within the comfortable ranges of children. Middle C, although used occasionally, tends to be a bit low for youngsters, while F or G at the top of the treble staff may be a little high for them.

Using a pitch-giving device, therefore, followed by a clear "ready, sing" or "ready, begin" sung on the beginning pitch of the song, helps to assure that everyone will begin simultaneously, and at the same pitch. Consistent use of this essential procedure not only increases the teacher's accuracy, but improves student musicality as well.

When a child has difficulty matching the teacher's pitch, a useful device is for the teacher to match the child's pitch, then go on from there. This procedure is helpful not only because it shows that the teacher accepts psychologically what the child is about, but it enables the child, perhaps for the first time, to hear exactly what constitutes matching of pitches. This can be an important first step to help students internalize this intangible but essential aspect of musical understanding.

So-called monotones—people said to have but one tone in their singing repertoire—do not really exist, since almost everyone can sing on more than one pitch level. If a child tends to dwell on one or two pitches, such exercises as imitating ambulance and fire engine sirens, or "singing way up high" and "way down low" can alleviate this problem. Since these activities can be presented in game formats, they need not be embarrassing for the individuals in question, especially if *all* the children, regardless of their singing abilities, are asked, one at a time, to engage in this experience.

Another valuable game to determine pitch accuracy in children involves a "getting acquainted" activity, which enables the teacher to learn students' names while also determing their singing abilities. On the pitch levels *so-mi-la-so-mi*, teacher sings "my name is such-and-such, what is your name?" to which the child individually answers, hopefully at the same pitches, "my name is such-and-such." If the child's response is not accurate, the teacher can repeat, perhaps at the child's pitch levels, the same patterns, to determine the child's ability to match pitches. It is *not* recommended, however, that children at this point be drilled into "getting it right." The purposes here are to determine musical status, and to provide experiences on which later presentations involving singing can be based. Many times, especially at the early childhood level, just experiencing and maturing in themselves bring on solutions. There is something to be said for allowing things to "sink in" over a period of time, rather than looking for immediate success.

Piaget would classify children up to around age eight as being in the pre-operational stage of development. In this stage, "the child uses symbols crudely but manipulates reality by intuitive regulation rather than by symbolic operations" (Leonhard, 1965a, p. 54). If one accepts the Piagetian theory that children at early stages of development simply are not ready to engage in certain experiences, teachers can patiently allow for time to do its job, not just with singing, or with music, but in all areas of the curriculum. It is with these kinds of insights that research and experimentation make such valuable contributions to education.

In terms of song material, children should have opportunities to sing a wide assortment under various musical conditions. For example, singing with and without accompaniment, singing with recordings, and singing with accompaniments provided by other children each present distinct advantages. Nye and Nye, in reminding teachers of children's interest in immediate goals and need for feelings of success, suggest songs about "everyday experiences such as mother and family, playthings, people they know, pets and animals" (1985, p. 11). One is reminded here of Froebel's prophetic writings in the last century, for it was he who called attention to the importance of mother and family, children's play, and respect for all living things in an era when what youngsters were about was hardly of major interest to most adults (Alper, 1980).

When teaching new songs to youngsters, teachers need to keep in mind certain factors in order to determine how the song material can be conveyed most effectively. For example, short, simple songs, with only a few words can be presented in their entirety. After hearing the song two or three times, the children are asked to sing the song or join in as they feel comfortable. This is called the whole-song method, and works well with repetitious and brief songs, including many of those having refrains. Introducing longer and more complex songs requires a different methodology. Children hear the entire song once or twice (live and/or recorded), then echo, phrase by phrase or segment by segment, until they have sung the whole song. Repetitions, it is hoped, with variations such as instruments and dramatization, help the song to become part of their repertoire. This echo method, if presented in large enough segments to avoid tedium, can be very effective in song presentation.

Four general factors for determining appropriateness of song materials for young children include: (1) length; (2) amount of repetition; (3) text; and (4) degree of musical complexity (Hoffer & Hoffer, 1982, pp. 51–52). Short songs, due to youngsters' limited attention spans, usually have more impact on them. If there is repetition of text and/or music, such as a refrain or repeated phrases, young children can grasp musical meaning more easily, thus facilitating learning. Texts need to be on their level and within their frames of reference, while the degree of musical complexity must be geared to children's limited experience at this stage of their lives. Up-to-date though these recommendations seem, they nevertheless relate to those of an earlier era. For example, the books of Eleanor Smith (1858–1942), an excellent children's song composer, acknowledged Froebel's philosophy by stressing children's natural abilities and inclinations, their aesthetic development, and the need for brevity in song materials to be used with very young children (Alper, 1980). Such lessons of history not only continue to teach about the future, but also help to determine its direction.

MOVEMENT

Rhythmic activities for young children always have been acknowledged as essential to a comprehensive educational program. As most teachers and parents know, it is almost impossible and perhaps even unnatural for youngsters to remain quiet and still for long periods. Realizing this, teachers need to provide children with many kinds of physical opportunities that can be related to music. An effective and readily perceived way to do this is to use an Orff-oriented pattern, in which youngsters keep time to music they sing or hear by "patsching" (slapping one's thighs or just above one's knees with both hands, usually while seated), followed immediately by clapping. In a duple meter, such as 2/4, the patsch-clap alternation pattern occurs as the children sing, thus improving their accuracy in rhythm and tempo. In a triple meter, such as 3/4, the pattern would be changed to patsch-clap-clap (Wheeler & Raebeck, 1985). Not only are such experiences perceived positively, they offer the additional benefit of implementing Orff's recommendation that children have opportunities to do two things simultaneously. Careful attention, however, should be given to articulation here: clapping must be graceful and aesthetic, totally in keeping with the feeling and mood of the music being used. Patsch-clap techniques are suitable also for use when *chanting* nursery rhyme-type poems, in which the objective is to improve skills in rhythm and tempo, leaving pitch and other melody considerations for another time.

The most desirable and aesthetic movement experiences for children are those that relate to factors inherent in music, such as form, tone color, melody, tempo, and the like. By eliminating the need to pretend to be something unrelated to music, such as an animal or thing, one can encourage a child to concentrate on music itself as the primary focus.

Singing games—songs like "Here We Go Round the Mulberry Bush" in which the words tell or imply specific kinds of movement activities in which to engage—have always played important roles in music experiences for young children. But even here, in "going around the mulberry bush," some basically musical factors enter. The song is strophic, that is, has the same music for all its verses. Each time the child changes an activity to correspond with the words, the fact that only the words have changed, and not the music itself, needs to be brought out.

On the other hand, in a song like "Shoo, Fly," which is in a ternary form—three parts, designated as A–B–A—the formal design can determine types and directions of movement. For example, in part 1 ("Shoo, fly, don't bother me") children might move in a circle from left to right while holding hands. On the middle part of the song (section B: "I feel, I feel, I feel," etc.), being different music, they might take small steps inward, raising their arms as they reach the center (corresponding to the end of phrase 1), then back out while continuing to hold hands for phrase 2. When section A returns, accompanied by the same circular movement patterns, the fact that this is the same music as sung initially, is reinforced intrinsically. The ternary (A–B–A) design of "Shoo, Fly" may begin to solidify in the child's mind.

It is desirable to use this kind of traditional song literature with young children, teaching through participation, even if students initially tend to concentrate on actions rather than on music. The objective is to develop proficiency in singing-and-moving simultaneously (Haines & Gerber, 1984, p. 66). More experiences with A–B–A form, such as with the minuets and scherzi of most symphonies by Haydn, Mozart, Beethoven, and Schubert, can help youngsters to internalize further about this commonly encountered design in music. Physical activity can enhance children's understanding of a form concept in music, in this case A–B–A, where movement serves as the means, and understanding a specific formal design, the end.

Movement, of course, may be used to achieve other goals as well. Children might make up suitable physical responses to songs they sing, interpreting and dramatizing the words, or reacting to contours of melody. Some of the Dalcroze-like activities listed earlier might serve as starting points to encourage imagination and ingenuity. Movement for its own intrinsic purposes constitutes yet another valid use of this indispensable experience. In an essay entitled "The Initiation into Rhythm," Dalcroze summarized its implications: "(1) rhythm is movement; (2) rhythm is essentially physical; (3) every movement involves time and space; (4) musical consciousness is the result of physical experience; (5) the perfecting of physical resources results in clarity of perception; (6) the perfecting of movements in time assures consciousness of musical rhythm; (7) the perfecting of movements in space assures consciousness of plastic rhythm; (8) the perfecting of movements in time and space can only be accomplished by exercises in rhythmic movement" (1921, pp. 39–40). Dalcroze's fourth observation about consciousness and physical experience anticipates current views on how young children learn, and his fifth poses an intriguing idea, traceable to Froebel, about the "outer" eventually penetrating and nurturing one's "inner" modes of perception. Froebelian also in Dalcroze's eight-tiered summarization is his choice of a hierarchy to define the total implications of rhythm and movement. The father of modern early childhood education thus influenced the renowned movement expert, who currently enjoys renewed popularity. Considering the fact that Orff techniques also are in extensive current use, the spirit of Froebel's philosophy still looms large, and is not confined to the early childhood level.

INSTRUMENTAL EXPERIENCES

Activities involving instruments should play an important role in young children's experiences with music. In addition to hearing many instruments, live and recorded, youngsters should perform on various kinds, including orchestral, as well as the familiar classroom percussion types of so-called rhythm instruments. In addition, children, with adult guidance, can make their own. In the latter activity, however, it is essential that the products have musical and aesthetic tone qualities. A "tambourine," for example, does not emit a musical tone quality if it merely sounds like a paper plate with bottle caps attached. Easily overlooked, but also important, are other "sound producers," like parts of one's own body, as well as such commonly found items as twigs, stones, keys, coins, paper, and the like.

Swanson categorized "raw" sound sources as (1) body sounds, (2) vocal sounds, and (3) striking or rubbing sounds (1981, p. 24). In her "Sources of Instruments" section (pp. 25–28), she offers suggestions on how to make a drum, sandblocks, maracas and guiro, rhythm sticks, and tone blocks. To implement Swanson's suggestions, however, older children or adults are needed, since very young children do not yet possess the necessary skills. Perhaps the only successful instruments, in terms of sound, that very young children can make themselves, are various kinds of shakers, using uncooked beans or rice within cardboard oatmeal containers or frozen juice cans, or perhaps drumlike instruments, if they sound good. Aesthetically speaking, one is better off buying high quality classroom instruments, if those that are self-made fail to reach a valid level of sound quality. Ideally, both types of instruments should be available; however, the manufactured variety is clearly preferable when considered for purely musical reasons.

Regular orchestral instruments, such as bowed strings, clarinets, or trumpets, often are overlooked by teachers as not being available, or as too difficult for young children. As a result of this view, many people go through their entire lives without ever experiencing the joy of physical contact with orchestral instruments. It is suggested, therefore, that teachers of early childhood request that band and orchestra teachers in their schools bring instruments to the classroom for children's exploration and lend a few instruments to the class for day-to-day use and experimentation.[2] For example, it is fun to "buzz" on woodwind and brass mouthpieces, with or without the instrument itself attached.[3] Making oral "raspberries" seems to come naturally to children, so they delight in applying this technique to a music activity in school. Learning to hold a violin or cello bow, then applying it to the instruments' strings is a thrill no one should miss. Having such contacts can result in (1) positive and successful feelings about orches-

---

[2]Opposition by band and orchestra directors to such suggestions may be encountered, mainly because these teachers tend to view very young children as having little relationship with their instrumental programs. When it is pointed out to them that today's youngsters become tomorrow's participants in band and orchestra, this view can change. Classroom teachers also might consider purchasing second-hand orchestral instruments with funds from curriculum budgets or the PTA.

[3]It is necessary, of course, to sterilize mouthpieces before each use.

tral and band instruments; (2) opportunities to realize possible latent talent; (3) perception by children that instruments are "fun"; and (4) enhanced knowledge of pitch, dynamics, and tempo when orchestral and band instruments are used to demonstrate these concepts.

Discussions of classroom instruments and how they can be used appear in many textbooks. Sally Moomaw offers a particularly clear discussion, and the accompanying illustrations provide further clarification (1984, pp. 53–58). She gives specific suggestions as to how teachers may go about introducing instruments to children and various ways instruments can enhance a comprehensive program. Moomaw classifies into three categories instruments suitable for children: rhythm instruments, to be struck or scraped, producing a variety of nonpitched sounds; melody instruments, producing specific pitches; and accompanying instruments, producing several tones simultaneously, thus creating chords that can accompany melodies (p. 53). Particularly helpful to classroom teachers are Moomaw's sections on ethnic or exotic self-made instruments (pp. 71–83) and her selected bibliography of books on and about instruments suitable for use at the early childhood level. With current recommendations that multicultural factors be included in education, Moomaw's discussion of ethnic and exotic instruments seems particularly timely and apropos.

The "Developmental Sequence" and "Suggestions to the Teacher" on playing instruments by Leeper, Skipper, and Witherspoon (1979) are interesting and helpful. These authors' recommendations recall the conceptual approach: the child manipulates and experiments with instruments, listens to an instrument, uses an instrument as accompaniment, listens to music and identifies an instrument, plays an instrument, learns names of instruments, and so forth (p. 453). Land and Vaughan (1978) offer pictures of most classroom instruments, including some unusual ones from Asia, Africa, and India. These authors' diagram of a seating plan for an orchestra and list of orchestral instruments provide further valuable information for teachers of early childhood.

Andress, Heimann, Rinehart, and Talbert offer unique suggestions for using instruments with young children, such as sound exploration carrels into which children place themselves with various sound-producing devices. The "sound plays" on instruments include a "feel me, hear me" box, in which the musical environment is arranged in various ways (1973, pp. 48–52). And one should not forget the possibility of using instruments and other sound producers in songs and stories presented to or by children, preferably where the children themselves decide which instruments to use, when, and in what combinations. This insures that they will consider timbres and dynamic qualities of available instruments to determine their suitability. Andress and colleagues also suggest setting up a music corner, in which an old piano with

its strings exposed might be placed. Such an instrument might be "prepared" by children, i.e., its tone quality altered by attaching, for instance,
paper, or rubber erasers, or metal pieces like paper clips or bottle caps, to its
strings. This technique, it might be pointed out to children, is used by
contemporary composers like George Crumb and John Cage. A recording of
prepared piano music (see Cage, Wergo #60074), therefore, might be
played for children to hear and react to, preferably after they have done their
own experimenting.

Possibilities and directions for instrumental experiences need be confined only by the limits of one's imagination, ingenuity, and willingness to
experiment, even if in "unknown" territory. All this is very much in keeping
with Froebel's view that, in addition to calling on receptive and reflective
qualities, early education should encourage creative and executive attributes
as well. This, of course, applies equally to children and teachers.

LISTENING

With the possible exception of singing, listening experiences are more
likely to be retained and utilized in later life than all others one encounters
in school music. Effectively teaching suitable listening techniques to children, therefore, should occupy an important place in each classroom teacher's methodology. One of the secrets of achieving this goal lies in: (1)
inventing and finding materials and methodologies that have aesthetic and
educational merit, (2) using compositions worthy of the time spent in
thinking about them, and (3) actively stimulating children to use their
mental and physical capabilities. Formidable though it may seem to implement this, it is not as difficult as one might think, for once children's interest
is captured, they learn with eagerness and the rest usually falls into place.

Some examples of techniques that are likely to capture children's
interest in listening to music include: (1) mirroring: children follow the
teacher's, then each other's, hand, arm, face, and/or torso movements which
correspond to the phrases of (preferably slow and legato) music, such as the
Intermezzo from Bizet's *Carmen*, (2) bounding or rolling large balls in time
to slow or moderate music, (3) moving in various ways or directions when
changes (in melody, tempo, dynamics, rhythm, harmony) occur in the music
being played, (4) using visuals (charts, pictures, diagrams) to increase
interest and to focus children's attention on specific elements, (5) outlining
melodic contour (children move bodies or arms to the general contours of
melody being heard, drawing outlines of these structures in the air), (6)
moving to music that is stopped suddenly or unexpectedly, at which point
children "freeze" into pretzel or other shapes, shortly after which the music

resumes, (7) placing on a chart or chalkboard in stick notation the rhythm of a melody which children follow by singing the pitches on TA and TI as they are heard on a recording, or children point to each note as it is played, and (8) using veil-like scarves as extensions of one's own body to illustrate, through movement, the mood, shape, or form of a particular piece of music. These are just a few of many possibilities for relating music listening to the spontaneous interests and experiences of children, without the encumbrance of telling stories or conjuring up pictures not really related to music. Music is about music. If it illustrates stories or pictures at all, it does so only tangentially.

Excellent and specific suggestions for presenting listening activities can be found in Lewis's (1983) booklets and recordings which, although specially arranged for this series,[4] include a variety of compositions suitable for use at the early childhood level. For example, children are asked to follow stick notation patterns which show the rhythm of a melody, and to sing on TA and TI as these are heard on the recording of an instrumental piece.[5] Or the teacher places two melodic patterns on the board, with tone syllables indicated under each note. Children initially sing each pattern using tone syllables—at this level, *so* and *mi*, possibly also *do* and *la*—thus helping to solidify the music in their minds before they are asked to utilize this new information. Children then raise one finger when they hear pattern 1, and two fingers for pattern 2. Other effective techniques in Lewis's series are, for third graders to step in three meters, that is, to begin feeling changes in meter from two, to three, to four, counting aloud as these changes occur, and moving accordingly.[6] Another interesting suggestion among hundreds in Lewis's series of books, is for first graders to: (1) raise hands when a certain melodic or rhythmic pattern occurs, (2) perform *so-mi* hand signs with these patterns when appropriate, (3) make a mark on a piece of paper or on the chalkboard each time they hear the pattern, and/or (4) play the pattern (if a simple one, like *so-mi*) on a melody instrument, such as bells or metallophone. Lewis's lessons, by dealing with music on an intrinsic basis—that is, in terms of melody, rhythm, form, and the like—tend to illustrate

---

[4]In order to render Lewis's recorded musical examples suitable for use with children, many have been specially arranged. When feasible, however, it is preferable to use recordings of musical compositions performed as far as possible as they were envisioned by their composers, without arrangement or simplication. One of many advantages to the now difficult-to-obtain RCA "Adventures in Music" series of recordings, is its variety of fine listening selections performed in their entirety.

[5]Certain types of (East) Indian music feature the *tabla* (drum) player singing the beats of the drum as he plays them with his hands. Children like listening to such recordings and enjoy trying to mimic the sounds.

[6]Note the implications for behavioral objectives in these activities. Teachers can *observe* exactly what students perceive, as reflected in their physical responses to music.

absolute expressionism or formalism, rather than referentialism. Rarely in Lewis's outlines do stories or pictorial elements interfere with essentially musical considerations. If it is deemed desirable to tell the story of, say, a piece of programmatic music, or to provide children with extramusical background information, the optimum time to do this is after children have explored the music through listening, movement, instruments, and notation.

CREATIVE AND IMPROVISATIONAL EXPERIENCES

Opportunities for children to invent, originate, or implement on their own probably receive inadequate time and attention in most classrooms. Whether this is due to fear of the unknown on the part of the teachers, trepidation about "losing control," or queasy feelings about not being able to predict an outcome, there are several activities in which children can initiate musical experiences, with minimum risk of things going awry. Among these is the technique of clapping patterns to individual children for them to respond to with a clapped "answer." Initially, some children will be reluctant or lacking in ideas, but enough can do this activity to keep it going. Everyone is asked to keep a steady beat by patsching/clapping, until their individual turn arrives. The teacher, of course, should demonstrate typical "questions" and "answers," before calling upon individuals. A "question" might be a clapped pattern such as TA TA TA TA or TA TA TI-TI TA, to which the child might respond with TA TA TA (*rest*) or TA TA TA TA. "Questions" and their "answers" can be clapped, vocalized with TA's and TI's, or both. Once children become comfortable with these activities, they can make up their own antecedent patterns for their peers to respond to with consequent models. This can turn out to be fun for everyone.

Bergethon and Boardman suggest that children learn to play a rhythm pattern of long ($\d$) and short ($\quarternote$) notes as given, then make up some new ones using long and short sounds in their own original combinations (1979, p. 79). These authors suggest also that children write simple rhythmic patterns, and then compose a musical story, after they have had experience with hearing existing examples (pp. 80–81). Other possibilities include encouraging children to create their own movement or dramatization patterns when the teacher plays steady beats on a drum, altering the tempo to emphasize that concept, or changing the volume to illustrate dynamics. Findlay gives specific suggestions for games with balls, after which children could make up their own variations or invent new games of their own (1971, pp. 73–74). Children might be asked to show how they move when they are tired; when it is dark; when it is slippery; when they are in a hurry; or when they come home from school (p. 54). Although such experiences are initiated by the teacher, exactly how individuals respond differs with each child, and these differences should be encouraged and acknowledged. Landis and Carder include a picture of youngsters physically illustrating the end of a musical phrase (1972, p. 15). If recognition of phrases and where they begin or end is to be the goal, teachers would encourage children to show these musical phenomena *in their own ways*. The possibilities for individual expression are great, but successful only in an atmosphere of safety, trust, and acceptance.

What, then, should music provide for youngsters at the early childhood level? It can be the door which, when opened, discloses realizations and insights about their lives, their relationships, themselves. It can be an important source for what Maslow (1968) termed "peak experiences," moments where one becomes complete and serene with, and within, oneself. Maslow viewed having many such experiences as leading to what he termed "self-actualization," an extremely positive process of "becoming," toward which most of us consciously or subconsciously strive. Although it might sound mundane, music also adds, from the many choices available to children, a further option for something to do. Because of its manifold phases and infinite possibilities for mental and physical activity, music helps to fill those gaps which, when overlooked, frequently lead to boredom. To recall Froebel once again, music offers to children a psychological and historical link with the past, something which the great German educator-philosopher believed they sense instinctively, as revealed in their simple yet spontaneous games and pastimes. Education in the arts can be difficult to explain or justify to those administrators and members of the community who tend to think solely in terms of tangibility and utility. What educators need to make more widely known is the fact that the arts, in providing insight, inner understanding, and appreciation of one's own being, contribute significantly to the facilitation of learning.

REFERENCES

Alper, C. (1980). The early childhood song books of Eleanor Smith: Their affinity with the philosophy of Friedrich Froebel. *Journal of Research in Music Education, 28* (2).

Andress, B. L., Heimann, H. M., Rinehart, C. A., and Talbert, E. G. (1973). *Music in early childhood*. Washington, DC: Music Educators National Conference.

Bergethon, B., and Boardman, E. (1979). *Musical growth in the elementary school*. (4th ed.) New York: Holt, Rinehart and Winston.

Cage, J. *Sonatas and Interludes for Prepared Piano*. Wergo : 60074.

Dalcroze, E. J. (1973 [1921]). *Rhythm, music and education*. (H. F. Rubenstein, Trans.) Aylesbury, Bucks (England): Hazell Watson and Viney Ltd.

Findlay, E. (1971). *Rhythm and movement: Applications of Dalcroze eurhythmics*. Evanston, IL: Summy-Birchard.

Gary, C. L. (Ed.) (1967). *The study of music in the elementary school—A conceptual approach*. Washington, DC: Music Educators National Conference.

Haines, B. J., and Gerber, L. L. (1984). *Leading young children to music*. (2nd ed.) Columbus, OH: Merrill.

Hoffer, C., and Hoffer, M. (1982). *Teaching music in the elementary classroom*. New York: Harcourt Brace Jovanovich.

Land, L. R., and Vaughan, M. A. (1978). *Music in today's classroom: Creating, listening, performing*. (2nd ed.) New York: Harcourt Brace Jovanovich.

Landis, B., and Carder, P. (1972). *The eclectic curriculum in American music education: Contributions of Dalcroze, Kodaly, and Orff*. Washington, DC: Music Educators National Conference.

Leeper, S., Skipper, D., and Witherspoon, R. (1979). *Good schools for young children*. (4th ed.) New York: Macmillan.

Leonhard, C. (1965a). Learning theory and music teaching. In *Comprehensive Musicianship, CMP2*. Washington, DC: Music Educators National Conference.

Leonhard, C. (1965b). The philosophy of music education—present and future. In *Comprehensive Musicianship, CMP2*. Washington, DC: Music Educators National Conference.

Lewis, A. G. (1983). *Listen, look, and sing (Grades 1, 2, and 3)*. Morristown, NJ: Silver Burdett.

Mark, M. (1982). *Source readings in music education history*. New York: Schirmer.

Maslow, A. (1968). *Toward a psychology of being*. (2nd ed.) New York: Van Nostrand.

Moomaw, S. (1984). *Discovering music in early childhood*. Newton, MA: Allyn and Bacon.

Nye, R., and Nye, V. (1985). *Music in the elementary school*. (5th ed.) Englewood Cliffs, NJ: Prentice-Hall.

Nye, V. (1979). *Music for young children*. (2nd ed.) Dubuque, IA: William C. Brown.

Reimer, B. (1970). *A philosophy of music education*. Englewood Cliffs, NJ: Prentice-Hall.

Swanson, B. (1981). *Music in the education of children*. (4th ed.) Belmont, CA: Wadsworth.

Wheeler, L., and Raebeck, L. (1985). *Orff and Kodaly adapted for the elementary school*. (3rd ed.) Dubuque, IA: William C. Brown.

CHAPTER 10

Social Studies
in Early Childhood Education

BLYTHE F. HINITZ
Trenton State College

"All that we take for granted in the pattern of our social lives, in our conceptions about people in the past, present and future, here and elsewhere, children have to learn" (Robinson, 1983, p. 263). This statement outlines the basis for the inclusion of the social studies in curricula for young children. Even though there is agreement that the social studies do have a place in early childhood education, there is a lack of agreement as to the definition and scope of these studies (Price, 1982, p. 175). The National Council for the Social Studies views the social studies as basic to all educational experiences, and defines them as:

> a basic subject of the K–12 curriculum that 1) derives its goals from the nature of citizenship in a democratic society that is closely linked to other nations and peoples of the world; 2) draws its content primarily from history, the social sciences, and in some respects from the humanities and science; and 3) is taught in ways that reflect an awareness of the personal, social, and cultural experiences and developmental levels of learners. (NCSS, 1984, p. 251)

Others as well have attempted to define the social studies. In 1975 the disciplines constituting the social studies were listed as: political science, economics, history, jurisprudence, anthropology, and sociology (*Fifty-sixth Yearbook of the National Society for the Study of Education,* 1975, p. 31).

Reflecting the ideas of both social studies educators and early childhood specialists, this chapter will present (1) the historical perspectives of social studies in early childhood, (2) economic concepts, (3) spatial and geographic concepts, (4) temporal and historical concepts, and (5) sociological concepts.

HISTORICAL PERSPECTIVES

The social studies were not stressed in the elementary schools prior to 1884. Before this time, geography, civics, and history were part of the elementary school curriculum; however, the disciplines were hardly distinguished from each other (Jarolimek, 1981; Handler, 1985). The teaching of subject matter was the school's major emphasis. The chief function of the curriculum was to transmit this knowledge. According to Hass, "Curriculum was a body of knowledge to be learned by those who came to school and its mastery at one grade was usually the basis for moving on to the next" (1983, p. 299).

In 1866 the National Education Association passed a resolution stating that the "common schools" (elementary schools) should "be required by legislation to teach the principles of American government, both state and national, in order to inculcate love of country and encourage respect for authority and obedience to the law" (Handler, 1985, p. 10). The NEA, together with the American Historical Association, officially adopted the term "social studies" in 1916.

At the same time, the "Kindergarteners" were focusing on the questions of the purpose and nature of the curriculum, including the body of knowledge called the social studies. A multidisciplinary approach to the curriculum, in opposition to those holding a strict Froebelian philosophy, was being advocated by Susan Blow and Alice Temple. Temple divided the kindergarten curriculum into three major subjects: (1) national objects and phenomena, (2) human beings and human activities—home and community life, and (3) the products of human intelligence—literature, art, and music (Weber, 1969, p. 93).

Carolyn Pratt's projects and Lucy Sprague Mitchell's work on geographic concepts heralded an era in early childhood social studies called the "here and now" curriculum (Hertzberg, 1981). Pratt's projects at the Bank Street School in New York emphasized child development. These projects were developed in reaction against the subject-centeredness of educational settings at the time. The ideas of John Dewey relating to group work and play as a means of socializing children into democratic living were incorporated into her projects.

Other educators were also changing their ideas on the nature of human beings, and thus the purpose and scope of the school's curriculum. The theories of such humanists as Maslow, Rogers, and Combs received wide acceptance in the education community beginning in the 1930s and 1940s.

Now the emphasis of the curriculum was based solidly on the learner, rather than on the subject matter, by both early childhood and elementary educators. Human beings were viewed as rational, rather than passive beings to be manipulated. Believing that human beings were motivated by social needs, educators looked to the social studies as the "integrating center" of the curriculum.

Comprehensive units were organized around social studies themes, and were planned to include all the other curriculum areas (Jarolimek, 1981; Charlesworth & Miller, 1985). There was stress on pupil involvement in activities and human relations education, even though somewhat superficially. Teachers were supposed to become "color blind" with regard to ethnic and racial differences, and teach the concept that people were more alike than different (Jarolimek, 1981).

During the 1960s social studies, like the rest of the curriculum, came under intense scrutiny. Curriculum reform and reconstruction characterized the period. Post-Sputnik demands focused on some of the weaknesses of the existing humanistic approach to social studies. Once again the discipline, or the subject, received a great deal of attention as educators and scientists sought to determine the "structure of accumulated knowledge" (Rowen, Bryne, & Winter, 1980).

Bruner's *The Process of Education* (1966) dominated the thinking of educators. "The disciplines were studied in increasingly greater detail and depth, using more sophisticated procedures of inquiry" (Robinson, 1983, p. 83). Curriculum development projects, such as "Man, a Course of Study," originated at several universities and were funded both by private foundations and the government. These had as their goal the identification of key concepts, or the structure of knowledge, as well as the major ways of knowing in each body of knowledge.

Bruner proposed a spiral approach to the curriculum. The big ideas, or key concepts, could be used to coordinate the knowledge or content sequences with the cognitive stages of the learner, so that at each successive stage children would be dealing with concepts they could understand, but in progressively greater complexity and depth.

Nevertheless, the attempt to make patterns and develop key concepts in each body of knowledge proved unexpectedly difficult. Young children's "ways of knowing" and learning processes were difficult to understand. Further, the structure of any given content area was equally difficult to identify. Spodek (1974) also noted the problem of integrating theories, methods, and knowledge among the social sciences without losing the integrity of each source of knowledge. Training or retraining teachers to take a conceptual approach to content, as opposed to the long-established fact or skill accumulation basis for curriculum was also a problem (Schwartz & Robison, 1982).

Jarolimek (1981) states that during this time the social studies were in disarray. The "new social studies" had little impact on the curricula of the nation's schools, with the exception of those curriculum development projects that were published in marketable textbooks. The period of social unrest from 1965 to the early 1980s led to calls for relevant curricula. The civil rights movement and the opposition to involvement in Vietnam affected all of society, including young children. Partly as a result of these social changes and the call for relevance, today's social studies curriculum incorporates both a humanistic and subject matter approach. Primary textbooks emphasize the pluralistic, multiethnic, and multicultural nature of our nation as well as focusing on key ideas of the disciplines of the social studies (Cartwright, 1979; Hinitz & Baker, 1979; Rice & Cobb, 1979). Jarolimek (1981) expects this trend to continue.

The back-to-basic movement is also reflected in the current social studies curricula, because knowledge, skills, and values are needed for children to function effectively in the culture of the United States and the world. The social studies are viewed as a thread through the entire school day for preschool and primary children (Charlesworth & Miller, 1985, p. 35). Children can acquire basic skills through social studies content using the traditional early childhood learning center environmental organization. Children are free to move at their own pace, make mistakes, and solve or adjust to possible problems. They have the opportunity to work cooperatively to develop social studies skills and concepts.

ECONOMIC CONCEPTS

"Economic concepts are more closely related to young children's lives than is generally realized" (Robison & Spodek, 1965, p. 39). Fox states that there are three things "that children of whatever socioeconomic status bring to school in their economic 'knapsacks': economic attitudes, direct experience, and cognitive capacities. The interplay of these three factors accounts for the formal economics children are able to learn and for the extent to which children become economic actors" (1978, p. 478). Young children's "knapsacks" are the result of their direct experiences and are relatively "unprocessed." The situations they encounter are only fully understood at a later time. Some economic experiences, such as buying, working, trading, owning, and saving, are examples of common economic experiences of children that are only later understood in terms of the concepts of profit and loss, or cost and selling price.

The ability to understand complex economic concepts appears to be related to growth and maturation (Mugge, 1968). "A more complete and more accurate understanding of economic concepts comes with age in the absence of classroom economics instruction. . . . These changes in understanding are influenced by cognitive development" (Fox, 1978, p. 480).

Schug and Birkey (1985) and Kourilsky (1985) have tied stages of growth in economic reasoning to developmental theory. Schug articulated three categories of economic reasoning which can be compared to Piagetian stages of cognitive development. These are: (1) the unreflective level, which approximates Piaget's preoperational stage, and is exemplified by highly literal reasoning based on the physical characteristics of objects or processes; (2) the transitional or emerging reasoning level, exemplified by higher-order reasoning, and similar to Piaget's concrete operational stage; and (3) the reflective level of economic reasoning, based on children's ability to use abstract ideas, and approximating Piaget's formal operations level.

Piagetian theorists believe that the egocentric, static, and irreversible nature of a preoperational child's thought affects children's ability to make sense of both direct experience and formal instruction in economics. Concurring with this view, Robison and Spodek (1965) report that a number of concrete experiences with profit and loss did not help kindergarten children understand these concepts. Kourilsky (1985) states that "although participation in The Mini-Society does appear to result in transfer of economic reasoning to everyday decision making, age is a potent factor in determining economic cognition . . . as they get older students appear to have a greater proclivity to utilize cost benefit analysis" (p. 12).*

On the other hand, a number of investigators do believe that economic concepts can be taught to young children (Davison & Kilgore, 1971, p. 24; Keoller, 1981; Kourilsky, 1977). In fact, Paul Samuelson, the Nobel Prize–winning economist, is quoted in the *Wall Street Journal* (Mackay-Smith, 1985, p. 1) as agreeing that "young children, and I speak as a father of a six year old, pick up basic notions of economics very quickly."

Senesh (1960) found that first-grade children, when motivated by teachers, enjoyed discovering the study of economics and were able to master concepts such as production of goods and services and the economic aspect of neighborhoods. Darrin (1968) studied more than 1,000 children from kindergarten through the sixth grade and concluded that some economic concepts, such as travel, communication, labor as related to production, and the wise use of goods and time, were able to be successfully taught to even the youngest children.

Kourilsky and Kehret-Ward (1984) found that kindergarten children

*The Mini-Society is a form of curriculum in which the classroom is structured to mimic the larger society. Stores, banks, post offices and so on are constructed, and children earn and then spend "pretend" money.

were able to link work and entitlement (distribution of rewards), although the linkage appeared to be stronger for males than females. Kourilsky and Hirshleifer (1976) also identified nine concepts as comprehensible to kindergarten and primary-age children:

scarcity
decision making
opportunity cost and cost-benefit analysis
production
specialization
distribution, consumption, and savings
demand and supply
business organization and business venture
money and barter.

In her work on the Kinder-Economy and the Mini-Society, Kourilsky (1985) introduced these and other basic concepts to children through concrete experiences, simulations, learning centers, worksheets, games and filmstrips.

No doubt an interaction between children's knapsack of economic experiences, growth and maturation, and educational experiences is involved in the teaching and learning of economic concepts. Further, educators and parents alike support the idea that early experiences in economics education can be of value.

Buffon (1979) holds economic concepts such as scarcity, division of labor, and production, can be taught to and used by young children. The Elkhart Project, a twelve-year experimental program begun in 1958, was based on the assumption that with proper motivation children at all grade levels can work effectively with economic concepts and that teachers can present these ideas to reflect the basic structure of economic knowledge. The project documented the success of including economics in the pre-school/primary curriculum.

The materials developed by the Iowa Council on Economic Education, the Center of Economic Education, and the Joint Council on Economic Education also endorse the inclusion of economic concepts in programs for children. These organizations have outlined the scope and sequence of economic concepts and give teachers practical suggestions for introducing these to children.

Kourilsky (1977) found that parents were highly supportive of the teaching of economics at the kindergarten and first-grade level. "Economics provides a unique opportunity for parents to discuss with their child a school subject that permeates their very existence" (p. 190).

GEOGRAPHY AND SPATIAL RELATIONS

Both geography and history are important to social studies education for young children. "It has been noted that to be an educated, cultivated, civilized, person one needs a sense of time and place in the social studies with time being the special province of history and place the special province of geography" (Helburn, 1985, p. 2).

The general public often perceives geography in a traditional sense, as a subject primarily concerned with factual knowledge. In contrast to this stereotyped perspective, others see the study of geography differently. Long ago Lucy Sprague Mitchell (1934) defined geography as consisting of facts (locational and physical geography) and relationships (human geography). Today's definitions of geography reflect these ideas. Gritzner (1985) defines geography as involving the study of "WHAT (physical and human features of the earth's surfaces), WHERE (locational data), WHY (explanation of processes or causative agents), and WHAT OF IT (significance)" (p. 1).

The most recent set of *Guidelines for Geographic Education* (1984) lists and defines five themes considered fundamental in geography. These are:

1. location or position on the earth's surface;
2. a sense of place;
3. understanding of relationships within places;
4. the movement of humans interacting on the earth and in regions;
5. how the earth is formed and changes.

Each of these concepts is studied and is believed central for young children. Teachers are familiar with such units as "Self in Space," "Homes and Schools in Different Places," and "Neighborhoods."

As with economic concepts, children's understanding of geographic concepts appears to be at least partially developmental. From early infancy, children learn concepts of geography. The infant develops an awareness of his or her surroundings, and during the first months of life differentiates self from nonself. Visual and tactile senses provide the means by which children understand their immediate environment. By age three, children are able to distinguish between objects that are near and can be grasped, and those further away, as well as the space boundaries of their immediate environment, such as the bedroom or yard.

Initially, children work out their own location and then go on to discern the whereabouts of other objects in the immediate environment. Through vision and increased mobility, children expand their space boundaries. As object permanence develops, children begin to comprehend the relationships that exist between objects and self, and between objects in themselves.

By the early preschool years, there is a growing awareness that other objects exist outside of the immediate environment. The spatial relationships between objects is also understood. Children express these concepts as they play with blocks, sand, and water, and construct with other materials. From preschool through the primary grades, children use language, as well as drawings of maps and other symbols, to represent their perceptions of their environment (Hewes, 1982; Catling, 1978).

Piaget outlined the stages of children's understanding of their geographic world. Children's thinking, according to Piaget, is dominated by artificialism and animism (1964). This means that children attribute life and consciousness to the earth, sun, moon, and stars, as well as to living things. Throughout the early years, children are even confused about what constitutes life. Three-year-olds will attribute life to anything that does or does not move. Until age seven or so, children believe that cars, planes, rivers, and clouds have life and consciousness. Around age eight or nine, children begin to distinguish between movement caused by machines or imposed externally and movement stemming from the internal life of organisms.

Until about the age of nine, children also retain the belief that every object, including natural bodies, was "made for" a purpose (Piaget, 1964). A natural object, such as the sun, a lake, or a mountain, is made for warmth, boating, or climbing, and because it has been made for humans it is closely allied to them. Children believe things were either made by humans or that the things created themselves for the purpose of humans.

According to Piaget, instruction is useless in fostering what is considered in Western culture as more accurate concepts of the physical world. He regards children as manufacturers of their own thought. "That is, the groundwork of the whole intellectual life of children is derived from manipulation and manual activism" (1964, p. 384). Thus no direct instruction can "prove to a mind inclined toward animism that the sun and the clouds are neither alive nor conscious. Neither can adult teaching undeceive the child for the child incorporates into his own mentality, even the best lesson, whatever the subject" (p. 165). Piaget uses the example of ten-year-olds who have been taught the process of evaporation in school, who then use this information to support their artificialistic thinking. After instruction, some children claim that the clouds get a bucket to fetch the water from the rivers.

Nevertheless, this doesn't mean that teachers just wait around for children to grow. Children appear to learn concepts of geography as they learn everything else, through their own experiences. Through free play in the home or preschool, and unstructured times spent out-of-doors, children develop a sense of their personal geography (Hews, 1982, p. 95). "Since children's experiences begin in the immediate communities in which they are brought up and since these communities are functioning in terms of the present day culture, it is the school's job to begin with the children's own environment whatever or wherever it may be" (Mitchell, 1934, p. 16). Mitchell, like others (Hewes, 1982; Seefeldt, 1984), advocates use of the laboratory method, thinking not training, the discovery method, and using facts, not merely knowing them, as the means of teaching geography.

Mapping, a vital tool of the geographer, provides an example of how children's understanding of geographic concepts and their natural explorations of their environment are used to plan and implement educational experiences. Piaget and Inhelder (1965) note that children must achieve formal thinking before they can understand mapping. Towler (1971) supports Piaget's theory and suggests that children's egocentric thinking negates their ability to read maps.

Spencer, Harrison, and Darvizeh (1980) report that children as young as three, without hesitation or need for prompting, interpreted aerial photographs and maps in geographical terms. They identified roads and decoded other environmental features. They could not explain perspective, or how the photos and maps were constructed or produced; yet they could read the photo as a map. They concluded that children, when not confused with the need to explain perspective or representation, do have concepts of maps.

Atkins (1981) tested three- and four-year-olds on their understanding of the shape of the earth, using the globe as a model, and on their understanding of directions, how to orient a map, distance and scale, symbols location, the earth-sun relationship, and abstract location. With the exception of abstract location, which children could not handle, the children already had acquired all of the other map and globe skills.

Mugge (1968) found that the majority of first-grade children studied were able to juxtapose streets, cities, states, and countries on the same plane instead of placing them in a hierarchical order. Children in second grade showed somewhat more maturity by placing those areas nearest to them, such as the street and the city, first in hierarchical order.

Others also have successfully introduced children to mapping skills. Working with disadvantaged kindergarten children, Portugaly (1967) found that these children could understand the relationship between the earth and sun and were able to develop some of the skills necessary to work with maps. McAulay (1962) demonstrated that many second graders could use simple maps to secure information, to transfer oral directions to map abstractions, and to make comparisons and judgments. Robison and Spodek (1965) introduced concepts of distance, direction, and scale to kindergarten children. They found the children were able to develop the skills needed to relate a map to a geographic area, to locate places using distance and direction, and to abstract information from map symbols.

Copeland (1974) outlined the stages of development in children's ability to make maps. Children in Stage 1 could use the concept of proximity and enclosure to locate objects. Between the ages of four and seven, children in Stage 2 could locate and develop reference points and locate items by *left, right, in front of,* and *behind.* In Stage 3, after the age of seven or so, children could locate or place items on another map without difficulty.

Cautioning that young children are limited in their ability to understand spatial and map relationships, Preston and Herman (1974) nevertheless maintain that it is important and feasible to introduce children to the concept of maps and to the skills of map reading. However, teachers must be aware of children's limited understanding of spatial relationships and be able to sequence experiences with maps according to the appropriate developmental level. Formal teaching of map skills is not recommended.

Experiences with mapping begin with the concrete: the building, making, or drawing of maps. All mapmaking stems from children's own experiences and should be on a continuum from the concrete to the abstract (Seefeldt, 1984). Using incidental experiences and children's interests, teachers can build further understanding of the concepts involved in mapping, those of symbolization, perspective, scale, and representation.

HISTORY AND TEMPORAL RELATIONS

The teaching of history and temporal relations to young children, like most geographic concepts, is "largely ignored" (Jantz & Klawitter, 1985). Although all may agree that the teaching of history is important to enhance students' comprehension of their social environment, and that history is valuable not only as a record of past events, but also as a means for understanding the present structure of society (Pietig, 1980), there is little information on how this can be done.

As the study of history involves understanding of time, the work of Piaget on children's understanding of temporal relations is useful. Piaget noted that children's ability to structure uniform intervals comes much later than ability to deal with temporal order. "Therefore, at the preschool level it is desirable to help children develop time concepts based on temporal order" (Hess & Croft, 1981, p. 167).

Piaget (1965) indicates that there are two types of time concepts exhibited by children. There is intuitive time, which is limited to successions and durations given by direct perception, and operational time, which uses logic as a basis for the operational understanding of time. Piaget examined the concept of time by investigating the concepts of succession, duration, and simultaneity. He states, "But if time as we suggest is the operational coordination of the motions themselves, then the relations between simultaneity, succession, and durations must first be constructed one by one" (1971, p. 3).

Applying Piaget's theory of development of time concepts to children's perceptions of time in terms of age, Copeland (1974) found that children at Stage 1 have primitive intuitions of their age in terms of a sibling's age. During Stage 2, some children did not realize who was born first, but they did know that the age difference between them remained the same. Other children could identify who was born first, but felt that as a younger sibling grew, he would eventually become the older because he would become bigger than the older one. Children at Stage 3 were at the formal operations level. They could understand the idea of succession of events in time in terms of order of births.

Elkind (1981), also using Piagetian theory, identified three important areas for the development of time concepts in young children: clock time, calendar time, and psychological time. Clock time is based on the formation of time intervals such as hour and minute. Children learn that these terms have definite meanings; by the time they reach kindergarten age, they are using these terms in their conversations even though an internalization of the duration of the interval has not yet been developed.

The development of clock time was described by Springer (1952) for four- to six-year-olds. Children first begin to associate activities with the regular daily class schedule. Soon they associate this schedule and time by the clock. Then they develop concepts of hour, half hour, and quarter hour. Later, children begin to set the hands of cardboard clocks to definite times. In this study, Springer concluded that specific instruction was more success-ful than incidental instruction in developing concepts of clock time in young children.

Calendar time is formulated upon the temporal or sequential order of events. Calendar time includes as a basis the development of indefinite time concepts such as *first, last, next, later, sooner, before,* and *after.* The development of these concepts is accomplished primarily by experiences. Jantz (1976) describes how Kim, two and a half, was beginning to develop the concept of *later.* One night her grandmother called on the phone and Kim asked if she could visit Grandma. She was told that she could go later. Her previous experiences with the concept *later* meant *never.* Even though things were promised to her in the future, she was unable to associate an event by the time it actually occurred with the previous promise. At age three, when told something would take place later, Kim wanted to know "how soon later?" or "how far later?"

Understanding calendar time might also be fostered through children's storybooks. Many folktales for young children begin with "once upon a time," which reflects an indefinite concept of the past, whereas other stories introduce children to the seasons and the passage of time. As they begin to grasp the idea of calendar time, children begin to form concepts of *week, month, year,* and *seasons* that eventually lead to the development of a true historical perspective. There is conflict, however, as to when this occurs. Mugge (1963) reported that second graders had little sense of historic time, while Wesley (1946) felt that many children can learn historical time concepts.

The third type of time Elkind identifies is psychological. Elkind (1981) suggests that time should be studied spontaneously for egocentric or self-centered motives and the desire to learn more about oneself. Accordingly, whatever is taught to children should be tied to their personal and immediate surroundings (p. 436). Unfortunately, the study of the time past seems far removed from children's daily experiences.

Whatever temporal and historical concepts are taught are "suggested by the bright eyed children themselves" (McMillan, 1919, p. 235). Beginning with self, children are introduced to the history of their own lives. The routines that take place during the day are interpreted and recorded for children. The changes that occur in the children themselves, their own growth, their development of skills, knowledge, and abilities, are recorded as well. The past is studied in relation to children. They discuss the things they did yesterday, as well as a past they have not experienced. Handling relics and objects of the past, comparing tools from long-ago to tools used today, as well as relating with elders, gives children an awareness of a more distant, historical past and an understanding of life before their time.

SOCIOLOGY

The study of society viewed as a system, a set of interacting parts, is sociology. One basic function of society is socialization (Robison & Spodek, 1965, p. 76). The study of sociology begins with the study of self—*Who am I?*—and continues to the study of group membership in the family, classroom, school, neighborhood, city, state, nation, and world.

Becoming a socialized person involves at least two dichotomies: first, the need for the child to develop a strong sense of self—that is, learning to become assertive, autonomous, and individual—and at the same time, learning to cooperate with the group, giving up some of the individuality and uniqueness the child has worked so hard to develop. Second, to become a socialized person involves the dichotomy between attachment and detachment. Psychologists have theorized that unless children have had a strong attachment to a nurturing figure in the early years, they will have difficulty becoming detached and be unable to reach out in trust to form relationships with others. Social growth is sequential and seems to develop in a series of stages. With greater physical and intellectual ability and emotional maturity, and with more and more experiences with others, children grow in their capabilities as social people and in their concepts of sociology.

It has been suggested that one's self-concept is the single most important factor affecting behavior. Individuals have the capability to develop a set of feelings and cognitions about themselves consisting of cognitive, affective, and behavioral components. Self-concept is an abstraction, an organization of ideas (Combs, Avila, & Purkey, 1971). The self-concept "is based upon the separation of one's self from society; it permits the individual to accept or reject society's evaluations of the self, and determines the value of the social world to the individual" (Jantz & Klawitter, 1985, p. 71).

Damon and Hart (1982) propose a developmental model to explain growth of the self-concept. The model proposes four levels of development: (1) infancy and early childhood, (2) middle and late childhood, (3) early adolescence, and (4) late adolescence. Children at all ages are believed to have some knowledge of the constituent self-schemes, but in the course of their development each scheme changes in character. During infancy the physical self and the fact of membership in particular social relations or groups is believed to develop. The active self, developing during middle and late childhood, is characterized by understanding that one's activities are considered with reference to the reactions by, and the approval or disapproval of others. Social and personality characteristics dominate during early and late adolescence.

The self-concept develops, but it is also learned behavior. Children learn who they are, first from the interactions with the parents, others in their family, then neighbors, peers, and the significant others in the school and the larger community. Through interactions with others, "each of us learns that he or she is liked or unliked, acceptable or unacceptable, a success or a failure, or respectable or of no account" (Combs, Avila, & Purkey, 1971, p. 48).

Once in a group setting, the self-concept is affected by the interactions of the teacher. Schempp, Cheffers, and Zaichkowsky (1983) found that children who were encouraged to participate in classroom decision making held more positive feelings about self than those in teacher-dominated classrooms. Teachers who were rated as highly interactive and positive were also found to be rated highly in fostering positive self-esteem (Benninga, Guskey, & Thornburg, 1981).

With a strong sense of self, children are ready to learn to relate to others (Turiel, 1983). Learning constructive social behavior involves a "gradual transition from the characteristic egocentric behavior of the three year old to the relatively more sociocentric behavior of the eight" (Walsh, 1980, p. 16). To do this, children must integrate social knowledge and concepts of human relationships (Bandura, 1977), developing the ability to (1) regulate themselves, seeing themselves as the principal agents of their own change, (2) use symbols, acquiring the capacity to use symbols to represent events, analyze conscious experiences, communicate, plan, create, and imagine, (3) observe and experience, and (4) take part in reciprocal interactions.

Social behavior can be learned through imitating a significant other person (Bandura, 1977; Denzin, 1982). It was observed that models who were willing to share increased children's sharing behavior (Harris, Wolf & Bear, 1967).

Teachers who themselves demonstrate sharing behavior, who respond freely and openly to children's needs, and who show more evidence of sharing themselves, seem to foster children's sharing (Prescott, Jones, & Kritchevsky, 1967). The physical environment also seems to influence children's sharing behavior. Children confined to small play spaces with limited equipment and toys are more frequently observed fighting than those in larger spaces with an adequate number of toys (Prescott, Jones, & Kritchevsky, 1967).

Cooperation, the opposite of competition, is another kind of social behavior that can be fostered through the example of other children as well as teacher behavior. Learning to cooperate means learning to work with a group. Sutton-Smith (1975) sees the repetitive or unison behavior of children—such as the copying of one another that starts with one banging a block on the table, followed by another child, until everyone is banging blocks—as the beginnings of cooperation and social coordination.

Reducing competition is believed to foster cooperative behavior. Playing games that do not have winners and losers, respecting each child as a unique individual, making sure each child has an opportunity to participate in special tasks, and using specific praise may foster cooperation. Other activities that require more than one child for successful completion, such as building a fort or a rabbit hutch, planting and maintaining a garden, making soup or baking bread, putting on a puppet show, or even building with blocks, are examples. Weingold and Webster (1964) asked two groups of children to work on à mural. In one group, each child was rewarded for the group product. In the other, children were told that only the child doing the best job would receive the reward. In the first group, there was an increase in friendly, cooperative behavior and peer interactions; in the other group, less attention was given to the product, and there was more boasting and depreciating behavior.

Learning about self and other ultimately should lead to the development of multicultural understanding. The general goal is to develop an understanding of, and appreciation for, all racial, ethnic, and cultural groups. "We need to teach children to embrace and value the many cultures that make up our nation not only for the transmission of beauty, but because we can't afford the cost in terms of human potential that any other course would demand" (Hornbake, 1984). Education that is multicultural need not be an "add on to an already overcrowded curriculum. Rather, it should be an ongoing, ever present attempt to promote among our students a recognition and understanding of the similarities and differences among people. A sense of self esteem and a genuine respect for other individuals and groups are encouraged at all times" (University of Maryland/Charles County Teacher Corps Project, 1981).

Lambert's and Klineberg's study (1967) provides the most complete explanation of how children learn from others. From their study of children in a number of nations, Lambert and Klineberg concluded that how the concept of "own group" is taught has important consequences. The process of establishing this concept sometimes apparently produces an exaggerated and caricatured view of one's own nation and people. The goal of education should be to teach the concept of belonging to a group without implying the inferiority of any other group.

SUMMARY

Historically the social studies have been a definite part of the curriculum in early childhood education. Nevertheless, teachers are continually faced with many decisions relating to what content to include and how best to introduce this content to children. The research base is uneven. Piagetian theory, the foundation of much of the research, offers strong support for an activity-based process of experiential learning that is presumed to lead to the formation of social studies concepts.

REFERENCES

Atkins, C. L. (1981). Introducing basic map and globe concepts to young children. *Journal of Geography, 30*, 228–33.

Bandura, A. (1977). *Social learning theory*. Englewood Cliffs, NJ: Prentice-Hall.

Benninga, J. S., Guskey, T., & Thornburg, K. (1981). The relationship between teacher attitudes and student perception of classroom climate. *Elementary School Journal, 82*, 66–75.

Bruner, J. S. (1966). *The process of education*. Cambridge, MA: Harvard University Press.

Buffon, C. M. (1979). *Economic education through literature: Primary grades k–3*. Topeka, KS: Kansas State Department of Education. ERIC Document Reproduction Service No. ED 177 572.

Cartwright, C. A. (1979). Global perspectives on early childhood education. In Pennsylvania State Department of Education & Research for Better Schools, *Curricular dimensions of global education*, pp. 63–82. Harrisburg, PA: ERIC Document Reproduction Service No. ED 187 629.

Catling, S. J. (1978). The child's spatial conception and geographic education. *Journal of Geography, 71*, 24–28.

Charlesworth, R., & Miller, N. (1985). Social studies and basic skills in the early childhood classroom. *Social Studies, 76*, 34–37.

Combs, A., Avila, D., & Purkey, W. (1971). *Helping relationships: Basic concepts for the helping professions*. Boston: Allyn & Bacon.

Copeland, R. (1974). *How children learn mathematics: Teaching implications of Piaget's research*. New York: Macmillan.

Damin, V., & Hart, D. (1982). The development of self understanding from infancy through adolescence. *Child Development, 53*, 841–64.

Danzin, N. (1982). The significant others of young children. In K. Borman (Ed.), *The social life of children in a changing society*. Hillsdale, NJ: Lawrence Erlbaum.

Darrin, G. (1968). Economics in the elementary school curriculum: Study of the District of Columbia Laboratory schools. Ph.D. diss., University of Maryland, College Park.

Davison, D. G., & Kilgore, J. H. (1971). A model for evaluating the effectiveness of economic education in primary grades. *Journal of Economic Education, 3*, 17–25.

Educators for Social Responsibility. (1985). *Taking part*. Boston: ESR.

Elkind, D. (1981). Child development and the social science curriculum of the elementary school. *Social Education, 45*, 435–37.

Fox, D. (1978). What children bring to school: The beginnings of economic education. *Social Education, 42*, 478–81.

Gritzner, C. F. (1985). Geography's role in the back to basics movement. *Social Studies Teacher, 6*, 1–5.

Guidelines for Geographic Education. (1984). National Council for Geographic Education and the Association of American Geographers.

Handler, B. S. (1985). *Women in the NEA and in the field of social studies, 1857–*

1912. Presented at the annual meeting of the American Educational Research Association, Chicago, IL.

Harris, F., Wolf, M., & Bear, D. (1967). Effects of adult social reinforcement on child behavior. In W. Hartup & N. Smothergill (Eds.), *The Young Child*. Washington, DC: National Association for the Education of Young Children.

Hass, G. (1983). *Curriculum planning: A new approach*. (4th ed.) Boston: Allyn & Bacon.

Helburn, N. (1985). Geography as basic. *ERIC Keeping Up*. Boulder, CO: Clearinghouse for Social Studies/Social Science Education.

Hertzberg, H. W. (1981). *Social studies in the elementary school*. (56th Yearbook). Chicago: National Society for the Study of Education.

Hess, R. D., & Croft, D. J. (1981). *Teachers of young children*. (3rd ed.) Boston: Houghton Mifflin.

Hewes, D. W. (1982). Preschool geography: Developing a sense of self in time and space. *Journal of Geography, 31*, 94–97.

Hinitz, B. F., & Baker, L. M. (1979). *Selected Bibliography for the International Year of the Child*. Philadelphia, PA: World Organization for Early Childhood Education.

Hornbake, D. W. (1984). *Guidelines for multicultural education*. Baltimore: Maryland State Board of Education.

Jantz, R. K. (1976). Social studies. In C. Seefeldt (Ed.), *Curriculum for the preschool-primary child*. Columbus, OH: Charles E. Merrill.

Jantz, R. K., & Klawitter, K. (1985). Early childhood/elementary social studies: A review of recent research. In W. B. Stanley (Ed.), *Review of research in social studies education: 1976–1983*, pp. 65–121. Washington, DC: National Council for the Social Studies.

Jarolimek, J. (1981). The social studies: An overview. In H. D. Mehlinger (Ed.), *The social studies. (80th Yearbook)*. Chicago: National Society for the Study of Education, pp. 3–18.

Keoller, S. (1981). Economics education applied to early childhood. *Childhood Education, 57*, 5, 293–96.

Kourilsky, M. (1985). Children's use of cost-benefit analysis: Developmental of nonexistent. Presented at the annual meeting of the American Educational Research Association, Chicago, IL.

Kourilsky, M. (1977). The kinder-economy: A case study of kindergarten pupils; acquisition of economic concepts. *The Elementary School Journal, 77*, 3, 182–91.

Kourilsky, M., & Hirshleifer, J. (1976). Mini-society vs. token economy: An experimental comparison of the effects on learning and autonomy of socially emergent and imposed behavior modification. *Journal of Educational Research, 69*, 376–81.

Kourilsky, M., & Kehret-Ward, T. (1984). Kindergartners' attitudes toward distributive justice: experiential mediators. *Merrill-Palmer Quarterly, 30*, 1, 49–63.

Lambert, W., & Klineberge, O. (1967). *Children's view of foreign people: A cross cultural study*. New York: Appleton-Century Crofts.

Leeper, S. L., Witherspoon, R., & Day, B. (1984). *Good schools for young children* (5th ed.) New York: Macmillan.

Mackay-Smith, A. (1985). Economics 101 goes to the first grade and the kids eat it up. *Wall Street Journal*, Jan. 4, 1985, p. 1.

McAulay, J. D. (1962). Some map abilities of second grade children. *Journal of Geography, 61*, 3–9.

McMillan, M. (1919). *The nursery school*. London: J. M. Dent.

Mehlinger, H. D. (1981). *The social studies*. (80th Yearbook). Chicago: National Society for the Study of Education.

Mitchell, L. S. (1971 [1934]). *Young geographers*. New York: Bank Street College of Education.

Mugge, D. (1968). Are young children ready to study the social studies? *Elementary School Journal, 68*, 233–40.

National Council for Geographic Education. (1984). *Guidelines for Geographic Education: Elementary and Secondary Schools*. Macomb, IL: Western Illinois University.

National Council for the Social Studies. (1984). In search of a scope and sequence for social studies. *Social Education, 48*, 249–62.

Pagano, A. L. (1978). Providing foundations for social studies in early childhood education. *Social Science Record, 15*, 3, 26–9.

Peitig, J. (1980). Lawrence Kohlberg, John Dewey, and moral education. *Social Education, 44*, 3, 238–42.

Piaget, J. (1964). *The child's conception of the world*. New York: Harcourt Brace Jovanovich.

Piaget, J. (1971). *The child's conception of time*. New York: Ballantine.

Piaget, J. (1965). *The moral judgment of the child*. New York: Free Press.

Piaget, J., & Inhelder, B. (1969). *The psychology of the child*. New York: Basic Books.

Portugaly, D. (1967). A study of the development of disadvantaged kindergarten children's understanding of the earth as a globe. Ph.D. diss., Columbia University. *DAI, 28*; University Microfilms No. 4056A.

Prescott, E., Jones, E., & Kritchevsky, S. (1967). *Group day care as a child rearing environment*. Pasadena, CA: Pacific Oaks College.

Preston, R., & Herman, W. (1974). *Teaching social studies in the elementary school* (4th ed.) New York: Holt, Rinehart & Winston.

Price, G. C. (1982). Cognitive learning in early childhood education: Mathematics, science, and social studies. In B. Spodek (Ed.), *Handbook of research in early childhood education*. New York: Free Press, pp. 264–94.

Rice, M. J., & Cobb, R. L. (1979). *What can children learn in geography? A review of research*. Boulder, CO: ERIC Clearinghouse for Social Studies/Social Science Education. ERIC Document Reproduction Services No. ED 166 1088.

Robison, H. F. (1983). *Exploring teaching in early childhood education*. (2nd ed.) Boston: Allyn & Bacon.

Robison, H. F., & Spodek, B. (1965). *New directions in the kindergarten*. New York: Teachers College Press.

Rowan, B., Bryne, J., & Winter, L. (1980). *The learning match: A developmental guide to teaching young children*. Englewood Cliffs, NJ: Prentice-Hall.

Schempp, P. G., Cheffers, J., & Zaichkowsky, L. (1983). Influences of decision making on attitudes, creativity, motor skills and self-concept of elementary children. *Research Quarterly for Exercise and Sport, 54*, 183–89.

Schug, M. C., & Birkey, C. J. (1985). The development of children's economic reasoning. Presented at the meeting of the American Educational Research Association, Chicago, IL

Schwartz, S., & Robinson, H. (1982). *Designing curriculum for early childhood*. Boston: Allyn & Bacon.

Seefeldt, C. (1984). *Social studies for the preschool-primary child*. (2nd ed.) Columbus, OH: Charles E. Merrill.

Senesh, L. (1960). The organic curriculum: A new experiment in economic education. *Counselor, 20*, 43–56.

Spencer, C., Harrison, M., & Darvizeh, Z. (1980). The development of iconic mapping ability in young children. *International Journal of Early Childhood, 21*, 2, 57–64.

Spodek, B. (1974). Social studies for young children: Identifying intellectual goals. *Social Education, 38*, 1, 40–45.

Springer, D. (1952). Development in young children of an understanding of time and the clock. *Journal of Genetic Psychology, 80*, 1973–94.

Sutton-Smith, B. (1975). Play as a novelty response. In J. Andrews (Ed.), *One child indivisible*. Washington, DC: National Association for the Education of Young Children.

Towler, J. (1971). Egocentrism: A key to map reading ability? *Social Education, 35*, 893–98.

Turiel, E. (1983). *The development of social knowledge*. Cambridge, England: Cambridge University Press.

University of Maryland/Charles County Teacher Corp. (1984). *Education that is multicultural: a curriculum infusion model*. College Park: University of Maryland.

Walsh, H. M. (1980). *Introducing the young child to the social world*. New York: Macmillan.

Weber, E. (1969). *The kindergarten: Its encounter with educational thought in America*. New York: Teachers College Press.

Weingold, H., & Webster, R. (1964). Effects of punishment on cooperative behavior of children. *Child Development, 35*, 1211–16.

Wesley, E. B. (1946). *Teaching social studies in elementary schools*. Lexington, MA: D. C. Heath.

CHAPTER 11

New Views on Movement Development and the Implications for Curriculum in Early Childhood

SANDRA R. CURTIS
Joyce Hakansson Associates

Research in movement development has benefited from technological advances in new and refined techniques for analyzing movement behavior. While studies employing these techniques have provided valuable information, such as data on spontaneous movement patterns in babies (Thelen, 1979), and interception of moving objects by babies (Von Hofsten, 1980), there has been a more important development. It is a change in perspective that has been coming over the last fifteen years. There has been a shift away from focusing on the tasks that children are performing to a focus on children themselves as movers.

The scales and normative data used for motor assessments by pediatricians, psychologists, and child development specialists were collected in the 1930s and 1940s by Gesell and Amatruda (1941), Shirley (1931), and Bayley (1935). These scales focus on very task specific behaviors: Does the child sit by herself? At what age did the child walk? In what manner does the child climb stairs? Current research and writing now look at children themselves and the process that occurs as they move. Many authors (Keogh & Sugden, 1985, Gentile, 1975; Wickstrom, 1977; Ridenour, 1978; Curtis, 1982) have expressed viewpoints in which children are seen as part of a dynamic interaction between themselves and their environment.

This change of focus is very compatible with current curriculum practices in early childhood education. Children are viewed as agents of change as they interact with their environment. They are themselves the dynamic process of learning. They are wholly involved in the learning process from their creative fantasies to the movement skills they express through their play.

The environment is viewed as the impetus for the child's interaction. The teacher becomes the facilitator of that environment. Children create, discover, explore, extend, challenge, and enhance their own development through their initiative, imagination, and interaction. One goal of early childhood education is to nurture creative, independent thinkers and problem solvers. Movement provides a vehicle for problem solving. The teacher can create movement situations in which children interact with their environment. In finding solutions to these movement problems, children facilitate their own development. Movement then serves the function of integrating children's interactive repertoire with their educational experience.

This chapter will examine current thinking in movement development and the implications for curriculum in early childhood programs.

MOVEMENT MODELS

It is valuable to include a theoretical paradigm for movement when discussing a total approach to early childhood programming. Movement is a dynamic component in young children's development. Since development is a process of change resulting from both internal and external influences, it becomes imperative to examine those influences and how they affect change. Models are then needed as reference points from which the changes can be evaluated.

Several authors (Teeple, 1978; Keogh & Sugden, 1985; Keogh, 1971) have provided models that focus on the interactive nature of children's development and the phenomena that cause change to occur. Figure 11.1 shows the factors influencing motor development. These factors, which include body size, neuromotor control, psychomotor information, heredity, and the environment, affect the child (performer), the task and their interaction, all in the context of growth at the time. Some factors, such as body size, greatly influence children's movement possibilities.

Keogh and Sugden (1985, pp. 7–10) conceptualize the production of movement in a similar manner. Figure 11.2 shows their conceptual representation. Movement is seen as a result of the neuromotor system causing muscles to contract and limbs to move in timed sequences. Human interactions take place in a psychological as well as a biological environment—the "inner surround," as the authors refer to them. The "outer surround" is the traditional environment in which human beings move.

Keogh (1971) has previously focused on the issue of movement control as an important unifying theme in motor development. He suggests that

Figure 11.1. Factors Influencing the Basic Components of the Motor Development Model

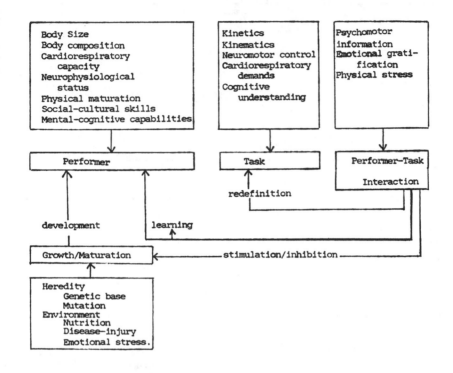

Source: J. Teeple (1978). "Physical Growth and Maturation," in M. V. Ridenour, ed., *Motor Development Issues and Applications,* Princeton, NJ: Princeton Book Company, p. 8.

part of the development process includes gaining control over body movements. Initially, infants are confronted with the task of moving themselves through their environment. As they grow, their task is to refine the accuracy of their movement responses in the environment. They learn to do movements faster and more forcefully, as well as slower and more gently.

Moving slowly is an important indicator of developing movement control. As an example, young children have great difficulty riding a bike slowly and maintaining their balance, yet the ability to accomplish slow, controlled bike riding increases with age. Several studies have looked at children's ability to control slow movements (Gipsman, 1973; Constantini et al., 1973; Constantini & Hoving, 1973; Maccoby et al., 1965). These studies

Figure 11.2.   A General Representation of the Production of Movement

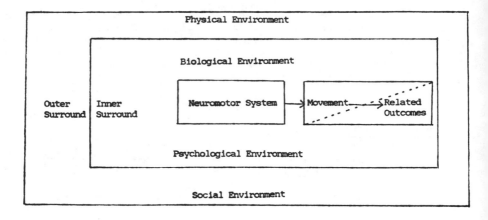

Source: J. F. Keogh and D. Sugden (1985). *Movement Skill Development*. New York: Macmillan, p. 8.

collectively show that the ability to control slow movements improves from age four to nine.

Gipsman's (1973) study made an interesting observation on how children use various strategies to perform movement tasks. In one task, each child was asked to walk along a defined path "as slowly as you can." Rather than actually taking slow controlled walking steps, some children's strategy was to take small but very rapid steps. It seems that the children perceived the solution to the task as one in which they were to take as long as possible to get to the end of the path. They solved the movement problem in a manner that did not result in an anticipated response. When children solve movement problems in unexpected ways, it is important for observers of children's movement to describe accurately these solutions and then to reflect on the cognitive, perceptual, and neuromotor demands of the task. Observers might also applaud the children's creative problem-solving approach. Gipsman's descriptive analysis of the strategy differences in solving a movement task is a good example of the shift in focus from the task (how slowly the child could walk the path), to what the child was actually doing while performing the task. It looks at the children's movement process, rather than merely the result, or the product of the children's movement (the time it took to complete the task).

Other components of movement control that Keogh and Sugden (1985) have elaborated on are: consistency, constancy, and competence. Movement consistency is "a reliable set of movements for coping with everyday recurring movement problems" (Keogh & Sugden, 1985, p. 199). These consistent movement responses become the building blocks of a movement repertoire. Movement constancy is the ability to use consistent movement responses in appropriate situations. These two components of movement control, consistency and constancy, act dynamically in relation to one another and reinforce each other. Young children can often be seen pouring water from different sized pitchers into different sized cups. In this, they are working to develop consistency and constancy in their movement response. For such a task, the motor control required to avoid spilling any water is a considerable task for any three-year-old. Using a large pitcher as opposed to a small pitcher presents a variation on the task and consequently changes the movement response.

Movement consistency and constancy must interact for children to achieve competence. The challenge to achieve competence is very strong in early childhood. Competence means achieving an effective solution to a movement problem, and can come in small or large increments. Pouring water successfully into one cup from a small pitcher versus any sized cup from any pitcher are two examples of the incremental levels of competence. These three components—consistency, constancy, and competence—interact to define a domain in which children and the environment create a dynamic interplay of continually evolving movement problems and solutions.

Griffin and Keogh (1982) have suggested another dimension in the development of movement control. Movement confidence is a combination of an individual's perception of his or her competence and factors related to the movement task itself. It is an "interplay of self-perceptions of competence, enjoyment of the movement sensations, and potential for physical harm." (Griffin & Keogh, 1982, p. 388). For instance, the excitement of skiing down a steep, narrow trail can improve an advanced skier's confidence if it is successfully accomplished. Considerable skill is required to complete the task. Conquering a movement challenge that is tinged with an element of risk contributes to an increase in movement confidence.

Falling backwards is an interesting task that gives some indications of movement confidence in young children. Children can stand with their backs to a mat or mattress and then fall onto their backs. Some children will fall back relaxed and gleefully. Others will have very anxious expressions and stiff bodies, while still others may turn at the last minute and land on their stomachs. While the precise interplay of movement confidence and the development of movement control is not clear, neither are the variables that might predict or enhance movement confidence. It does, however, provide another parameter from which to view the development of movement control.

Four additional components have been discussed by Gentile (1975) and Spaeth-Arnold (1981) that add layers of complexity to the broader picture of movement control. Gentile proposed that movements were divided into situations where the body is stable (body stability) and those in which the body is moving (body transport). The functioning of arms and legs provides another factor which complicates a movement. Running would be classified under body transport, with no limb manipulation. If the child were kicking a ball while running, then there would be limb manipulation. If the child were running on a grass soccer field alone, the environment conditions themselves would be stable. However, add a team in a soccer practice and the environment conditions will be changing constantly. Spatial dimensions become critical when the runner tries to kick the ball through an opposing team. The temporal requirements impose yet another layer of difficulty. Timing a kick to pass and outrun another player to get to the ball, or timing a fake to throw the defending player off balance so as to run past, become movement problems that demand high skill levels. The environmental and spatial-temporal components clearly complicate the factors affecting movement control.

Motor development specialists (Espenschade & Eckert, 1967; Wickstrom, 1977) agree that all fundamental motor patterns emerge by age five. After this age, no new patterns develop. However, the process of refinement of these rudimentary skills takes from ten to fifteen years. Wickstrom did extensive research on the development of fundamental motor patterns (walking, running, jumping, kicking, throwing, and catching). He views these patterns as the basic language of movement. Just as notes are the basic language of music and become musical compositions, fundamental movements develop into mature patterns that become the basis of sport skills.

Changes occur in the fundamental movement patterns with opportunities to practice the movements and with maturation. This is where the interplay between consistency, constancy, and competence becomes evident. Figure 11.3 describes the developmental changes that occur as the fundamental pattern of throwing progresses from the initial stage through the mature stage.

Robertson (1977) has looked further into the issues regarding movement stages. She has investigated the process of change in certain movement sequences, determining whether the change is consistent for all children or is a matter of individual difference. From her work in analyzing overarm throwing patterns, she concludes that although there may be an orderly sequence of movement phases, there is considerable variation in the

Figure 11.3.   Throwing

Stage 1	Stage 2
1. Feet are stationary.	1. Some body rotation to side opposite throwing arm.
2. Ball is held near ear. Child pushes ball straight down.	2. Hand holds ball cocked behind the head.
3. No rotation of body or step forward.	3. No foot movement.

Stage 3	Stage 4
1. Arm and trunk movements are the same as in Stage 2.	1. As movement is begun, body weight shifts to side with ball.
2. Child steps forward on foot that is on same side of body as throwing arm.	2. Arm is brought up and back behind head.
	3. Weight is transferred by a step to foot that is on the opposite side of body as throwing arm.
	4. Trunk rotates to opposite side.
	5. Ball is released as elbow is straightened with a whipping motion.

Source: S. Curtis (1982). *The Joy of Movement in Early Childhood*. New York: Teachers College Press, p. 24.

order of changes for different body parts. For example, trunk changes may precede or follow changes that occur with the arms or legs. Since there does seem to be considerable individual variation as motor skills develop, Robertson's ideas coincide with other researchers' conceptualizations on development including those of Gesell (reciprocal interweaving) and Piaget (equilibration). Their collective works argue for not viewing development as a sequence of age-ordered tasks.

Cognitive and perceptual components of movement tasks limit the development of movement control. However, they also provide for much of children's growth potential, since children's processing abilities improve with age. Todor (1979) has looked at general processing abilities in relation to a movement task through an application of the neo-Piagetian theory of Pascual-Leone (1970). First, he analyzed what an effective versus an ineffective performance would be on a task in which a crank handle is turned around to a bumper, then released, and the hand is then moved to touch a target. The most inefficient strategy, with the slowest performance time, would treat the three movements consecutively. Todor hypothesized that according to Pascual-Leone's work, the mental capacity (M demand) needed for the ineffective strategy would be $M = 1$. In other words, one item can be attended to at a time. More efficient strategies would chain the movements together and increase the M demand to $M = 2$ or $M = 3$. He then made performance predictions based on the M demand and children's ages. The ability to deal with increased M demand purportedly improves with age. His findings supported his hypotheses.

While Todor's work seems promising for future investigations, Connell's (1980) work suggests some cautions. From testing she conducted with five- to eight-year-olds on reaction time tasks, short-term memory and schema learning, Connell found that mental capacity seemed to influence task performance on complex processing tasks more than on simple ones. She points out the difficulty of assigning schemes within the neo-Piagetian context when the performer and/or the environment are moving.

Movement relies heavily on input from the perceptual systems, primarily from visual and kinesthetic resources. Keogh and Sugden (1985, pp. 295–97, 383–85) have proposed a three-step approach to solving movement problems that takes into consideration the perceptual demands of tasks and how children of varying ages respond to them. (See Figure 11.4.) Step I calls for reading and specifying the requirements for the body and the environment. Step II concerns selecting and generating a movement plan. Step III is for executing the movement plan. The authors combine Steps I and II into the movement preparation phase and Step III as the movement execution phase. Babies and young children are able to accomplish Step I but they are limited in generating and in executing movement plans. As they grow, children are able to use more sources of perceptual information and can be more precise in executing movements.

McCracken (1983) illustrated the performance difference between younger (six-year-old) and older (ten-year-old) boys on a movement task that relied heavily on the visual perceptual system. He had the boys do a tapping task where they alternately touched two target circles as rapidly as possible. The most effective strategy was used by the older boys. They looked at only one target or between the two targets as they performed the task. They did not, however, look back and forth to the circles as they tapped each one, which was the strategy used by the younger boys.

McCracken's findings correspond with research by Curtis (1985) on use of computer games with children. She found that the most effective players manipulated the joystick for moving, picking up, shooting, or dropping off objects without looking at the joystick and, at the same time, fixing their eyes on a large or significant area of the computer screen. Young children were ineffective performers largely because they looked at their joystick as they moved it, and they also looked at many different areas on the computer screen.

To summarize, many factors have been identified that influence movement development during the early childhood years. Current ideas on the nature of movement control and the components that influence its emergence have been discussed. Several frameworks have been presented for conceptualizing movement. The common factor among these frameworks is their view of the dynamic, interactive relationship between the child and the

Figure 11.4.   Three Steps and Their Functions in the Solution of a Movement Problem

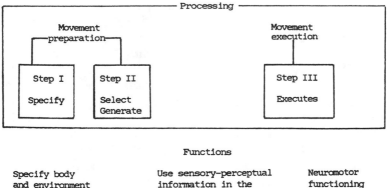

Processing

Movement preparation

Movement execution

Step I	Step II	Step III
Specify	Select Generate	Executes

Functions

Specify body and environment in terms of spatial-temporal requirements and related conditions.

Use sensory-perceptual information in the selection of the movement to be made and in the generation of response specifications.

Neuromotor functioning to execute the intended movement.

Source: J. F. Keogh and D. Sugden (1985). *Movement Skill Development*. New York: Macmillan.

environment. Internal factors that relate to perceptual, cognitive, psycho-logical, biological, psychological, and neurological growth influence how individuals move through their environments. The environment itself and the dynamics of change within the environment interact with the mover to create a variety of movement problems to be solved. The challenges are limitless. Many opportunities for facilitating change exist and while the dynamics of these changes are not completely understood, some interesting curriculum applications can be suggested.

IMPLICATIONS FOR CURRICULA

Given how children interact with their environment, and given that one goal of early childhood education is to foster creative problem solvers, a real challenge to teachers and child care providers is how to structure the physical environment so that it stimulates creative problem solving. The movement domain, while typically not viewed from this perspective, can be a useful avenue to this goal in many early childhood settings. It provides additional benefits in fostering movement development.

Mosston (1966) has developed a clear and concise teaching method that can be effectively adapted for use by early childhood educators. He stresses creative problem solving in physical activities, focusing on individualized instruction and enhancing cognitive processing. His progression of teaching styles from "Command to Discovery" gradually shifts decision making from the adults to the children. The unique features of his approach encourage children to seek simple solutions to movement problems and to be part of the decision-making process.

Curtis (1982) has elaborated on ways to incorporate Mosston's teaching styles into a movement education program. Movement education was developed in England after World War II. The aim was to give children a broad and comprehensive base of movement experiences, in order to develop each child's movement resources to their fullest potential. Her approach avoids observing development from the perspective of age-ordered tasks. Rather, she focuses on the process of change over time. She devotes a major portion of her book to activities that stimulate creative movement situations for young children to become involved with, and which will enhance their movement development.

In many early childhood settings, the teacher is seen as the facilitator of learning experiences. This facilitator model works well with a movement education approach. The facilitator sets up the environment to present movement challenges to the children. By finding creative solutions to the movement problems, children expand their movement repertoires.

Herkowitz (1978) suggests several ways to design playspaces for young children that provide for increasing physical challenges. Her ideas incorporate a diverse mix of motor, intellectual, and social functioning opportunities for children. Reinforcement and novelty are stressed. The playspace can be restructured through equipment that is changeable. She proposes three guidelines that provide many movement opportunities for children at many different skill levels: (1) equipment that has the same form but varies in size should be grouped together (such as ladders that have rungs at varying intervals), (2) equipment should be used that children can adjust to their own levels (for example, a ball suspended on a string that children can raise or lower), and (3) single pieces of equipment should be structurally built to challenge children of different levels (such as a balance board that is wide at one end but gradually narrows to the other end). The design of playspaces can and should be evaluated on criteria such as the degree of socialization they encourage, the popularity of equipment, relationships of equipment to open spaces, the relationship between hard surfaces that are for riding toys, and running surfaces with stationary apparatus. Unique considerations come into play for the special demands of each particular early childhood setting.

While technological advances have become valuable tools for researchers studying movement development, practitioners continue to be restricted to using their eyes, ears, and knowledge of child development in order to make assessments of change. Good observation skills will always be valuable assets for evaluating change in children. For the early childhood educator who desires to implement a movement program that will facilitate development, it would be helpful to have easy-to-use guidelines on current expectations for young children, a description of how the progression of abilities proceeds, what kind of expectations one should have, and how a movement program can be implemented. Curtis (1982) has provided these guidelines as well as observational checklists for assessing various movement patterns. Her approach is highly dependent on the teacher's responsiveness and perceptiveness in seeing what children are doing in their movement and then setting up environments to challenge their abilities.

FINAL COMMENTS

Research in the field of movement development is emerging from a new perspective that focuses on children and how they move. Many questions have been raised, yet few have been answered definitively. Gradually new information is becoming available as research in this diverse area of study is being undertaken. Much work, however, remains to be done.

The area of central processing ability and its relation to movement skills may stimulate interesting studies that follow up on Todor's and Connell's work. Techniques for analyzing movements into schemes may lead to the development of teaching strategies that can facilitate development and maximize learning within a child's mental processing ability for specific movement tasks.

Keogh's work on movement confidence provides another promising area of research. In what ways might it be possible to improve young children's confidence through experiences in their school and home environments? What are the possibilities for positively effecting future skill development?

Longitudinal research is needed to help provide insight into many questions that have been raised regarding individual variations in performance and the progression of motor skill development for specific movements. Other questions that need investigation are: How do boys and girls differ in performance as a function of age, the environment, and/or innate biological differences? Are there constant differences in performance between boys and girls on some skills like jumping or running, yet differential variations between them on others, such as throwing or balance tasks? Understanding the changes in perceptual abilities and their relations to performance has been and will continue to be an interesting area of study, particularly when viewed longitudinally.

Playspaces and their constructions form another area in which valuable information can be learned. Are there certain equipment configurations that encourage the enhancement of particular movement skills? What types of equipment and movement problems promote creative problem solving? What new techniques for analyzing movement skills can help teachers facilitate the development of new abilities? Will analyzing movements from new perspectives provide new insights into development? These are merely a few examples of the rich area of research from which important applications may some day be applied to enhance movement development within early childhood settings.

REFERENCES

Bayley, N. (1935). The development of motor abilities during the first three years. *Monographs of the Society for Research in Child Development* 1, Serial No. 1.

Connell, R. A. (1980). Cognitive factors and development of movement control. Unpublished, University of Leeds.

Constantini, A. F., Corsini, D. A., and Davis, J. E. (1973). Conceptual tempo, inhibition of movement and acceleration of movement in 4, 7, and 9 year old children. *Perceptual and Motor Skills* 37: 779–84.

Constantini, A. F., and Hoving, K. L. (1973). The relationship of cognitive and motor response inhibition to age and IQ. *Journal of Genetic Psychology* 123: 309–19.

Curtis, S. R. (1985). Formative evaluations on computer games designed for children ages 3–14 years. Berkeley, CA: Joyce Hakansson Associates, unpublished.

Curtis, S. R. (1982). *The Joy of Movement in Early Childhood*. New York: Teachers College Press.

Espenscade, A. S., and Eckert, H. M. (1967). *Motor Development*. Columbus, OH: Merrill.

Gentile, A. M., Higgins, J. R., Miller, E. A., and Rosen, B. M. (1975). The structure of motor tasks. *Mouvement* 7: 11–28.

Gesell, A., and Amatruda, C. S. (1941). *Developmental Diagnosis*. New York: Harper.

Gipsman, S. C. (1973). Control of range of movement rate in primary school children. M.A. thesis, University of California, Los Angeles.

Griffin, N. S., and Keogh, J. F. (1982). A Model for movement confidence. In J.A.S. Kelso and J. E. Clark (Eds.), *The Development of Movement Control and Coordination*. New York: McGraw-Hill.

Herkowitz, J. (1978). The design and evaluation of playspaces for children. In Ridenour, M. V. (Ed.), *Motor Development Issues and Applications*. Princeton, NJ: Princeton Book Company.

Keogh, J. F. (1971). Motor control as a unifying concept in the study of motor development. Presented at the Motor Development Symposium, University of California, Berkeley.

Keogh, J. F., and Sugden, D. (1985). *Movement Skill Development*. New York: Macmillan.

Maccoby, E. E., Dowley, E. M., Hogen, J. W., and Degerman, R. (1965). Activity level and intellectual functioning in normal preschool children. *Child Development* 36: 761–70.

McCracken, H. D. (1983). Movement control in a reciprocal tapping task: a developmental study. *Journal of Motor Behavior* 15: 262–79.

Mosston, M. (1966). *Teaching Physical Education: From Command to Discovery*. Columbus, OH: Merrill.

Pascual-Leone, J. (1970). A mathematical model for the transition rule in Piaget's developmental stages. *Acta Psychologica* 32: 301–45.

Piaget, J. (1973). *Memory and Intelligence*. New York: Basic Books.

Ridenour, M. V. (1978). Contemporary issues in motor development. In M. V. Ridenour (Ed.), *Motor Development: Issues and Applications*. Princeton, NJ: Princeton Book Company.

Robertson, M. A. (1977). Stability of stage categorizations across trials: implications for the "stage theory" of overarm throw development. *Journal of Human Movement Studies* 3: 49–59.

Shirley, M. M. (1931). *The First Two Years: A Study of Twenty-five Babies*. Vol. 1, *Postural and Locomotor Development*. Minneapolis: University of Minnesota Press.

Spaeth-Arnold, R. K. (1981). Developing sport skills. *Motor Skill: Theory into Practice*, Monograph 2.

Teeple, J. (1978). Physical growth and maturation. In M. V. Ridenour (Ed.), *Motor Development: Issues and Applications*. Princeton, NJ: Princeton Book Company.

Thelen, E. (1979). Rhythmical stereotypes in normal human infants. *Animal Behavior* 27: 699–715.

Todor, J. F. (1979). Developmental differences in motor task integration—a test of Pascual-Leone's theory of constructive operators. *Journal of Experimental Child Psychology* 28: 314–22.

Von Hofsten, C. (1980). Predictive reaching for moving objects by human infants. *Journal of Experimental Child Psychology* 30: 369–82.

Wickstrom, R. (1977). *Fundamental Motor Patterns*. (2nd ed.) Philadelphia: Lea and Febiger.

CHAPTER 12

Conclusion

CAROL SEEFELDT
University of Maryland

Early childhood education—whether in a child care center, nursery school, kindergarten or primary grade—is available to more and more children today. It has been estimated that nearly 5 million children are enrolled in some type of early childhood program. Nearly all children in our nation attend a primary grade: 82 percent of the fives are in a kindergarten, and 46 percent of fours and 27 percent of the three-year-olds are in some form of nursery group (Hymes, 1983).

Head Start is enrolling over 400,000 children yearly. The census bureau reports that the under-age-five group is the third largest growing segment of the population and estimates that more than 5.5 million children will be in some form of early childhood program by the mid-1980s.

Increases in enrollment in early childhood programs continue as economic conditions dictate that both parents be employed outside of the home, and more children live in single-parent homes. Social forces have affected the field (as illustrated in Hinitz's chapter on the social studies); however, the wide acceptance of early childhood education as valid and beneficial for all may be equally responsible for this growth. Today, society recognizes that early education benefits children and families. Early educational experiences are sought because there is agreement that these experiences do in fact, contribute to children's physical, social intellectual, and emotional growth.

Nevertheless, while there is agreement that early education benefits children, there is often little agreement as to what this education should consist of. The curriculum, what children actually do during their time in an early childhood environment, differs dramatically from setting to setting.

THE DIVERSITY OF EARLY CHILDHOOD EDUCATION

There is a great diversity of program types, administrative units, and sponsoring agencies in the field of early childhood. Certainly, this plurality results in varied curriculum practices. Administrative units include the primary grades, kindergarten, nursery schools, day care and Head Start centers, home-based programs, and others. Some programs are sponsored by the public schools, while others are supported with local, state, or federal funds. Nonprofit as well as for-profit programs are run by parents, churches, or other agencies in order to meet a community's needs.

At one time this diversity of program types and sponsoring agencies led educators and psychologists to search for the one perfect curriculum model that would ensure unity in the field. One model curriculum could provide children and teachers, in whatever setting, with all that was required for optimal intellectual, social, emotional, and physical growth and development. Throughout the 1960s and 1970s a variety of program models were implemented in Head Start, Follow Through, and other program units.

Model programs, such as the Weikart Perry Preschool Project, Gray's Early Training Project, and Karnes Curriculum Study, were designed and implemented (see Evans in Spodek, 1982). Sparked by the theories of Hunt, Bloom, Piaget, and others, who believed that mental growth is cumulative, and that later intellectual development depends, in part, on early educational experiences, these model curricula were developed to foster cognitive growth. The success of these model programs was assessed by examining their effectiveness in increasing children's intellectual abilities.

During this time, students of early childhood development became familiar with the philosophical and theoretical underpinnings of each of the models, their stated goals and objectives and curriculum plans. Graduate programs in early childhood education frequently focused only on the examination of the models, to the neglect of other important developments in the field.

The search for one perfect curriculum seems simplistic and unrealistic today. There is the recognition that differences in curriculum practices, such as ideas of what the curriculum is and how it should be implemented, stem from the way individuals view children and how children learn. "Each teacher is different and each teaching situation is different" state Margaret Lay-Dopyrea and John Dopyrea in Chapter 2, "Strategies for Teaching." They point out that individual teachers often bring a preferred orientation toward children that influences their decision making and behavior.

Some teachers and sponsoring agencies hold an interactionist point of view, and believe children learn as they interact with their physical, social, and cognitive environment. These teachers endorse the theories of the cognitive psychologists. Others support a behavioristic perspective and provide for more adult-initiated activities and a more structured learning environment. Still others, who support the maturationists, find that an understanding of normal patterns of child growth and development, and trust in the goodness of each individual child direct their behavior. These teachers may take a more passive approach, and see themselves as providers of learning opportunities and as a guide for children's learning rather than as teachers.

These differing views are reflected in each of the chapters of the text. Barbour, in "Learning to Read" (Chapter 5), begins with a discussion of the impact of the theories of the cognitive psychologists, behaviorists, and the maturationists or nativists, on how reading is taught. Other chapters in the text refer to these theoretical approaches, documenting how each is reflected in the art, music, or science curriculum.

Regardless of the differing orientations of teachers and programs, our nation is a democratic, pluralistic nation. Diversity is not only a fact of life, but something we respect, treasure, and strive to protect. Early childhood educators have always attempted to respond to the culture, values, and desires of parents and the community. Today's early childhood educator is faced with new pressures to protect this democratic diversity. In exerting their viewpoints, the right wing conservatives are demanding a homogeneous nation with one all-embracing set of values. It seems, as if to validate their own beliefs and values, the conservatives work to force these values and beliefs on others.

Because educators are intent on involving parents and the community in the school, it seems natural that curriculum practices would differ from program to program. Celia Genishi, in the chapter on language, points out that one role of the teacher is to meet the persistent challenge of respecting each child's cultural and linguistic background by making modifications in the curriculum. This implies that differences in curricula and teaching practices are required in order to provide a match between a child's home background and the culture of the school.

THE UNITY OF EARLY CHILDHOOD EDUCATION

High-quality programs clearly demand teachers who are active decision makers and who are knowledgeable about children, learning theories, and curriculum content. Although there is great diversity among the curricula of early childhood education, there is unity of agreement. First, no one doubts the relationship of the curriculum to the total quality of an early childhood program. Program quality and effectiveness depend on a well-planned curriculum. The curriculum, "a systematic way of operating class-rooms" is a critical element in early childhood programs. It is the curriculum that "defines and clarifies so many other issues, including teacher behavior and questioning style, classroom organization, relationships with families, directive teaching versus child centered learning and so on. The big dividing line between effective programs and ineffective programs is that the staff of the latter have not made a decision about the curriculum" (Weikart, 1986, p. 8).

Play, the "unifying cauldron" that Doris Fromberg discusses, is the basis for teaching and learning in each curriculum area. Early childhood educators generally agree that play serves an important function for young children. Play is viewed by each author as the basic mode for children's thinking and learning. Forman and Kaden in "Research on Science Education" express the widely held belief that a playful mode is necessary for learning. Hinitz, writing on social studies education, Seefeldt on art, and Curtis on movement, all support this belief.

There is also agreement on the fact that children can not be separated into mind and body, but are whole beings, and that cognitive activity is one and the same with social, physical, and emotional activity.

Even though this text presents separate chapters describing the research, theory, and implications for practice in separate curriculum content areas, the idea of an integrated approach to the curriculum is present. The idea of a whole curriculum, rather than a separate subject approach, underlies each chapter. Williams traces this belief to the philosophies of Rousseau, Frobel, and Dewey, and discusses how the ideas of each of these thinkers are present in curriculum today.

No author endorses dividing the child's day into separate subjects, but rather each supports an integrated curriculum. While each curriculum area includes a specific set of contents, a body of acquired facts and knowledge that give rise to different activities and methods of teaching, each author nevertheless endorses a total, unified approach to the curriculum. Alper describes the need for an undivided approach stating, "Experiences in music must become, therefore, not isolated . . . but integral parts of children's total learning process."

Piaget's work has had an enormous unifying effect on the field of early childhood education. Each content area reflects the thinking of Piaget, and supports the assumption of the theory of equilibration. As Forman and Kaden point out, children, who appear to have an intrinsic need not to contradict themselves, learn (1) when they sense that a contradiction has occurred, and (2) when they construct a new way of looking at the concept in order to eliminate the contradiction.

One way of fostering children's ability to see the contradictions between their thinking and the reality of the world is to provide for action. The ideas of Castaneda, who reminds us of the need for children to physically act on objects in their environment, are reflected in each of the other chapters as well.

An active teacher, one who makes decisions, initiates plans, and interacts with children, is called for. Teachers make decisions as they set the stage for children's learning, but they do more than provide materials and set the stage. Based on their understanding of children's thinking, and the content of each of the curriculum areas, they exploit children's daily encounters with their physical and social environment, to stimulate the thinking process.

Activities are planned and implemented in ways that lead logically to conceptualization (Biber, 1977). The main activity of the teacher is to understand the child. A teacher who understands children's thinking understands how to provide structure and routines, when and how to ask questions, and how to help children formulate and then verbalize their ideas and thoughts. Children's cognitive search for relationships is met as the active teacher juxtaposes and balances direct contact with people and the processes of the environment, with opportunities for reflection and thought.

THE FUTURE

Early childhood education today is reaching maturity. Each chapter illustrates the vast amount of information we have about how children learn specific knowledge, skills, and attitudes, and about how to teach children. Yet there is still much to learn. "The early childhood educator soon learns that much of the research that is relevant to her field deals with limited aspects of children's functioning. Too seldom is that functioning viewed in the context of the child's total experiences" (Almy, 1975, p. 245). Much of what we know about teaching strategies and implementing the content areas of teaching art, social studies, science, and other areas is often based on research conducted in the middle grades, or on older children. In fact, much of the research reviewed in this text is taken from the field of elementary education or related fields. Few studies on the development or effectiveness of curriculum in the content areas for children under age five are reported.

Yet much more research within early childhood classrooms is required. As the profession reaches full maturity, early childhood educators must begin to assume responsibility for production of the necessary research. Piaget questions why teachers do so little of the work of researchers. "The general problem is to understand why the vast army of educators now laboring throughout the entire world with such devotion and in general, with such competence, does not engender an elite of researchers capable of making pedagogy into a discipline" (Piaget, 1969, p. 10).

Early childhood educators can no longer afford to distance themselves from the research process. First, it is the teacher who is most knowledgeable about the practice of early childhood education. It is the teacher who is best able to identify the problems and critical issues as well as successes of the educative process. It is the teacher, who from this base of knowledge, should be asking the questions that will direct research. It is the teacher who must become the double specialist, putting theory into practice and practice into theory.

Then too, current demands for educational accountability and effectiveness suggest that early childhood educators must become involved in research. First, when teachers formulate hypotheses, gather and consider evidence, and decide how results can be implemented in practice, research is seen not as an esoteric process removed from practice, but as a means to the end of improving the teaching/learning process.

The problem may be not merely the lack of research in the curriculum areas of early childhood, or convincing educators that they must begin to think of themselves as researchers, but utilizing the research findings available to us. Certainly, as the authors in this text have demonstrated, there is a vast amount of knowledge available on which to base decisions about teaching. When schools for young children are using work sheets and dittos, introducing early academic skills earlier and earlier, the next important question may be how to use the research findings we do have and the knowledge we have, rather than the need to create additional knowledge.

At the same time, early childhood educators must develop a clear sense of values. "Neither the individual who takes little pleasure in exploring ideas and their consequences nor the one who plunges ahead on each new idea, seeing no necessity for either reflection or the marshalling of evidence, seems appropriate" (Almy, 1975, p. 265). Values integral to a democratic society must serve to guide educators as they select the research they will implement in their classrooms.

REFERENCES

Almy, M. (1975). *The early childhood educator at work*. New York: McGraw-Hill.

Biber, B. (1977). Cognition in early childhood education: A historical perspective. In B. Spodek and H. Walberg (eds.) *Early childhood education: Issues and insights*, Berkeley, CA: McCutchen.

Evans, E. (1982). Curriculum models and early childhood education. In B. Spodek (ed.) *Handbook of research in early childhood education*. New York: Free Press.

Hymes, J. L. (1983). The satisfactions. In *Annual editions: Early childhood education 1983–1984*. Guilford, CT: The Duskin Publishing Group.

Piaget, J. (1969). *Science of education and the psychology of the child*. New York: Viking Compass.

Weikart, D. P. (1986). What do we know so far? *A magazine for educators: High Scope ReSource*, Winter.

About the Editor
and the Contributors

CLIFFORD D. ALPER is Professor of Music at Towson State University, where, since 1960, he has taught in the Early Childhood Program and coordinated the graduate program in music education. He has authored articles on early childhood music in periodicals such as the *Journal of Research in Music Education* and the *Music Educators Journal*.

NITA BARBOUR is Chair of the Department of Education at the University of Maryland, Baltimore County, where she previously directed the Early Childhood Program. Dr. Barbour has experience teaching in early childhood, the grades and secondary schools. In addition, she was Director of the Child Development Associate programs for Head Start at the University of Maryland Baltimore County.

ALBERTA M. CASTANEDA has taught kindergarten and first grade, and currently is Associate Professor in the Department of Curriculum and Instruction at the University of Texas at Austin. Co-author of two kindergarten mathematics programs and a kindergarten curriculum, her research includes evaluation of mathematics programs for five- and six-year-old children.

SANDRA R. CURTIS is Director of Research at Joyce Hakansson Associates, where she coordinates formative evaluation of entertaining and educational software products for children aged 4–14. She has been the concept developer, project manager, writer, and coordinator of media products for children, including the Magic Window Series Entertainment Video for Children. She received her doctorate from the University of California, Berkeley and is the author of *The Joy of Movement in Early Childhood*.

JOHN E. DOPYERA has taught in the teacher education programs at Syracuse University, The Pennsylvania State University and at Pacific Oaks College where he also served as Dean of Faculty. He has over 30 years experience in conducting needs assessments and in designing, conducting, and evaluating training programs for education, human services, and business and industry.

279

GEORGE FORMAN, Professor of Education at the University of Massachusetts, has been active in developing curriculum for young children since 1970 at George Peabody College, the University of New York at Buffalo, and the University of Massachusetts. He founded the School for Constructive Play—a preschool for 3 to 5 year olds—based on Piaget's theory, and is a past president of the International Jean Piaget Society.

DORIS PRONIN FROMBERG is Professor of Elementary and Early Childhood Education and Director of Early Childhood Teacher Education at Hofstra University. She has been a curriculum and administration consultant to school districts and the Director of a Teacher Corps project which developed field-based inservice consultation for teachers, administrators, and the community. Her latest books are *The Successful Classroom: Management Strategies for Regular and Special Education Teachers* and *The Full-Day Kindergarten*.

CELIA GENISHI has taught at the secondary, preschool, and university levels and is currently Professor at the Ohio State University in the Department of Educational Theory and Practice. Her areas of interest are related to language acquisition and early childhood language arts, and she has published primarily on the subjects of children's oral language, and bilingual children. Celia is co-editor with Anne Dyson of *Research Currents*, a monthly column in *Language Arts*, the Journal of the National Council of Teachers of English.

BLYTHE F. HINITZ is Assistant Professor of Early Childhood Education at Trenton State College, New Jersey. Blythe has served on the Child Care Task Force of the Mayor's Commission for Women in Philadelphia and consulted with the Ministry of Education in Israel. She is active in the World Organization for Early Childhood Education, and the National Association for the Education of Young Children, and is currently interested in computer literacy in early childhood.

MELISSA KADEN is an intern supervisor at the University of Massachusetts, Amherst. She is a doctoral candidate in early childhood education at the University of Massachusetts, and has been an instructor at Greenfield Community College and the University of Massachusetts. Ms. Kaden has taught young children in a variety of settings, including day care, preschools and the public schools.

MARGARET LAY-DOPYERA has 12 years of teaching experience with young children in the public schools and laboratory schools. A faculty member at Syracuse University since 1967, she has had major responsibilities in designing and implementing model teacher training programs, and is currently Associate Dean for Academic Programs in the School of Education. With her husband, John Dopyera, she co-authored the textbook *Becoming a Teacher of Young Children*.

CAROL SEEFELDT, (editor), is Professor of Early Childhood and Child Development at the University of Maryland, where she received the Distinguished Scholar/Teacher Award. She has worked in the field for over 30 years, teaching day care through third grade. In Florida, Dr. Seefeldt opened and directed a private preschool and served as Regional Training Officer for Project Head Start. She is active in the National Association for the Education of Young Children and the Association for the Childhood Education International. Her research emphasizes early childhood curriculum, intergenerational attitudes, and the effects of competition on child growth and development.

LESLIE R. WILLIAMS is a curriculum designer and teacher educator who focuses on the refinement of teaching practice in experienced teachers. Her special interests include multicultural education and infant study and practice; currently she is researching the all-day kindergarten movement in the United States, and coordinating annual all-day kindergarten institutes at Teachers' College, Columbia University, where she is Associate Professor of Early Childhood Education.